The
BIG BOOK
of
HUNTING
STORIES

STEVE CHAPMAN

HARVEST HOUSE PUBLISHERS
EUGENE, OREGON

Cover design by Bryce Williamson

Cover photo © da kuk, A-Digit, PREDRAGILIEVSKI, DenisKrivoy / Gettyimages

Includes new stories as well as some stories from these books by Steve Chapman, previously published by Harvest House Publishers:
A Look at Life from a Deer Stand
Another Look at Life from a Deer Stand
Tales Hunters Tell
Great Hunting Stories
With Dad on a Deer Stand
A Hunter Sets His Sights

The Big Book of Hunting Stories
Copyright © 2020 by Steve Chapman
Published by Harvest House Publishers
Eugene, Oregon 97408
www.harvesthousepublishers.com

ISBN 978-0-7369-7844-6 (pbk.)
ISBN 978-0-7369-8019-7 (eBook)

Library of Congress Cataloging-in-Publication Data

Names: Chapman, Steve, author.
Title: The big book of hunting stories / Steve Chapman.
Description: Eugene, Oregon : Harvest House Publishers, [2020]
Identifiers: LCCN 2019034740 (print) | LCCN 2019034741 (ebook) | ISBN
    9780736978446 (trade paperback) | ISBN 9780736980197 (ebook)
Subjects: LCSH: Chapman, Steve. | Hunters--United States--Biography.
Classification: LCC SK17.C43 A3 2020 (print) | LCC SK17.C43 (ebook) | DDC
    639/.1092 [B]--dc23
LC record available at https://lccn.loc.gov/2019034740
LC ebook record available at https://lccn.loc.gov/2019034741

Printed in the United States of America

20 21 22 23 24 25 26 27 / BP-RD / 10 9 8 7 6 5 4 3 2 1

Contents

1

First to Last

Have you ever noticed that there is something about "firsts" that intrigues us all? We find ourselves spellbound by them, and for some reason we focus on them and often refer to firsts as the highlights of our lives. Consider the importance we place on the following:

firstborn
first step
first word ever spoken
first grade
first date
first kiss
first car
first man on the moon
first cup of coffee
first impression
"The First Time Ever I Saw Your Face"

On and on the list could go. As I pondered our affection for firsts, I began to realize that we are drawn to these initial events because they seem to have a unique ability to set the course for the journeys we take, whether good or bad.

In my forty-plus years of avid hunting, I still look back at my first morning in the woods as my most favorite outdoor experience. To this day I truly believe it put me on a path which I hope to travel as long as I'm able to get around. Maybe you have a fond memory of a similar experience that set you on the same course.

For me, the journey began when I was fourteen years old. My dad was pastor of a church in the rolling hills of West Virginia, and among the members of his congregation was a gentleman named Kenneth Bledsoe. One Sunday after the service, he invited me to join him on a squirrel hunt the following Saturday. I could hardly wait for the end of the week to come.

Friday finally came, and my folks took me to his home. It sat along a rural highway on top of a ridge surrounded by gently rolling hills. His land was graced with large patches of woods and beautiful meadows. It was the middle of October and all the leaves on the trees were ablaze with incredible autumn colors. The red, brown, orange, and yellow hues seemed to glow in the bright sun with an invitation to simply stand in awe of God's ability to paint a scene. The view that spread out before us was like a huge canvas, and we were fortunate to be living creatures on it.

I went to bed that night and quickly drifted off into a deep slumber. Little did I know that from that evening on, I would never go to sleep so easily on the night before a hunt. For the rest of my life, the anticipation of a repeat of the morning to follow would always make me anxious for the alarm to sound.

At 5:30 a.m. we were sitting down to breakfast. It hadn't happened often that I was up at that hour. Perhaps Easter sunrise service or leaving early to drive with my folks to Grandma's house were the only reasons you would find me up before daylight. But there I was, wide awake with anticipation and already dressed for the day.

In the dim light of the carport, Kenneth handed me the gun he had shown me how to use the night before. It was a .22/20-gauge over-and-under masterpiece. He put a handful of 20-gauge shells in my pocket, and we walked across the paved road at the end of his driveway and headed down a hillside into the darkness of the woods. My friend knew his way very well through the forest. Nearly every step of the way, he gave me instructions that would ensure our safety. When we came to the first fence, he held out his hand to take my gun. He said, "Never cross a fence while holding your gun. Too many guys have died that way." Also, he warned me about choosing my steps carefully in the dark. "Falling with a gun is no fun, especially for those around you!"

I was getting my first safety course that day, and I felt secure with such a veteran hunter as Kenneth. I couldn't have chosen a better teacher. Many times throughout my hunting life, I have applied the lessons I learned that morning. Years later, when I finally took an official hunter's safety course here in Tennessee with my son, I was amazed at how much ground had already been covered by my friend, who had never seen the textbook. Someone had taught him well, and I was grateful that the heritage was handed down to me.

About twenty minutes before daylight, we stopped by a large oak. With his big boot, Kenneth scraped away the dry leaves on the forest floor to reveal an area of dark, soft ground about three feet wide and three feet long. He said softly, "You'll need a quiet place to sit. You don't want to be making a lot of noise while you hunt. You're in the critters' territory. They know sounds. Unfamiliar noises are a sign of danger to them. Now, have a seat here and try to move only when it's time to take a shot." Then, as if I were being left on a deserted island, he walked up the hill behind me and out of sight. Just before he left, he whispered, "I'll be around the hill. Stay here till I come back and get you."

It was the next thirty to forty minutes that forever sealed the joy of hunting in my heart. There I sat, outside and under a tree, as the world came to life. Creatures began to respond to the rays of the sun that crept over the top of the ridge. With each passing minute, an excitement started to build inside me. I heard all kinds of sounds I had never heard before. Crows were cawing in the distance, speaking an unknown language. Leaves were mysteriously rustling on the ground somewhere nearby, a hoot owl made its call, and an amazing variety of birds began to sing their tunes. Like a city going to work, the animals that didn't work the night shift (like raccoons and possums) began their foraging for food. It was amazing to me that such a kingdom existed and that I was sitting in the middle of it.

All my five senses seemed heightened that first morning. The wonderful taste of an early breakfast of eggs, bacon, toast, and jam that Evelyn Bledsoe had prepared still lingered on my tongue. The crisp, cool October air felt refreshing on my skin.

The scene of the growing light made me grateful for eyesight, and my hearing was experiencing a virtual orchestra of new sounds. The experience brought a sense of great joy to this young city slicker. For some odd reason, however, the fifth of the senses that was blessed seemed to be the one I remember the most. It was the incredible smell of the autumn woods. There is no other aroma like it in the world. There's no way to explain it. To this day, the smell of the forest floor triggers more memories and a stronger desire to head to the woods than any of the other senses.

An hour must have passed as I sat there. I never did see a squirrel. Perhaps I shifted around more than I should have and scared them off. Also, it's possible that a dozen squirrels may have scurried right above me in the canopy of branches and I just didn't see them. I was still sitting in my quiet spot that Kenneth had prepared for me at the base of the tree when suddenly I got a tap on the shoulder. It made a shiver race up my spine that took years to go away. It's a wonder I didn't fire the gun I was holding across my lap. I quickly turned around, expecting to see the bear just before it ate me, and felt greatly relieved to see it was Kenneth standing there. He saw what he had done to me and chuckled as he softly said, "The hunt is over."

"How did you do that? I never heard you coming!" I said in much too loud a voice for the great hunter.

He simply whispered, "I can teach you to do that." And so he did. On the way back to the house, he began to teach me the art of stalking through the woods. He showed me how to pick a place void of fallen twigs, put the toe down first, and then set the rest of the foot down gently. He instructed me to not forget to stop often and keep the eyes moving like radar across the woods. The techniques I gleaned from his seasoned wisdom that morning have yielded some impressive mounts that hang on my walls today.

That first morning in the woods opened a door to a whole new world and left pleasant and permanent tracks in my memory. When you think about your initial hunt, there's a lot more to it than one has time to share. Yet, all who hunt will cherish the "first," and it will always hold its rightful place in your thoughts. I know this is true because there is a head mount hanging over our son's fireplace. It's a white-tailed deer. The six-point rack is not large, but the plaque beneath it reads, "Nathan's First Deer."

My first deer had even a smaller rack but was nonetheless important. I had it mounted, and it still brings just as much joy as the six-by-six elk rack I brought home from Montana. The memory is as sweet. I'll never forget that day. Not only did I enjoy taking my first whitetail, but there were other firsts that I treasure.

For example, my very first ride in a four-wheel-drive vehicle took place the morning of my first deer hunt. It was frightening, but I survived it. The driver was an elderly gentleman whose flame was fueled by the fear in his passengers. He seemed to be intoxicated by the challenge of getting that old, olive-green Army-issue Jeep up that steep West Virginia mountain. I repented of every sin I could think of and even started in on my friends' sins as we bounced up "death road."

Another first I experienced that day is what is known as a "drive." It's a hunting tactic used most often in the later part of the season to push the deer out of the dense brush into the open woods by driving them with a line of hunters walking through the thickets. A deer usually heads for a low gap in the ridgeline called a "saddle," and that's where I was standing when I took my first shot at a buck. What an incredible moment it was. It's as exciting to think about it now as when it happened. If it's a memory you share, you understand the rush of feelings I can still remember years later.

Also, with the help of my host, Max Groves, I gutted a deer for the first time. (I should say "field dressed" the deer for those who are squeamish.) It's a disgusting but necessary process.

That wonderful day ended with another first. Mrs. Groves prepared the evening meal using venison that I had "harvested." It was a gastronomical jubilee! She pan-fried the backstrap and then made a gravy to pour over it. She graced the tender meat with mashed potatoes, green beans, corn, hot yeast rolls, and a steaming pot of fresh-brewed coffee. (Just try not to drool on these pages.)

It is true that we humans are enamored with firsts. However, as wonderful as they are, I do have one problem with them. The fact that there are firsts indicates that there will come a last. A beginning represents an ending that must follow. It would be hard to number how many midmorning departures from a deer stand I have dreaded to make. With a reluctance that tempts me to forsake all other responsibilities, many times I have stood up, gathered my gear, and headed to the truck. I often whisper to myself as I'm walking away, "All good things must end." As much as I would like to be able to, I can't keep the curtain from falling on a great day afield.

Life is a lot like a day in the woods. It has a beginning and an end. We take the alpha with the omega. The firstborn will leave home. Someday there'll be a final step. There'll be a last kiss, a last word, a graduation, a goodbye, a sunset, and—brace yourself—there will even be a last hunt. When will it be? Who knows?

What we do with all that is between the crib and the casket is an awesome opportunity and an incredible responsibility. Maybe some of us have deviated from the course that had a great and worthy beginning. Maybe we have forgotten our "first love." Perhaps some of us have given so much attention to other interests that we have forgotten how much we would enjoy an autumn sunrise or a quiet November deer stand.

How easy it is to get caught up in the cares of this life and forget to go outside.

For some of us, there are other things besides hunting that had a wonderful and true beginning, but because of various distractions, we have forgotten how to enjoy them. For example, how long has it been since we enjoyed a date with a spouse that resembles the first date? What about those first hours with a new baby? Have we hugged our children like that since? Perhaps a friendship needs to be rekindled. For some of us, maybe it's been a long time since we communed with our Father in heaven the way we did when we first gave our lives to Him.

May I suggest that you stop for a moment and take in a deep breath? In the way that the smell of an autumn morning brings back the precious memory of a first hunt, perhaps you could catch the aroma of another part of life that had a wonderful beginning. I pray that if you do, you will once again enjoy it. May you do so before time slips up behind you, taps you on the shoulder, and says, "The hunt is over."

2

The Ultimate Sacrifice

If you are a serious hunter like me, you have come to understand the word "sacrifice." The list of things one must give up to fill the big-game tag attached to a hunting license is significant. Yet because of the thrill of a challenge, deer hunters press on and willingly pay the price. It's a form of rigid self-discipline that has its rewards. However, a problem can arise when other people are pulled into the river of our sacrifices.

I vividly recall one hunt when I was a teenager that two gentlemen had a right to regret. It involved the father and a brother of the girl I would eventually marry. I met Annie in 1963 in junior high school. I was thirteen years old and she was twelve. (It was love at first sight—for Annie!) We were in different grades, but at sixteen and fifteen, we shared one class together: the school choir.

One November day in the chorus room, Annie began telling me about the deer her brother had taken on her dad's farm. When I perked up, she was delighted. Little did I know that she had a crush on me and that my immediate interest in the deer story was possibly a key that could unlock love's door. She hinted that I might be welcome to hunt on the farm, so I seized the moment and asked her if her brother might be willing to put me in the stand where he had experienced success. Annie responded with a cautious yes. Not wanting to miss a golden opportunity,

I set a time to be there and spent the rest of the week dreaming about the upcoming hunt.

Sleep is high on the list of things that hunters sacrifice. When the next Saturday finally came, the alarm roused me from my warm bed at 2:30 a.m., and I was out the door and on my way to the Williamson farm by 3:30. The real reason for my early departure was I was afraid I wouldn't be able to find their farm in the pre-dawn darkness. And it would have been tragic to have missed such a grand hunting opportunity. Therefore, giving up my sleep to arrive there at the right time seemed the safe thing to do. As it turned out, I drove up their lane around 3:45 a.m. Not wanting to disturb anyone that early, I sat in the car for a few moments, trying to decide whether to go to the front door. Everything seemed so calm. I hated to be a bother. I was hoping a light would come on and signal me that they were aware of my presence. Still, no one stirred.

Being driven, however, by the prospects of a large buck passing under that tree stand, I cast aside politeness, exited the car, and walked up to the porch and approached the door. I gave it an old-fashioned knuckle knock. Nothing happened. I waited a few cold minutes and then tried again. No response. I rapped one more time with vigor, and—aha!—the lights snapped on. About a minute later, I heard the locks turn from the inside. The door slowly opened to reveal an older man who I assumed was Annie's father. He looked a little bewildered and rather concerned.

Feeling pretty awkward, I quickly introduced myself and felt relieved to see him put the pieces together and realize that I was Annie's guest. I said, "Annie told me that your son has agreed to take me to his favorite tree stand this morning. I sure do appreciate it, and I'm ready to go." He gave me a "Do you know how early it is?" look and then said, "Have a seat, and I'll get my son up."

In a few minutes a younger man came into the living room. He seemed like the quiet type and was rubbing his eyes. He simply said, "Let's go." Justifiably so, Annie's brother was not too pleased to partake in my sacrifices. Regretfully, in all my excitement to bag a big one, I was unable to detect his suffering.

Comfort is another item hunters trade for the taste of venison. Annie's dad had briefly given up a warm bed to answer the door. However, his son and I were about to make a greater sacrifice. The temperature was around fifteen degrees, and the windchill put it in a dangerously frigid range. Any sweat we worked up as we trudged along in silence immediately froze on our clothing. Our lungs also paid a price as we climbed the hill toward the ridge. We had left the house around 4:00 a.m., and by 4:30 we were standing at the base of the tree looking up at the stand. After making sure I had safely climbed the wooden steps that were nailed to the forks of the tree and was standing securely on the plywood platform, my host left me in the dark. As I watched the dancing beam of his flashlight disappear into the distance, I had no idea that I was about to face a near-death experience.

Being somewhat naive in my career as an outdoorsman, I had not yet learned the effectiveness of layering my clothes. When I had tumbled out of bed that morning, I had thrown on one of the thickest sweatshirts I could find, two pairs of pants, a coat, and a pair of my dad's thin work gloves.

In those days, blaze orange had not yet been introduced to the hunting community, so hunters wore reds and other bright colors. I knew that safety was a factor, so I did the best I could. I borrowed my dad's yellow rain suit, which fit loosely over my clothing, and at least I felt safer. However, I had not counted on one problem. The frigid air made the plastic brittle, and every time I moved I sounded like breaking glass, so I had to remain as motionless as possible. Consequently, I couldn't enjoy the warming effect of moving around, and I quickly became quite cold and miserable. The frightening thing was that it was around 5:00 a.m.—nearly two hours before daylight.

Time had literally frozen too. It came to a standstill because the cheap watch I was wearing had stopped working around 4:40 a.m. It just couldn't operate in such cold weather. As a result, the encouragement that came from checking the time and anxiously awaiting the sun's first rays was sadly lost.

As the pain began to set in, I thought about abandoning my tree stand and leaving. It was only 5:30 a.m. (I guessed). However, I couldn't do it. I didn't dare take the risk of the Williamsons seeing me drive away and turning their sacrifices into a worthless effort. Also, I couldn't go back to the car, start it up, get warm, and then return to the stand. I knew I would never be able to find it again. I was stuck.

I wiggled my toes and fingers inside my boots and gloves. I tried flexing different muscles and then relaxing them to create some movement and warm myself. Nothing seemed to work. I was freezing to death. All my burial would require would be to melt me and pour me into a jar. After all these years, I have never experienced a more painful battle with cold weather than I had that morning.

I'm not sure how I survived to see it happen, but finally the sun began to peek over the ridge. It was a welcome sight. Around 6:45 (I guessed), I was standing in a spotlight of sun rays. Even though it was slight, I could feel their warmth. It gave me enough hope to press on. By 7:30 (I guessed), I was able to think rationally once again, and I began to recall my purpose for being there.

Suddenly, I heard a twig snap. I could feel the adrenaline start to flow, and a bead of perspiration formed on my brow. This was it!

Somehow I knew the twin brother to the buck Annie's brother had taken was coming up the ridgeline. Slowly, I felt for the hammer of the lever action .30-30 that I gripped in my hands. As I prepared for a shot, I mentally began to rehearse the speech I would give at the local hunting club, since I would probably receive the award for the biggest rack. Suddenly, out of the mist came the source of the noise. Walking right up to my tree stand, my "trophy" looked up at me and said, "Seen anything this morning? Sorry to bother ya! Guess I'll be going now…"

What a brutal addition to the discomfort I had endured already! As the unwelcome intruder crunched away in the frozen leaves, I honestly thought of firing a few angry rounds at his feet just to watch him dance. Instead, I exercised self-control and simply wished that the fleas of a thousand camels would infest his hunting coat.

My sacrifice of sleep and comfort yielded nothing in the way of table meat that cold and miserable day. What's worse, I had involved others in the losses. I will forever appreciate Annie's brother's willingness to guide me that cold morning to the tree stand. But I will always regret appearing so selfish as to arrive at such an ungodly hour on a day so bitterly cold that even the watchdogs were not foolish enough to leave their warm beds to bark at my car as I drove up the driveway.

The inconveniences and discomfort that I put my future in-laws through that morning years ago were significant. However, they are small-scale when compared to the sacrifices I have been known to require of those now closest to me. I speak of my wife and children. Through time and tears, I have thankfully learned that it is unwise and dangerous to drag them into an unbridled and relentless pursuit of the whitetail. If I'm not careful to keep things in balance, I will drown out their appreciation and approval of my interest in hunting.

How many of us have knowingly left behind "deer widows and orphans" for the sake of a hunt? Have we, in our untamed enthusiasm for a close encounter with a whitetail, allowed our families to experience the loss of emotional rest, mental comfort, precious time with their husband and father (or wife and mother), and financial resources? It is indeed a temptation that is hard to resist. Perhaps some of us, however, have felt the bitter-cold wind of the potential loneliness that would result and have awakened in time to make critical adjustments to our outdoor lifestyles. Those who have done so know that it is not by any means an easy change to make.

I have decided that my wife and children are much more important than any animal, fish, golf ball, job, or any other pursuit that would require too much of their lives. By the grace of God, this hunter has come to grips with the fact that while getting close to a whitetail buck is an incredible challenge (that I enjoy with a passion), a much greater challenge is to see how far away from a deer I can get when I realize that pursuing it is costing my family too much. For a hunter, that is the ultimate sacrifice.

3

The Arrow and the Bow

I really didn't mind that by the time I reached the stand of trees and set up my portable tree stand, I was in a drenching sweat. I was happy just to be on that wooded hillside in Cheatham County, Tennessee. At that time in my life, I was a novice bowhunter. I immediately was consumed by it. I knew very little but wanted to learn it all. So I spent days—even weeks—getting ready for the season. I loved every part of it—even the sweat. I found a Bear Whitetail compound bow at a pawnshop and some arrows at a garage sale.

At the time, our children were very young. In fact, one was "in the oven." Heidi was due in a few months, and Nathan was not yet three years old. I'm not sure how many children it takes to fill a quiver, but ours was full with two. I am grateful for them and love them both with all my heart. Early on in my fatherhood, I had a strong desire to be the best dad I could be, but I couldn't see a mistake I was making. I was allowing my new interest in archery to threaten the time and attention that belonged to my children.

Sitting in that tree stand, I waited from sunup till about 9:30 a.m. There was no movement, no noise—just dead silence.

I was having a problem staying awake. I know I dozed off several times. In fact, during one snooze that probably lasted thirty seconds but seemed like an hour, I found myself dreaming. When I opened my eyes, all I could see was the ground about twenty feet below. I thought I was falling, and it startled me to the point I gasped loudly. I immediately realized where I was and began to laugh.

I needed a way to stay awake, so I took the opportunity to check out my equipment. The compound bow cams, cables, grip, sights, and silencers all seemed to be in order. I glanced at the broadhead tip and then eyed the arrow for straightness—and that's when a phrase passed through my head. It sounded so good in my thoughts that I said it out loud: "The arrow and the bow." Somehow it sounded melodic to me, more so than "bow and arrow." As a songwriter, I'm always considering how words are metered together, and this phrase grabbed my attention. I thought to myself, *I'd like to use those words in a song someday.*

The woods continued to be silent, and the humidity felt like I was sitting in a steam room. Under my camo head net, the sweat poured off my forehead and into my eyes. Pesky little gnats and mosquitoes made a high-pitched buzz around my ears and swarmed menacingly around my eyes. (I hate that. Every time I deal with those disgusting pests, I think, *Thanks for nothing, Adam! These nasty creatures are a product of sin!*)

Wishing for more enjoyable thoughts, my attention went back to that phrase "the arrow and the bow." I began to ponder the meaning, and a sobering analogy came to mind. *The bow is like the parent, and the arrow is like the child.* A flood of thoughts followed. First, there will come a day when I'll have to let my children go. In the same way that I draw back the arrow and release it at the right moment, I should release my children at the right time. I don't look forward to that day, but if things go normally, they'll eventually leave. The "drawing back" starts early in their lives. Second, at what target am I aiming my arrows? If I want their lives to be placed in the center of God's will, then that's where I must aim. What am I doing to help make it so?

Also, am I, as the bow, rightly tuned and in good working order? And in whose hands am I? Furthermore, am I willing to let go? I once heard of some parents who learned that their son desired to go to a foreign mission field. Out of fear for their own welfare and a selfish clinging to the child, they manipulated the situation and blocked the response to the call God had placed on that young heart. The child eventually chose a vocation unrelated to the mission field. As his feelings of failure and resentment grew, his spiritual life took a dangerous turn. Only then did his parents realize what a terrible mistake they had made to discourage their child from entering the ministry. They were overwrought with regret.

I don't want to be guilty of standing in the Lord's way when it comes to His desire for my children's lives. I must be willing to release them to His call. He knows what's best for their lives. Besides, who knows how many lives will be touched with the gospel through our children? An old saying goes, "You can count the seeds in an apple, but you can't count the apples in a seed." In the same way, we can count the kids in our house, but we'll never know how many children of God will be added to His family as a result of our kids' devotion to Christ.

Also, will I do well at letting them go to another's love? I think of my sweet Heidi. It's going to be tough to let her go to some young twit. Excuse me—I mean, some young man. I agree with whoever said, "Giving your daughter away in marriage is like giving a fine, priceless violin to a gorilla!" I don't look forward to the day when a preacher asks, "Who gives this woman to be married to this man?" I hope I am sensible in that moment.*

But I must let go. It wouldn't be fair to my arrows to keep them protected in a quiver. To make that mistake would prevent them from fulfilling their purpose. The following is a lyric that was born that morning in my tree stand.

The Arrow and the Bow

Here is wisdom for the moms and dads
That time has proven true
The day your children learn to walk
They start to walk away from you

For at first you hold all of them
Cradled safely in your arms

---

* By the way, Heidi eventually married a young man named Emmitt Beall. Their wedding was on November 25, 2000, which fell on the first day of our state's deer/gun season. I hinted to Annie that Emmitt and I could go to the woods to hunt that morning and be back in time for the wedding. Her response was, "If you do it, you'll never get out of the woods." Needless to say, I missed the first day of the season that year.

Then one day their hand is all you'll hold
Then soon it's just their heart

And there'll even come the time
If your love for them is true
You'll have to let their hearts go free
To let them love
Someone else, not only you

Can the sparrow ever learn to fly
If the nest is all it knows?
Can the arrow ever reach its mark
By remaining in the bow?
You have to let it go

Here is wisdom for the moms and dads
That time has proven true
The day your children learn to walk
They start to walk away from you[1]

Now my children are older, and fortunately I listened to better judgment. I backed off in the amount of time I was spending in the field, and instead of losing a closeness to my son, he has now become my hunting buddy. Whenever I buy new equipment, I have to purchase it in pairs, and I do so with pleasure. I also hunt with Heidi, by the way. Her game, however, is a little different. Let's put it this way: Nathan likes to wear hunting clothes, and Heidi likes hunting for clothes. The "neat" part of Heidi's hunt is that the game is already hanging and cleaned when we shoot it.

To close, may I suggest a prayer for fathers who hunt:

O Father in heaven,
Make me to be a fine-tuned bow in Your hands.
Use my life to make the arrows You have given me
    to fly accurately and confidently
      to the destinations You have chosen.

Help me to bend well under the tension of parenting.
And someday, should that incredible miracle happen,
    and You turn my arrows into bows,
        may they too understand the act of letting go.
In Jesus's name, amen.

4

He's Comin', Daddy

When we pulled up in front of the rustic-looking cabin, the first thing I noticed was its matchbox size. It wasn't much larger than the pickup we were in. I noted that there were no electric wires running to a pole nearby. It meant that there would be no convenience of an electric stove and no after-dinner TV that evening. Somehow, though, it didn't matter. My son and I, along with two other fellows, were there to hunt deer. So what if we didn't have an inside toilet or running water. So what if our refrigerator was a cooler and a bag of melting ice and that we would be sleeping head-to-toe. That was part of the fun! Getting ready for the sack by the light of a Coleman lantern was pure adventure. "Bring on the primitive lifestyle!" we declared. "We're men!" (Besides, we knew that in less than 48 hours we would be on our way back to an easy chair in front of a fire!)

This was the fourth year for Nathan, my son, to go after his first elusive white-tail. The property we were going to hunt on was leased by a group of gentlemen who had formed a hunting club, and we were there as guests. Their choice of territory revealed their understanding of the deer's ideal habitat.

The mountainside was covered with huge hickories and oaks. The woods were mostly clear and open yet edged with inviting thickets for cover. It looked like a place that deer dream about. It held great prospects for Nathan's success that year.

I had suspended my pursuit of deer for the previous three years to help Nathan. We first went through a hunter's safety course together. I highly recommend it and think it very wise to require youngsters to take it. It best teaches the most important element of hunting—safety. Even adults can benefit from the course.

We then shopped for a good gun that best suited the region we would hunt most, as well as a caliber that Nathan could handle at his young age. We settled on a .30-30 lever action. That gun came in his second season. The first year he hunted, he carried an old 12-gauge single shot and "slugs." His move to a high-powered rifle was, to say the least, an exciting event for him.

For three years, we faithfully trekked into the woods together in various places with no yield of venison. *This year*, we thought, *it's gonna be different.*

The alarm went off at 4:00 a.m. and hurt my slumbering ears on that first of two mornings we would hunt. We had to be on our way at 4:30. The walk would take forty-five minutes or more…uphill all the way.

After breakfast we set out at a careful pace. It was dark, which made for slow going. Fortunately, our host had a four-wheeler and could carry our packs with dry clothes to the top. We were left to carry our heavy guns up some steep terrain. Before long, my lungs were burning as the path kept turning sharply up and up. We weren't prepared for this kind of pain.

At one point, Nathan stopped and bent over double with his face near the ground. The fellow we were climbing with said, "Nathan, are you okay?"

"Yes…" he huffed. "I'm just checking the leaves!" For the rest of the trip, we each used that line more than once, accompanied by a chuckle.

Drenched with sweat, we finally reached the top as dawn began to lighten the sky. As we changed clothes in the cold November air, we did the "chill-bump cha-cha." We also were dancing a little to ease the leg cramps caused by the climb. A pitiful sight!

Nathan and I took a westerly route into a wooded section. We had never been on the property, so at random I chose a place for us to sit as daylight gave more distinct form to the trees and valleys beneath us. After an hour I left Nathan sitting and walked around a little to check things out.

I found a few tracks along a possible run. But the morning passed with no gunfire. I returned to Nathan, and we walked back to a designated spot on the ridge for a noon snack with the other two hunters.

Eating is one of our favorite things to do during a hunt. No food is off-limits in the wild. All concern about fat grams, cholesterol, and calories is cast aside. Somehow we talk ourselves into believing that we burn it all off during the hunt. I don't think my "caloric calculations" would support what we want to believe. My average deer-hunt lunch probably has about 87 grams of fat and 7,028 calories. As for "burn-off," the average deer hunt probably accounts for only 822 calories and burns maybe 2.3 grams of fat. These are, of course, my estimates, but they are probably close to accurate (give or take a thousand calories or so).

Soon lunch was over, and it was time to return to the stands and fight the "sugar blues." (Not to fear, we each had a Butterfinger bar we could inject intravenously at about 3 p.m.) I returned with Nathan to the area we had hunted that morning and sat with him on a flat facing north. The day was getting on, and we had not seen even the flick of a whitetail. About 2:30 I instructed him to stay there till I returned, and I again went to check out the surrounding area. This time, I discovered some serious deer signs. Three well-worked scrapes and some rubs gave away what I thought to be a buck's territory. I made some mental notes on how to find the place again. Right about dark, I returned to Nathan. He looked glum. I felt the same.

The whole day had passed without even an opportunity to feel the heart race. Tomorrow was it. The final day of the season.

I lifted Nathan's spirits with the news of a much better place to take our stand the next morning. Then we headed back down the mountain. The trip back to the cabin was just as painful as the trip up had been. Muscles were awakened that had been asleep for years. I could almost hear the cartilage in my knees shredding as we pounded down the rocky path. And the gun slung over my shoulder was giving me a stiff neck.

That night, we consumed probably an additional pound of saturated fat and a ton of calories. We laughed about killing ourselves with chips, cookies, candy, and hamburgers slathered in mayonnaise. To appease our guilty consciences, we drank diet pop.

We also engaged in another most enjoyable part of a group hunt. Everybody had stories about the events of the day. This guy had a great sighting—three white-tails disappearing into a wooded stand. The next guy saw a huge rack. I should have kept my mouth shut when my turn rolled around. Instead, with full details I shared my discoveries of deer signs. Based on my experience and mostly guessing, I announced where I thought a buck was working and that Nathan and I would like to check out that area when morning light came. I didn't pay attention as the eyebrows went up all around.

After the day we had spent trudging up and down the mountain, sleep came quickly. We were all exhausted from so much fun.

Morning came quickly too. Our host offered Nathan a ride up the mountain on the four-wheeler, but he refused. A little challenge didn't seem to bother him. Actually, I think his hesitation to ride came from hearing that the driver had flipped the machine the week before.

Up on the mountain, we changed into dry clothes again. My heart was racing a little with anticipation as we went to the new stand I had chosen. About ten minutes before daylight, we sat down…and the wait began. Around 8:05 a.m. we heard a real reason to get excited. This noise wasn't chipmunks or squirrels. This sound was different. The leaves had that certain crunch. A buck grunted. In another moment the deer we could not yet see would probably emerge on the flat just below us.

Nathan began to shake with buck fever. "Get ready," I whispered. We waited as blood rang in my ears.

Suddenly the woods exploded with the blast of a high-powered rifle. Probably a .30-06. Crashing hooves went in all directions. In a moment, everything was silent. And then in the distance, we heard the telltale snort.

We sat there devastated. Someone had shot "our" deer. Yet we were oddly excited that something had happened so close to us.

After five minutes or so, we heard a victory yelp about 150 yards down the hill. Some men do that when they've killed a deer. Someone from another club, or perhaps a local landowner, must have come onto the property. We decided not to interrupt the moment.

We didn't see the others in our party all that day. We had planned our own lunch and told the guys that we would not rendezvous till dark. Since this was the last day of the season, we wanted to take full advantage of every hour. After the big disappointment, we quietly moved to another spot, and I decided to stay with Nathan for the remainder of the hunt. I will never forget the end of that day. Even now it hurts to think about it.

Evening came and the sun began to fall. As the light slowly faded, so did the ability to see very far into the woods. I finally said what had to be said. "Son, it's time to go."

Nathan repeated his response each time I said it. "No! Let's wait. He's comin', Daddy!" At last I said, "Nathan, raise your gun and look down the barrel. Can you see the sights?"

"No, Dad."

"Then don't you think we better go?"

It was a cold, silent trip down that mountain. An occasional moan broke the silence because of the pain in our legs. Both of us were also nursing a pain in our hearts from another year without success. It would be a long drive home with nothing to show for our efforts.

When we neared the cabin, we could hear the voices of the two club members. They greeted us with smiles. On the ground next to their car lay a large deer. A nice rack of eight points (a four-by-four, for you Westerners) graced the animal. It was a beautiful whitetail. I asked, "Who's the proud owner of this trophy?" The answer came from the member who had not invited us on the hunt. "He's mine!" We offered congratulations, and then I inquired, "Where did you find him?" As he answered, my blood ran cold.

Of course there was no way to prove what I suspected, but since that evening, I've always wondered if it were true. We did determine that the gun blast that morning came from his .30-06. And we learned that the "victory yelp" was part of his tradition.

The fact was, his club dues entitled him to the deer. But the question was, Did I direct him to that buck with my conversation the night before? Did he intentionally intercept a first deer that he knew a young hunter could have downed? And did it matter to him if he did? The problem was, it was this guy's third kill that year. I'll never really know the truth, but I'll always wonder.

As I stood there in the glow of the parking lights, my heart ached for Nathan. We helped lift the huge buck onto the trunk lid of the man's car and then quickly packed to leave.

As we offered our farewells, I watched Nathan go over to the deer and, with his tender thirteen-year-old hand, stroke the eight points one by one. Then, as if resolved to wait another year, he put his gear in the back and quietly climbed into our truck.

While we drove away, Nathan's eyes were locked onto that deer. Even when we could no longer see it, he continued to stare out the window. I knew why. He didn't want me to see the tears. I hoped he wouldn't look my way because I didn't want him to see mine either.

We bounced lightly in our seats as we drove across the huge field to the dirt road that would lead us back to the main road and then home. Before we reached the pavement, I was struck with the reality that my son and I were sharing one of the most incredible moments I would ever spend with a man. We cried together. The tears didn't last long, but the effects of it will last forever. So will the memory.

A nonhunter might be thinking right now, "What's the big deal? Why get all bent out of shape over a deer?" Well, it's much more than that. Nathan had worked so hard, had dreamed so much, and now had nothing to show for it. For some kids, it's a strikeout that causes the last game of the series to be lost. For others, it's a slip on the ice that loses the medal. For my son that day, it was the one that got away. The same deep disappointment comes for all.

I was grateful to have been there for him when it happened—again. I was able to let him know that the rest of life would not be much different. There would be other disappointments to face, more dreams shattered, and the inevitable feelings of resentment and betrayal that would likely accompany them. From personal experience, I knew the temptation to seek revenge and the desire to give up that would crop up again somewhere along the way. However, I told him that when those hard times came, it would be important to confess those feelings to a brother like we had done that day with our tears. I told him that the only way to stop the destructive cycle of ill feelings that often leads to greater trouble was to forgive.

Before we pulled onto the interstate and headed for Nashville, we visited "cholesterol canyon." We found a pizza joint and drowned our sorrow in a deep-dish, thick-crust, greasy pizza. We washed it down with real Coke. We sat in the booth and discussed everything but deer. (We promised each other to start a diet the next day.)

On the two-hour drive home, Nathan fell asleep. As the miles rolled by, I occasionally looked over at him, and waves of emotions washed across my heart and soul. *He acted like a man today. He showed strength in the face of failure. He's learned so much from this day.* I silently thanked the Lord for this friend and for the bond that had grown stronger as we experienced this small disaster together.

Watching someone you care about go through tough times is never pleasant. As parents, we often want to protect our children and help them avoid the trauma of disappointment. However, there is something valuable in our tough times and losses if we go through them and come out stronger on the other side. That night in the truck I recalled an incident that my wife, Annie, talks about in our book *Gifts Your Kids Can't Break*.

> I have found that I need not fear the struggle my kids go through as they grow and learn. It's the struggle that makes them strong enough to survive. Back on the farm in West Virginia, we hatched baby chicks each spring. I'd see those peepers fighting to peck their way out of the shell, and my heart would melt. So to help the tiny things, I decided to peel the shell away for them. To my disappointment, each chick I helped in this way soon died. I didn't know they were developing the strength they needed to survive during that struggle to free themselves from the eggshell. When I denied them the struggle, I robbed them of the stamina they needed to live in the outside world. My kindness killed them![2]

As Nathan slept that night, I prayed that somehow the day's disappointments would yield the fruit of long-suffering in other areas of his life. I also thanked God for the opportunity to learn important lessons like these while deer hunting with my son.

Over the fireplace in Nathan's den, by the way, there now hangs the mounted head of a buck Nathan took the next year on the second day of the season.

5

The Vapor

One thing I like about bow and muzzleloader season is the weather. A slightly cool morning without the need for heavy clothing is a favorite time to hunt. Although the bugs can be a midday bother here in Tennessee during the early part of the season, the problem can be solved with proper netting.

I would much rather experience the mid-autumn mild temperatures and endure a few gnats and mosquitoes (but I hate snakes) than sit in bitter-cold weather. However, because my blood type is "doe positive" instead of O-positive, I'll go out and freeze just for the chance of even a sighting. There have been a few mornings that I've been known to look a little like the man in *Jeremiah Johnson* who was found frozen to death with a 50-caliber Hawken clutched to his chest.

For me, hunting from a tree stand in extremely cold weather is out of the question for two reasons. First, the wind up there seems to pass right through even the best of clothing. And second, if I were to fall, I'm afraid I would break like a china plate on a concrete floor. I would rather snuggle up on the ground against a tree and pursue some degree of comfort, especially for my feet. If my toes hurt, I cannot concentrate.

So my stand is on the ground in the dead of winter, even though the risk of detection is greater.

The times are too numerous to mention when, during one of those bitter-cold days, I've heard that familiar crunch in the leaves or caught a flickering glimpse of a whitetail in the distance. As my heart rate begins to rise to hummingbird levels and the deer approaches, I usually begin that habitual rehearsal of what to do. First (if I can remember my name), I need to repeat *Calm down!* to myself several times. Then, according to the type of equipment I'm using, I quickly visualize the steps to make the best shot. I then scan the woods for more deer. If there is a lead doe, I wait to see if she is showing any signs that a buck is behind her.

As hard as I try to do everything right, one thing has always frustrated me about being on the ground in frigid weather. It's that annoying choo-choo-like puff of vapor that escapes with every excited breath. I've tried holding it in, but fainting is no fun. I've tried blowing down over my chin toward my chest, but I look like a pot of boiling water on a stove. I've tried breathing only through my nose, but the "freezing of the nose hair bringeth pain."

I'm convinced that deer can spot the movement of fog in the air, and that can alert them to the presence of something unusual. I may be wrong about it, but I still try to avoid the "vapor trail." As hard as I try, I'm never successful.

I can't remember when I first noticed the lesson in the vapor. I'm sure it was not during a deer sighting, but rather in those hours of waiting when I didn't see anything. It was just me, my cold feet, and the fog I manufactured. I was sort of playing with it, seeing how far out I could blow the vapor. Which direction will the wind take it? (That can be helpful.) What shapes can I make with it? *Hey, that looked like a plate of biscuits and gravy!* (Whoever said sitting on a deer stand is boring?) *But enough playing around,* I thought, *I better get back to hunting. That's why I'm enduring this pain. Right?*

The next breath of vapor somehow caught my attention. Why that particular one? I don't know. But what happened next was special. That vapor of breath hung for a moment and then disappeared. I did it again, and it too went away. The next and the next vanished as well. That's when the Scripture in James 4:14 crossed my freezing brain. "You are just a vapor that appears for a little while and then vanishes away."

I didn't want to think of that! There I was having a wonderful time, when suddenly I had to be faced with a noble thought. Can't this wait till Sunday morning?

It wouldn't go away. That vapor was me out there appearing and disappearing. That was Annie, Nathan, Heidi, my parents, in-laws, brothers, sisters, neighbors, all of us. (It was about then that I could have used a distraction from the impending depression. Something like a ten-point buck would have been nice, but he didn't appear.) I couldn't believe it. Here I was on a deer stand and thinking things like, *I'm only here for a little while, a blade of grass in the yard. I'm a leaf headed toward October, an ocean wave that washes up on shore and is never seen again.*

Unable to escape the thoughts, I began to seriously consider my own brief life—my "hang time." The realization that my life was like the brief appearance of vapor that quickly disappeared had captured my thoughts. *What will I do with the time I have here? I must make it count for something worthwhile.* In doing so, perhaps a part of me could go on in time.

Like the lady who taught a twelve-year-old boy how to play the guitar, and her music now echoes through his own melodies. Now he has a son who plays tunes heard years before when his grandmother used to play. That lady is my own mother. I long, as she did, to do something to ensure that others in the future will know that I was once visible.

How wisely will we use our time? Have we ever considered what a valuable gift it is? I once heard a challenging scenario that describes time's value. It goes as follows. Suppose I was a banker and I said to you, "If you'll come to my bank each day, I will give you $86,400 to spend any way you wish. The only condition is that at the end of each day you return the portion you do not spend. It will not be added to your account in savings, but instead, it will be destroyed. You must promise to spend the money wisely. Do you agree?"

Sure you would! "Mama didn't raise no fool!" you would probably say. I have a feeling you would make every effort to spend the entire amount and as wisely as possible.

The sobering thought is that each of us goes to the bank of heaven each day and receives 86,400 seconds. When the day is finished, that which we didn't spend or that which we used unwisely is lost forever.

I pray that God would help us, in our hang time, to be a breath of fresh air to our spouses, kids, family, and neighbors. I pray that He would help us not to waste precious time and to take careful notice of how we act toward those we love. I also pray that in our short days, His purpose for us in this world will be accomplished.

A momentary encounter with real truths, like the one I was pondering that morning, always yields eternal fruit. I knew I would leave the deer stand that day a different person.

Just how quickly does a man's life seem to pass through time? Perhaps it seems as brief as the time it would take you to read the following lyric.

Seasons of a Man

I am the springtime
When everything seems so fine
Whether rain or sunshine
You will find me playing
Days full of pretending
When a dime is a lot to be spending
A time when life is beginning
I am the springtime

I am the summer
When days are warm and longer
And the call comes to wander
But I can't go far from home
When the girls become a mystery
And you're barely passing history
And thinking, *Old is when you're thirty*
I am the summer

I am the autumn days
When changes come so many ways
Looking back I stand amazed
That time has gone so quickly
When love is more than feelings
It's fixing bikes and painting ceilings

The Vapor

It's when you feel a cold wind coming
I am the autumn days

I am the winter
When days are cold and bitter
And the days I can remember
Number more than the days to come.
When you ride instead of walking
When you barely hear the talking
And goodbyes are said too often
I am the winter days

But I'll see spring again in heaven
And it'll last forever[3]

6

Open to Suggestions

Planning a multiday deer hunt is a process that can occupy the thoughts, conversations, and daydreams of anyone who enjoys big-game hunting. Such was the case for my four-day stay at my father-in-law's farm in West Virginia. I made a checklist as long as my arm of all the things I would need, from boots to bullets. I checked it twice and didn't miss a detail. I schemed and plotted my course of action. I had "it" bad. By the time the first day rolled around, my expectations for a successful hunt were so high, I nearly ran up the mountain to my stand.

The place I had chosen to hunt was on the remote west end of the property, away from houses and humans. My stand was well placed. Deer signs were all around. The weather was great, and I had a .30-06 bolt action that was sighted in and could make three shot patterns the size of a half dollar at 100 yards. I was ready! However, at the end of the third day, I hadn't fired a shot. I didn't understand it. I hadn't seen one single deer.

When the fourth and final morning rolled around, I didn't have much hope as I trudged back to the same stand.

When 10:30 a.m. came and still no whitetails appeared, I packed up my gear and headed back.

I returned to my in-laws' house for lunch, and Mr. Williamson joined me at the table. He could tell I was frustrated coming back each day without filling my tag, so he offered me some advice. "Steve, if you want to see deer, I suggest you hunt up here behind the house. Quite often I've seen a buck or two come out right at the corner of the fence on top of the hill. Hardly anyone has hunted around the house. I recommend you walk into the woods about seventy-five paces and set up facing away from the field. Around 4:30, be watching."

Believing that being open to suggestions is a virtue, I decided to abandon my fruitless plans and follow his. At about 4:15 I settled onto a stump near the place Mr. Williamson pointed out. Within fifteen minutes I heard a familiar sound— the light crunching of deer hooves pressing into the dry November leaves. Sure enough, there he came. I watched the buck for a few minutes. Finally, his eyes disappeared behind a tree, and I slowly raised my rifle. I took aim on his vitals and pulled the trigger.

The buck dropped a few yards from where he was standing. I took in a deep sigh of relief, for it all seemed to happen so fast, and I needed to gather my thoughts. Then I remembered that a part of the process of harvesting an animal is to record the time of the kill on the game tag. I found my pen, and just as I was writing down the time, it hit me. My watch said 4:35. I had made the shot about five minutes before, which put it right at 4:30 p.m. Mr. Williamson's words echoed through my head. I sat there amazed.

How did he know that my best chance for success would be in this place? I also wondered, *How did he know for sure the deer would be here this evening?* The answer was simple. For years he had walked every inch of that land until he knew that farm like the back of his hardworking hand. He probably knew when a tree fell on the back side of the property. Why shouldn't he know the habits of the deer that roamed around the farm?

As I stood there looking at the nice-sized buck, I was grateful for his advice. I was also glad I had chosen to follow it. I shiver to think what I would have missed had I not been willing to listen to him. It was necessary for my success. In fact, any knowledge I possess of hunting is simply a collection of bits of wisdom I have gleaned from other hunters through the years. From conversations in pickup trucks over thermoses of hot coffee to the informative articles in the hundreds of outdoor magazines I've read, I've managed to gather enough know-how to be a successful deer hunter in nearly all of the thirty-plus seasons I've enjoyed in the woods.

Not only in the art of deer hunting is the advice of others a valuable treasure, but even more it is necessary to accept guidance in areas of life beyond the woods. As a father, for instance, I have always needed help. From changing a dirty diaper (field dressing a deer is not half as gross!) to explaining what it means when I say, "This is going to hurt me more than you," I need input from the experts. Fortunately, my best source of instruction was my own dad. He taught me well by being a great dad himself. He had no idea he was teaching a future father some effective techniques as he rubbed the back of my little head while driving down the highway. When he gently placed that same hand on my shoulder as he prayed for me, he was offering another lesson that I still use today as a dad.

Think of all the skills needed in life to succeed. All of us need leadership in our roles as spouses and sportsmen, fiancés and financiers (these sound similar, don't they?), friends and family members. In each of these fields, someone who is knowledgeable, whether a professional or a wise friend, is of great value.

For example, what kind of mates would we be without the helpful hints from other men? As a husband, I am always willing to learn. Of course, not all advice has been useful. One fellow summed up his philosophy on marriage by saying, "I don't try to run her life, and I don't try to run mine!" It seemed to work for him, but I have found a bit of wisdom from another brother to be more beneficial. He said, "In all you do, seek to please your wife first. Be a servant to her, and your marriage will improve daily." His godly advice has stood the test of time and trials. I'm a better husband because of it. My role as a man is not threatened by making a bed or washing the dishes. Instead, I realize that these types of service testify to one's manhood. I know this because of the wisdom a friend shared from Matthew 20:26: "Whoever wishes to become great among you shall be your servant." Now *that's* good advice.

The exchange of wisdom between two people is a blessed event. Good advice, the fruit of experience, tastes sweet to those who hunger for wisdom. Of course, that exchange takes place most often in times of crisis. You may have heard this tale about a man who was skydiving. He jumped out of the plane, but when he attempted to open his parachute, it didn't operate. As he rapidly fell toward the hard earth below, he scrambled to try to make the thing work. That's when he noticed another fellow coming up quickly from the direction of the ground. As they passed in midair, the skydiver screamed, "Hey! Do you know anything about parachutes?" The other fellow yelled back, "No! Do you know anything about gas stoves?"

The two fellows in that story were more than willing to seek help. To get some advice earlier would have been the best thing to do. Those who can cast aside any reservation caused by hindrances like pride or self-consciousness and seek insight from others are to be commended. And just as Mr. Williamson noticed my silence in the face of a disappointing turn of events and offered his help, we need to keep our eyes open for those around us who may be facing a difficult time and need some wisdom. Just maybe we can help someone open the chute before it's too late. (As for the guy with the gas-stove problem—I'm open to suggestions!)

7

Sunrise

Something about walking by myself to a deer stand before daylight makes me a candidate for goose bumps. Not the little ones caused by a brisk wind shooting down the collar. No, I'm referring to the big bumps that jump up because of the fear of what might be hiding behind the next tree. The kind that makes your skin resemble that of a freshly plucked chicken. I've been in the woods long before dawn often enough to know that the old imagination factory can really process some interesting stuff when the woods are black as coal.

Somehow, a flashlight in the dark is no comfort to me. Whatever is out there will detect my presence even sooner because of the light. So usually I enter the woods with my eyes wide open and pupils dilated to the size of dimes.

Remember the character played by Don Knotts in the movie *The Ghost and Mr. Chicken*? That's what I can look like as I walk alone to a stand. I look like Mr. Macho dressed to kill, yet I'm prepared to pick my heart up off the ground at the first strange sound.

I don't have to be alone when fear grabs ahold. I'll never forget the morning my friend Mark Smith and I headed up a hillside in Tennessee with our bows. I was in the lead, and we were being unusually quiet. It was unbelievably dark. A thick cover of clouds hid a crescent moon, and the woods looked like the inside of a closed casket. Even with Mark a few steps back, I felt jumpy that morning. I stopped to take a breather. Mark took the few extra steps to catch up and then stopped. Suddenly, the silence of the woods was split wide open with an ear-piercing screech. I felt as if I were going to have a coronary on the spot. Straight overhead in the oak tree perched a creature that can take more years off a life than high cholesterol. It was a vicious, two-legged beast that has a most effective device when it comes to stopping a heart. It was what we call a screech owl, and screech it did.

If you've never heard this bird let out a frightening shriek in the middle of the night, then you're in for the scare of your life. It screamed right above me. I screamed too. It was a horrifying sound, and my flesh crawled on my bones.

My audible response was not repeatable. Actually, I don't really know what I said. You would have to ask Mark. As I stood there consuming a liter of poisonous adrenaline, my friend was thoroughly enjoying life's best medicine: laughter. I think I had tears on my cheeks as that cursed bird winged its way into the darkness. (I've always wanted to ask Mark if I maintained some level of verbal decency in that moment, but to be honest, I'm not sure I want to know. I do know he's still laughing about it!)

One nice thing about darkness is that it makes you appreciate the light. During one hunt in a recent season, I parked at the end of a long meadow on Bear Creek Farm in Tennessee about an hour before daylight. I closed the door to my harbor of safety, hid the ignition keys, and walked up the field alone in the pitch black. All the leaves still clung to the branches on the trees, and the thick canopy made the woods seem even more dense and foreboding. I arrived at my stand about thirty minutes before daybreak and settled in. I was grateful to still be alive and to not have been eaten by a ferocious camo monster. The stars still shone bright overhead, and I knew the morning would present a beautiful skyline. Also, I knew that once daylight came, I could relax, hunt, and not feel hunted.

Slowly the first golden rays of sunlight peeped over the horizon. As I've said before, this is one of my favorite times to be in the woods. As if someone were manually rotating a dimmer light switch, the growing daylight made the shadows give way to distinct shapes of trees and other forest growth. I could see that what had looked like the swamp creature of Cheatham County in the predawn darkness was just an ivy-covered oak.

About 30 minutes after the initial show, as though the warm-up act had completed its part, there to the east came the main attraction. Slowly rising above the horizon—so slow in fact that its movement could be noticed only in sections of time—came that huge ball of brilliant fire.

Finally, it was *sunrise*! Just saying that word brings comfort from the dark as well as relief and warmth. It's a welcome event. In fact, I've heard that the morning light has caused some who were dying to hold on for another day. Something about a sunrise moves our soul. When it happens, it makes me grateful for my sight.

There is a similar dawning that I've come to view as just as enjoyable and incredible. It's the moments when, after wandering around in the darkness of misunderstanding, the light comes on and a truth is revealed. Just as there's relief for this worried hunter when the sun comes up, there's a certain freedom that follows the revelation of truth in other areas of life.

In some cases, the light of understanding suddenly reveals a fact that is valuable but not necessarily earth-shattering. Like discovering that the two tabs on the top of an audiocassette can be removed to protect a valuable recording.* Or finding out that you can put Scotch tape over the place where the tabs once were and record over the contents of a cassette. Do you remember small discoveries like that? Aren't they fun?

However, some revelations are lifealtering, even to the point of yielding a freedom that changes one's entire character and personality. The following song lyrics describe an example of a newfound liberty in a life. In this case, the person was bound by unforgiveness until an important revelation transformed his thoughts.

The Key

I cannot tell you how I was hurt but I'll tell you I've had some tears
I cannot tell you who it was that turned my trust into fears
So I took the pieces of my broken heart
I built some prison walls
And there I've held that offender for years

---

* Remember cassette tapes? If so, you, too, were around in the 1900s!

And this is what I thought
He'll never know freedom
As long as I live, I'll never give him freedom

Then one day the Visitor came to this prison in my heart
He said, "You ought to know the truth about the one behind the bars
Yes, he's weak and he's weary, he has not smiled in years
And you have been successful at keeping his eyes filled with tears
But oh, how he longs for his freedom
These words are the key
They first came from me
"Father, forgive them"
Come, let me show you how to use them"

He said, "Don't you know the offender is rarely the one in pain.
Instead the one who will not forgive is the one who wears the chains"
So I opened up the prison door, I used forgiveness as the key
And when I let that prisoner go
I found that it was me

And oh how sweet is the freedom
It came on the day
When my heart prayed
"Father, forgive them
Father, forgive them"[4]

How this heart must have danced for joy when the light finally came on. Also, don't you know that the ripple effect of forgiveness caused a cleansing that began in that soul and divinely extended to those around him? When a heart is inundated with the powerful light of liberty, that's when the evil and destructive forces that torment a soul will flee like roaches that scatter in a kitchen when the light comes on. Destruction ceases. The light of truth begins to heal. Darkness cannot win over light. The glow of one small candle cannot be snuffed out by all the darkness in the universe.

In many hearts, the bitterness, the anger, the unforgiveness, and a host of other possible sins have caused the bondage of night to last much too long. The sun needs to rise. A revelation cries to take place. What would it take for the light of truth to begin to peek over the ridge? The only answer to that question is found in what takes place each morning here on the earth.

The next time you're in your deer stand as daybreak arrives, consider this: The sun does not actually rise. The event we have always called "sunrise" is a divine illusion. What happens is far more spectacular than we may have realized. Instead of rising, the sun remains stationary. It doesn't revolve around the planet. Instead, it is the earth that makes the move. As it spins on its axis, the earth bows to the sun. What a beautiful picture of the only solution for a human heart that suffers from a void of heavenly light. It must humble itself in the sight of a never-changing God. And at that moment, His light rises up, warms the heart, and blesses all who see it.

God longs to be revealed in every heart, including yours. If you have not allowed Him that divine action, please remember that Jesus said, "I am the Light of the world; he who follows Me will not walk in darkness, but will have the Light of life" (John 8:12). Today is the day of salvation! Let Him into your heart. Then He will gladly say of you, "You are the light of the world" (Matthew 5:14). May the Lord give you courage to allow Him to be the Sonrise in your heart.

8

Things Aren't Always as They Seem

The alarm woke me at 3:45 a.m. Because I was going to be spending a day in the woods, I had no problem getting out of bed. On the mornings of a planned hunt, you would think there was a catapult built into my mattress, triggered by the alarm clock.

Of course, on days when our concert schedule calls for an early morning departure, getting up can prove to be quite painful. It's not that I don't like my work. I just don't find it enjoyable to risk my life once again on an airplane that was probably built by the lowest bidder. (Flying is no fun for me. I agree with the fellow who said, "I wish they wouldn't call airports 'terminals!'") Also, I don't care to drive in rental cars on strange highways where people are talking on the phone, doing their hair, and going through file folders. Furthermore, I'm not crazy about laying my head on another hotel-room pillow that I know has been drooled on by dozens or maybe hundreds of other people. I prefer my own drool, thank you!

But this was a morning I was going to get a break from that routine by being in the wild, so waking up was no problem. By 4:10 I was happily on my way to Hickman County, Tennessee, and at 5:30 a.m. I was comfortably perched in my portable treetop easy chair and enjoying my early start at engaging in "think time."

As I sat there in the brisk morning air, searching my mind for interesting memories, I had to be careful not to do what I used to see my Grandpa Steele do while he sat on the front porch of his house. I can still picture him sitting for a long while and not uttering a sound. Then suddenly, he would start to laugh out loud. Whenever I was there, I would ask, "What are ya thinking about, Grandpa?" I always enjoyed his answer because there would be some humorous story in his thoughts.

The same thing has happened to me in the quietness of a deer stand. I have recalled some events in my life that have generated a chuckle or two. In the woods, I have to control myself, however, lest by laughing out loud I give away my presence and scare away the deer.

That morning I had one of those fond recollections. It involved my Grandma Chapman. I remembered she was sitting on the back porch of the big house where she raised her eleven kids. All of them had moved away—about 100 yards. My dad and mom lived even closer than that in a nearby small frame house until I was ten years old.

It was a summer day in my seventh year. Grandma was snapping the green beans resting in her apron and dropping them in a pan on the floor next to her chair. My mother decided it would be a good day to complete the job of cleaning the eaves of the house. With a broom and a kitchen chair in her hands, she headed out the front door with my sister and me in tow. We had been given brown paper bags to use for gathering the cobwebs and old birds' nests Mom knocked to the ground with the broom.

She climbed onto the chair and proceeded to gouge the broom into the eaves on the backside of that little white house. Suddenly, Mom got the surprise of her life when she stuck the broom into a hornet's nest. The angry hornets came swarming toward us, making an ominous sound. It was a frightening sight as well. They looked like "quarter pounders" with massive wings. We all screamed and threw our arms about and danced around, trying to avoid the hornets' revenge.

I don't know how I thought of it, but as fast as my little six-year-old legs could carry me, I ran toward the dirt road near our house. I knew it would lead to Grandpa Chapman's store, where I would find safety. When I took off, one lone hornet decided I was going to be the object of his retaliation. Someone was going to pay for destroying its home. I could hear it angrily buzzing behind me. I screamed at the top of my lungs and pumped my legs like an Olympian running the 100-meter dash.

Right at my heels, I was thankful to discover, was my mom. Realizing her son was under attack, she decided to rescue me by killing the hornet with the broom.

As I dashed down the little dirt road toward the store, my mom swatted repeatedly at the hornet while running close behind. By this time, we were in full view of Grandma. She heard me screaming as I ran, and she saw my mother wildly swinging the broom behind me. However, she couldn't see the hornet. I always get a chuckle out of imagining what she must have thought. I'm sure it was the worst. In fact, the next green bean she snapped was probably, in her imagination, my mother's neck!

I made it to the store and was still an "unstung hero." Unfortunately, the porch was too high for me to jump onto quickly. When I slowed down to do it, I felt the hornet bury its fiery stinger into the back of my leg. It felt like a baseball bat had knocked me to the concrete. I went sliding across the porch, gathering "road rash" on my little belly. I remember crying in pain as I lay on the porch of the supermarket.

About that time, my Grandma appeared on the other end of the storefront. She marched over to my mom and promptly gave her a good talking to about what she had just seen a few moments earlier. Oh, how I wish now that I would have had the wisdom and composure to quickly stand up, brush my little self off, dry my tears, and say, "Grandma, things aren't as they seem!" However, she eventually realized the truth of what had happened, and all was well (except for the throbbing pain in the back of my little leg).

After all these years, I still shiver when I remember my bout with that hornet. But that morning on the deer stand, I enjoyed a controlled chuckle once again when I thought of my grandmother's perspective of my predicament. Though it was traumatic, the years that have passed have helped me glean some valuable insights from the story.

As hard as I ran from that angry hornet, it still caught me and inflicted its pain in my life. I wish I could have outrun it, but I suppose there was something to learn from it. Perhaps I needed to realize that other painful experiences would some-day overtake me. And while going through them, I would need someone to bat-tle on my behalf and be there to comfort me if hard times knocked me down. As it turned out, I found myself in another terrifying situation only two years later.

At the age of eight, I became quite sick and developed a swelling in my throat that was accompanied by a loss of weight and a darkness under my eyes. Alarmed at the symptoms, my parents took me to see the doctor. They held me tightly as he examined me and then announced that an operation would be necessary. I spent three fear-filled days in the hospital as they did several tests on the tissue they had removed from the lymph nodes in my neck. The frightening buzz of the word "cancer" gripped my parents. They saw me running scared.

Just as my mother tried to kill the hornet that day with the broom, I know my parents were flailing the weapon of prayer at the attacker that was trying to harm their son. Yet for some reason—still unknown—the "hornet" did its dastardly deed. What then? All that remained for them was to stay close and offer comfort and help. And that they did by placing me into God's hands as well as the care of a compassionate and knowledgeable doctor.

We were all relieved to hear that the entire tumor had been removed and that my life would go on. The doctor said that had we waited a few more weeks, the outcome would have been far different.

Going back to the hornet horror, Grandma was puzzled by the scene in the distance as I ran screaming down the road ahead of my mother. In the same way, others will stand by in bewilderment and watch as loved ones go through tough times. Tragedies like divorce, illness, injury, or the loss of a job or self-respect will leave us all with questions. Sometimes we will learn the truth, just as Grandma Chapman learned the truth about the bee and me. But sometimes we will never know the reason for the "sting" in the lives of loved ones. When the hard times come, they need to know they're not alone. We need to be there for them when they buckle under the pain.

As I enjoyed my recollection of my grandmother that morning on the deer stand, I began to really miss her and my other grandparents. The joy of their mem-ory often intensifies the sadness of their absence. I miss my Grandma Steele. I long to sit beside her again in the porch swing. I miss hearing my Grandpa Chapman say to us, "Put out your feet and be a good horse!" I miss Grandpa Steele's funny stories. And I miss those three special, heartwarming words my Grandma Chapman would always say to me when I went to her house: "Want a sandwich?"

I often grieve over their absence. Yet I know I can do so with hope. I believe we all will see our departed loved ones whose lives belonged to Christ. I have an assurance that the painful grief in the hearts of the living who are left behind by those who pass on will be eliminated on the glorious day described in 1 Thessalonians 4:16-17 (KJV):

> The Lord himself shall descend from heaven with a shout, with the voice of the archangel, and with the trump of God: and the dead in Christ shall rise first: Then we which are alive and remain shall be caught up together with them in the clouds, to meet the Lord in the air: and so shall we ever be with the Lord.

I look forward to that day! I have a feeling that you do as well. And until that wonderful day arrives, may we be found faithful in the race against all that would knock us down. And if someone has been knocked down by the hardships of life, let's give him a hand and help him up.

I wondered that day in the tree stand what I might have been able to see if my spiritual eyes were opened. Could I look into the heavens and see the great cloud of witnesses mentioned in Hebrews 12:1? I felt that were I allowed to do so, I would see my Grandma Chapman leaning over the balcony of heaven saying, "Steve, hold on. Don't give up. Be faithful to finish the race. Lay aside every weight that would easily ensnare you. What you see with your eyes may sometimes look bleak, but remember, I have a different view of things. Things aren't as they seem. God is in control!"

Thank God for deer stands and "think" time!

9

The Great Surprise

I looked at my watch and whispered, "Seven-twenty. They should be here in about ten minutes." On a couple of other mornings, I'd observed a herd of deer enter the lower end of the field I was hunting around 7:30, but each time they were too far away and out of range for my muzzleloader. Choosing to set up closer to that spot and on the ground under a wide-trunk oak, I closed the gap a good seventy-five yards on where I thought they would show up. If they did, the range for the weighty .50 caliber bullet would be a manageable eighty to ninety yards.

Though they were a little late, five females appeared. One by one they stepped into the open and began browsing. They had no idea I was watching as they spread out and fed. When their eyes were focused on searching for edible grasses, I slowly raised the heavy-barreled gun to my knee. I studied the group. There were two mothers, two youngsters, and a doe that appeared to be "dry"—old enough to be a mom but without an offspring. She would be my choice since, I admit, I can be a softie when it comes to separating moms and kids.

I had my eye on the fawnless doe, but she seemed to deliberately keep the others between us. I wondered if she possessed some sort of special sense that she was being considered as a candidate for freezer wrap. Finally she meandered away from the foursome. Now all she had to do was turn broadside, and I'd have my bead on her. That positioning seemed to take forever, but at last it was time to pull the hammer back and drop it on the cap.

When the charge exploded, the area beneath the oak became a container of smoke so thick I had to quickly crawl out to the side a couple of feet just to get a reading on how many deer were running toward the woods. Were there four...or five? Their departure happened so fast I couldn't tell.

When the breeze finally carried the smoke wall away, I stood up and dug for my binoculars. While scanning the area where the deer had been feeding, I saw a tuft of white fur.

"Aha! One down!" I said. I confess it felt good to have a plan, stick with it, and watch it work out successfully. Since there was no one else around, I engaged in a little self-congratulating as I gathered up my backpack and headed across the field to check out the reward of my well-schemed hunt. Yes, even the words "Yoo da man!" tumbled out of my mouth. I grinned, not knowing my gloating was going to be short-lived.

When I got a mere twelve feet or so from the downed doe, she suddenly stood up, looked at me, turned her head toward the woods where her friends had gone, and bolted away. It was like she'd been shot out of a giant slingshot! So much for my assumption that she'd quickly expired as a result of a well-placed shot.

And what did I do in that moment? Nothing. Why? Because when I'd seen her through the binoculars looking lifeless, I'd decided she was dead. Because of that errant judgment, I hadn't reloaded. Was that a costly decision? Yep. And it wasn't laziness or an attempt to conserve powder and bullets. Nope. It was simply a bad call on my part. I should have approached the doe ready to react with a deal-closing shot if necessary.

As I stood there feeling the pain of being snookered by a female, I listened hard. I was hoping to hear a crashing sound in the dry leaves where she had escaped. You know, the audible evidence that would tell me her "dead run" was just that. Unfortunately, no sound like that happened. With that, I knew the rest of the morning would be spent back at the cabin waiting a couple of hours and then coming back to search for a blood trail.

The problem with the waiting was the replaying of the scene in my head. There was all the kicking my own behind that I had to endure for being so careless. How could I have failed to reload the muzzleloader after the shot? I *always* did—but not that day.

Almost three hours passed before I headed back to the field to track the wounded doe. I didn't find any red stuff until I entered the woods. And then the drops were few and far between. With each passing minute, my dejection sank lower and lower. I was caught in the mire of regret. When the trail completely stopped, I sighed deep and faced the defeat. I'd invested nearly four hours in the search and was finally convinced my shot had not mortally wounded the doe. Instead, it obviously just addled her for a few minutes—just enough time to allow me to show up so I could learn a hard lesson.

If I had a dollar for every time the sight of that doe standing up within a few feet of me has played in my noggin, I'd be a wealthy man. Each time it rewinds and rolls again, I feel the sting of my blunder. But there is at least one redeemable thought that came to me during one of the replays—a comparison that has helped heal the wound of the experience. It has to do with my reaction to the resurrection that took place in the field that morning and the reaction of those who discovered another resurrection that took place more than 2,000 years ago.

That doe looked very dead when I walked up to it. She was lying there completely motionless, seemingly ready for my post-kill surgery. In my mind's eye I can still see that flash of a slight flinch in her side when I got close—just before she sprang to her feet and looked right at me.

I do believe if there had been a recording of my face when that critter bolted upright, I'd be a doubly rich man. I could have sold the footage to any number of ad agencies who were searching for a model of utter surprise for a commercial. I'm sure my jaw dropped, my brow tensed, and my head went forward. I may have even gasped an exasperated, "What? Hey! Where you goin', girl?" as the doe sped away.

When Jesus was crucified by the Romans, the apostle Peter knew his Lord and friend was dead. Peter had no cause to believe otherwise. And unlike the doe that was only addled, Jesus had physically died and was even placed in a tomb. When Mary went to the resting place of Jesus's body early on the first day of the week while it was still dark, she saw the stone in front of the opening had been rolled away. She ran to Simon Peter and John to report that Jesus's body had been taken, and she didn't know where they had carried it.

Hearing Mary's announcement, the two men took off running to the gravesite. The more fleet-footed John won the race and peered inside the tomb, but he didn't go in. No doubt his face showed amazement and maybe even bewilderment as he surveyed the inside and surrounding area.

But Peter, in typical fashion, didn't stop at the door. He boldly shot right by John and entered the tomb to verify firsthand that Mary's report was accurate. John then followed him inside, and they found that the tomb did not contain a body. Only the graveclothes were in there.

Here's my point. Even though my look of surprise over the doe that seemingly came back to life might be a weak comparison, I believe that experience gave me a small glimpse at what astonishment must have been evident on Peter's and John's faces when they realized their Master had risen from the dead. Can you imagine?

I sincerely hope that when I reach the other side and am in that place where time is no longer a concern, God, who is not bound by time, will take me back to that moment. I would love to see the expressions of total awe that had to be visible on the disciples' faces as a result of such a great surprise. Yes, my look of surprise was different from theirs in that mine was spoiled by the knowledge of failure. Their faces, on the other hand, were most assuredly brightened with joy, victory, relief, and blessed hope that never disappointed them once they realized what had happened. And this is true for everyone who chooses to believe in and accept Jesus as their Savior and Lord!

10

Good Waiting

After a season closes, deer hunters wait about eight long months for the opening day of the next season. With so many days on the calendar to put X's through, it's no wonder that those of us who cherish the hunt have a lot of trouble leaving the woods at the end of that first day. But the reluctance to exit a stand doesn't stop on opening day for me. Throughout the season, leaving the woods is rarely something I want to do. A meeting that can't be postponed, a flight to catch, looming darkness, lightning bolts, loggers taking the tree I'm sitting in, a son or daughter getting married, and another season closing are just a few reasons to have to wrap up the day and head to the house. Though I am very much aware that I can easily make trouble for myself if I don't go home when I need to, I am very often guilty of trying to squeeze as many minutes in the deer stand as I possibly can.

This short in my wiring has been sparking for a long time. I recall when I was sixteen years old and deer hunting in the McClintic Wildlife Station north of Point Pleasant, West Virginia. I stayed on a ground stand until I couldn't see the sights at the end of my .30-30 barrel, which was a short carbine, hardly twenty inches long. I unwillingly stood up and, because I didn't have a light, began stumbling back to the gravel road where my folks' car was parked.

As I neared the light green Chevy, which seemed to softly glow in the evening darkness, I thought I saw the dark form of a human standing next to it. I halted.

The form didn't move…I didn't move. The silhouette and I were in a standoff. I gripped my rifle tightly and slowly began to raise it to my hip. My heart rate shot up, and I gasped for breath as I searched for the hammer with my thumb. I pressed on it gently and waited in full alert.

Suddenly the silhouette spoke.

"Gettin' back to your vehicle a little late, aren't you, mister?"

Obviously the title "mister" revealed the stranger didn't know he was facing down a kid who was trembling from head to toe like a nervous Barney Fife. I swallowed hard and offered as confident a reply as I could muster.

"Yep."

Any more words than one and the tremble in my voice would have been easily detected.

"Is there a reason you're so late?"

"Is there a reason you're asking?" I shot back.

That's when the flashlight abruptly came on. Little did I know, as I stood there totally blinded by the light he must have taken from the front end of a locomotive, I had just challenged the integrity and authority of a game warden.

When he got a good look at me and my stance with the rifle he must have seen that I was tense and needed a bit of calming.

"Young man, I'm an officer with the West Virginia Department of Natural Resources, and I must ask you, is that rifle still loaded?"

"Yes, sir." (Somehow my manners returned!)

"Then please unload it right there where you're standing."

"Yes, sir."

As I put the four cartridges in my jacket and dug through my pants pockets for my license, I explained to the officer that the reason I was so late getting to the car was that I really liked to wait as long as I could before leaving the stand. He was very kind to listen to my excuse, but he showed no sympathy as he offered a brief but stern lecture about the dangers of being alone in the woods after dark. Thankfully, he sent me on my way without further consequences.

I'd like to report that his warning did some good, but quite honestly, it didn't connect. To this day I'm still likely to wait until the last possible millisecond before leaving a deer stand. But the good news is, I think I finally figured out the main reason I'm wired in such a weird way. It's because I enjoy "good" waiting.

Like most Americans these days, I do enough waiting that is tedious. You know, the kind that yields little in the way of delight. For example, I frequently get in airport security checkpoint lines where the only happy people present are those who haven't flown since September 11, 2001 (rare birds they are!). They seem to be totally oblivious to the fact that their waiting might result in being randomly chosen for a complete body search. They appear ignorantly blissful, not realizing that when they finally reach the TSA agent's control, all their personal belongings might be removed from their bags and strewn around the area for the disgustingly curious to see and for sticky-fingered thieves to assess. That kind of waiting I can do without.

Or how about the unfortunate and frustrating standstills that many of us have driven up to on interstate highways? Isn't that some of the worst waiting we must endure? We're driving along, getting somewhere quickly, when suddenly the red brake lights come on ahead of us and remain illuminated, warning us that the world up there is coming to a stop. That's when the sinking feeling hits us and we whisper a hopeless, "Oh, no! How long is this gonna take?" And you know it's really bad when you pull up behind the last car and the people who were total strangers prior to the standstill are out playing rummy on the hoods of their vehicles, cooking hamburgers on their tailgates, and exchanging addresses because friendships have developed. That's not good waiting either.

And there is nothing pleasant when sitting in a doctor's holding room. After tolerating the delay in the main lobby and dreading the inevitable probing, poking, and pinching, then having to sit alone in a smaller room for who knows how long and look at disgustingly ugly pictures of the insides of sick people—that's lousy waiting. (And to think we pay big bucks for the privilege too!) Then there are the lab test results. With all the technology available, why must we wait two weeks after a biopsy to find out if that lump is cancer? That's one I've yet to figure out. I'm sure some lab person will seek me out now to explain it to me, but whatever he or she says, it won't make the drawn-out, nail-biting vigil by the phone any more fun.

But there is a good kind of waiting. It's when there's something positive at the end. Thankfully, there are plenty of lines in which to linger that offer better rewards—enough of them at least to balance out most of the bad waiting. One of my more memorable experiences of voluntarily waiting in a line because of the thrill on the far end took place in Ohio around 1979.

I was in a band that was invited to perform during "Christian Day" at King's Island near Cincinnati. We arrived plenty early in the day because part of the benefit for the band members was a free pass to the amusement park. I was especially excited because of a ride called "the Beast."

Back then I was a roller-coaster junkie, and the Beast was one of the most famous rides of the times. For a full six minutes or so, a person could enjoy a neck-popping, vocal-cord-stripping, hip-bruising ride on a state-of-the-art machine that boasted some of the highest peaks and lowest valleys known to those who thirsted for a violent, near-death experience. But to enjoy those six precious minutes, the riders had to stand in a line that resembled the winding path bowels take through the human abdomen.

Packed with people bunched together tightly and moving slower than a snail with a limp, the line snaked around the parallel metal pipes for what seemed hundreds of yards. It's the kind of line that allows people to pass each other again and again—so many times that faces are memorized down to the moles and stray hairs, T-shirt messages become absolute truth, and conversations overheard come in bits and pieces, some being so interesting (or appalling) that it is hard to wait until you get close enough to hear again.

For a good forty-plus minutes, I shuffled through that line. And I did it six times that day! Why? Because there was something on the other end that I found exhilarating. It was something I wanted, a challenge I dreamed about. And once I did it the first time and the ride lived up to my expectations, I couldn't get enough. I was finally forced to leave the Beast because there was a concert to do.

To balance out the waits in life that are not so enjoyable, there are other places besides amusement parks where waiting has its sweet spoils. On the high end of life, there are glorious places, like maternity waiting rooms, where family members excitedly anticipate the announcement that a new little one has arrived. I went to one of those rooms as a first-time grandfather not too long ago. That was some really great waiting! (Her name is Lily Anne, by the way, the latest fawn in the Chapman herd.)*

In the everyday category of places where waiting can be enjoyable are locations such as movie theaters, concert halls, NASCAR events, a favorite restaurant, and checkout counters at Bass Pro or Cabela's. The lines at these places are not at all toilsome. I gladly bear them because of what I expect to find in the distance. But of all the places that involve waiting, the deer stand is definitely my favorite.

I can confidently say that as far as I'm concerned, sitting alone on a deer stand has not once felt like drudgery. Even when I head home empty-handed, I still feel refreshed for having been out there. This view of how pleasurable even a shotless hunt can be reminds me of what the granddad of the late singer Harry Chapin said to his grandson. He said something to the effect of…

> Harry, there are two kinds of tired. There's a bad tired and a good tired. When you come to the end of the day exhausted because you've labored throughout all of it to help someone else fulfill their dreams, that's a bad tired. But when your day ends and the hard work you did was for the sake of your own dream, even if you didn't make any money, that's a good tired.

Good deer-stand waiting, like a good tired, means that even if the critters don't show up, there is always something about it that makes the waiting worth the effort. One reason most hunters agree this is true is that hunting is something we *want* to do. And though we might go home with an unpunched tag, that doesn't mean we're leaving the woods empty-handed. There have been times when I've left the stand with the memory of a sunrise that genuinely melted my emotions, a sight so lovely that I was reminded to say a quiet thank-You to the Creator. Is that a trophy? You bet!

On more than one occasion I have unloaded my bow or gun and headed to the truck with the refreshment of a few hours of blessed solitude. During these valuable breaks from the rest of the world, I am often able to concentrate on praying

---

* We now have a total of six new additions to the "grand-herd." There are four doe and two bucks.

for those I love. Or I get to go through some things I need to think about. Is that a good use of time? Yes, sir!

If you and I redeem the time on a hunt in this way, we're doing the kind of waiting mentioned in the Old Testament book of Psalms: "Wait for the LORD; be strong and let your heart take courage; yes, wait for the LORD" (27:14). On the surface, this passage seems to imply that when it comes to waiting for God, all we need to do is find a park bench and sit there quietly with folded hands, and sooner or later He will come strolling by. That is not the meaning at all.

To "wait" has a proactive meaning in this verse. The original word (*qavah*) means to "bind together by twisting." Essentially, those of us who effectively wait for God will redeem the time by "wrapping ourselves around" Him. To get that tightly intertwined with God requires an active approach to a relationship with Him. Conversing with Him in prayer, listening to Him through His Word, studying and worshipping Him, allowing Him to influence every aspect of our lives...this is good waiting.

Deer hunters, for the most part, don't have a problem grasping this scriptural insight. We rarely sit on a deer stand thoughtless and brain dead. We "wrap ourselves around the hunt" by constantly watching the woods, carefully looking for the slightest movement. We mentally rehearse our shooting methods, and we take note of weather and wind. Our minds are busy. This active approach creates pure excitement from the first moment of a hunt to the last. And more importantly, it tutors us about how to wait on the Lord. What a deal!

While there are some unquestionably wonderful byproducts of keeping a vigil on a deer stand, such as learning how and why to redeem the time, seeing deer is the ultimate reason I gladly linger there. The anticipation of sighting the subtle movement of brownish-colored fur amid the thicket or catching the flicker of a white-tipped tail in the distance—pure heaven. This unique aspect of deer hunting has taught me more about how to enjoy the rest of life than nearly anything else.

Life is very similar to a deer hunt. It's a wait. The question to ask is, What will be the reward of my waiting? That expectation will dictate whether my waiting is bad or good. If I believe the wait will yield something dreadful or even nothing at all, then life will surely be void of true joy. However, if I expect the wait to result in something wonderful—something even better than a huge trophy buck—then the sweetness of anticipation makes life much more enjoyable.

I will be forever grateful that I have something wonderful to look forward to as I wait on the "deer stand" of this life. The very thought of the divine sighting that I fully expect makes living feel like one uninterrupted day in the hunter's woods, when every moment is filled with the hope of seeing the prize I search for!

> Behold what manner of love the Father has bestowed on us, that we should be called children of God! Therefore the world does not know us, because it did not know Him. Beloved, now we are children of God; and it has not yet been revealed what we shall be, but we know that when He is revealed, we shall be like Him, for we shall see Him as He is. And everyone who has this hope in Him purifies himself, just as He is pure (1 John 3:1-3 NKJV).

> For the grace of God that brings salvation has appeared to all men, teaching us that, denying ungodliness and worldly lusts, we should live soberly, righteously, and godly in the present age, looking for the blessed hope and glorious appearing of our great God and Savior Jesus Christ, who gave Himself for us, that He might redeem us (Titus 2:11-14 NKJV).

If these passages describe your expectations as they do mine; then, my friend, we are enjoying some really great waiting!

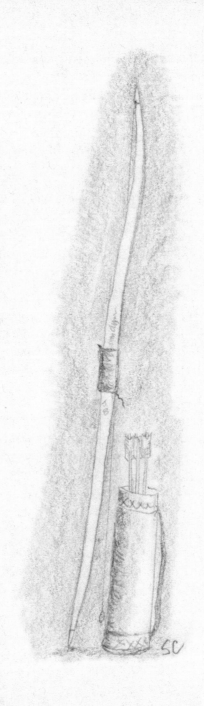

11

Crooked Bows

I don't remember exactly what I was doing in the yard that early summer day when I saw the square brown delivery truck coming down our driveway. However, I'll never forget what the driver put in my hands. As he headed back toward the paved road, I stood in my yard holding a long, sturdy, cardboard tube that was addressed to me. I wondered what on earth it was.

I headed into the house to get a knife so I could open up the package to see what came. As I ripped the tape off the top to get to the prize inside, I felt like a youngster tearing into a box of Cracker Jacks. I was excited! The packing tightly filled the innards of the round container, and though it wasn't easy, I was finally able to pull the contents from it.

I couldn't believe what I was holding. It was a beautiful, handmade longbow. The return address showed that it had come all the way from Long Pine, in the great state of Nebraska. When I read the note inside, I realized the gift was from the skilled hands of a gentleman I had met there several months before named Joel Barrow. He shaped and finished the wood, made the string, boned the tips with deer antler, and even added a wind direction thread that was mounted to the black leather grip. It was, without question, one of the nicest gifts I have ever received. Knowing what a tremendous amount of time and effort it took to build such a thoughtful offering, I was humbled to be holding it in my hands.

Almost before the brown truck could drive out of sight, I strung the bow and ran to my garage to retrieve my collection of cedar arrows and a protective finger tab. I keep a shooting block target in my backyard, and in about the time it takes a buck to turn and run once it "winds" a feller, I was coming to full draw with the longbow.

Not being a frequent user of the traditional-style archery equipment, I started close to the target—about five yards. That distance might sound easy to some folks, but a fifteen-foot shot with a bow that requires the archer to depend only on God-given instincts to hit the intended target makes a two and half by two-foot foam block seem like a matchbox. Furthermore, I didn't want to miss because I don't enjoy crawling around in the yard on all fours while gingerly patting the grass with the palm of my hand. That's the process I use to feel for that slight hump that indicates there might be an unintentionally misplaced arrow that has slid just under the surface of the lawn. Seeing me crawl around is a sight I'm sure makes the neighbors wonder about my sanity! So I was compelled to make each shot connect with the block.

I have to admit, though I may never win contests at traditional archery competitions, I do think I have a pretty good feel for shooting instinctively. With surprising consistency, I was grouping the arrows in a respectable area about the size of a dinner plate…at five yards. So I summoned a little bravery and backed the distance to about ten yards and then about fifteen. That decision made it necessary to pat the yard a couple of times, but thankfully, after shooting for a while, I managed to still have the same number of shafts I started with.

About twenty minutes into enjoying the new addition to my archery arsenal, I took a rest to give my shoulders a break and to admire the wooden work of art in my hands. As I looked closely at it from tip to tip, I discovered something I failed to see when I looked it over when it first arrived. In my excitement, I didn't notice that it had my name on it! Joel had not only scribed his own sign in the bow but also personalized it for me near the grip. What a true treasure!

I shot a little more that day and grew increasingly impressed with how smooth the release of the string felt, how quiet it was, and how natural the feel was in my hands. The fifty pounds of pull was not overly taxing on my aging joints. In regard to finishing with my quiver still full, I will admit that the second session of shooting resulted in one cedar seed being permanently sown somewhere. The only consolation is that maybe someday I'll step outside and find an arrow tree growing near the house. And when the tree is fully mature, it will yield wooden shafts that will be fletched with feathers, preknocked, field-tipped, and fully crested with orange and white (in honor of the Tennessee Volunteers!). Annie will be grateful that I'll never have to dip into our coffers for another dozen arrows.

As I was putting my "Barrow longbow" away in its shipping box to be safely stored until I used it again, an interesting feature caught my eye. I was quite surprised that I had not already seen it. The bow was barely down into the tube when I noticed that it was not exactly straight. At first I wondered if it was my imagination, so I pulled it out and checked it over closely. When I took it by the grip and held it out from my body as far as I could, I said out loud, "Yep, this bow is sure enough crooked."

I couldn't believe my eyes. After just experiencing about thirty or forty minutes of smooth releases, nicely flying arrows, and a lot of good hits on the foam block, I realized that all along, I was using a crooked stick. I thought, *No way should this bow be yielding such precision.*

I was absolutely amazed. My compound bow that has a high-tech aluminum riser made with a computer-generated machining device, perfectly matched fiberglass limbs, and wheels and cables that have been scientifically engineered for utmost operational consistency didn't feel any sweeter than the Barrow bow. I realized that even though an incredible span of time separates the discovery of the technology that goes into the building of each type of bow, the two were nearly identical in terms of their potential accuracy. I tucked that discovery away in the file cabinet of my brain that is marked "There's gotta be a lesson in this somewhere."

As the days passed, I couldn't help but string up the longbow and poke more holes in the foam block in the backyard. It was more fun than a fellow should be allowed to have while outdoors. Though I used it often and would occasionally note its wandering shape, the fact that the bow was crooked didn't yield an insight until one Saturday afternoon later that summer. It happened while I sat in a sound booth at a church, listening to my wife deliver the keynote address at a women's conference. She was teaching about the life of Abraham from the Old Testament.

Annie told the group of women, "Without question, Abraham—or Abram as he is known when we first meet him in the later portion of Genesis 11—is considered one of the great patriarchs of our faith. However, he was not a perfect man." Using a metaphor that the ladies would understand, Annie continued, "He did some things that require us to view him through a 'soft lens' in order to see him as God saw him. To explain, the 'soft lens' was a movie camera attachment first used many years ago in the movie-making industry before computer technology replaced it. The soft lens gave the picture a slightly blurred effect. While the purpose of the lens may have been to generate a certain emotion in the movie viewer, it also did something for the beauty-conscious actresses of the day that some of them probably demanded. On a close-up shot, a soft lens would practically erase all wrinkles and other imperfections on their faces."

Moving on, Annie further explained, "In spite of his flaws, Abraham was viewed by God through the 'soft lens of grace.' Because God had tested him by directing him to pack up and leave the pagan culture of his homeland, and the fact that Abraham obeyed the call, God considered him to be a man whose heart was true and willing to be obedient. However, Abraham's actions didn't always show it.

"Most of us know, for example, two of the notable blunders he made. One, because he feared that the Egyptians would kill him in order to take his beautiful wife, Sarah, he asked her to tell a lie for him and say to the Egyptians that she was his sister. This scheme involved a half-truth since Sarah was his half-sister. Yet a half-truth is a whole lie. Abraham's plan did prolong his life, and he was treated well by the Pharaoh. That is, until the king and his house were struck with plagues because of Sarah. As a result, Abraham and his wife, along with all that he owned, were thrown out of Egypt. They were fortunate not to be killed. But God spared them because He had a plan for their lives."

Annie continued, "A second familiar mistake Abraham made is found in Genesis 16. It involved the impatience he showed regarding God's promise to make of him a great nation. He knew that in order for this to happen, Sarah needed to bear him a son to propagate his lineage. Sarah, however, was beyond the childbearing years and unable to provide a son. Taking matters into her own hands, she talked Abraham into having a child with her maid, Hagar. Her weak and impatient husband decided to listen to the manipulations of his wife, and the result was Ishmael, a son, a boy who became a wild man and the father of the Arab tribes, Israel's fiercest enemy to this day. This is proof that God's way is the best way, but Abraham fell short of embracing it. Yet God kept His promise, and in time, Isaac came along."

As I continued to listen to Annie tell about Abraham's human imperfections, I was amazed, along with the ladies who listened, that God would have ever chosen to use such a man. Yet what Annie said next really captured my attention as well as my imagination.

"Abraham's flesh may have been a little bit bent, but his heart was straight!"

As you can probably imagine, my mind left the building and raced a few states away to the room in my house in Tennessee where the Barrow bow was stored. I quietly rejoiced as I whispered, "Wow…God shoots straight with crooked bows!"

What an incredible picture. Even the great patriarch of our faith had a history that didn't line up with perfection. Yet the arrows of God's truth flew accurately from his life. How could this be? The answer to that question can be found in Joel Barrow's workshop.

Skilled bowyers, especially those who work with elm wood—the kind Joel used to make the bow he sent to me—will agree that a perfect bow never begins with a perfect stick of wood. The fact is, there is no such thing as a flawless stave from which a bowyer begins the process. Instead, the key to a great shooting bow is in the amount of understanding the bowyer has of the wood and his or her ability to work with it.

The same can be said of people. Romans 3, verses 9 and 23, is an assessment of the quality of each of us as spiritual staves: "There is none righteous, not even one," and "for all have sinned and fall short of the glory of God." Except for Christ Jesus, there has not been a perfect example of humanity since Adam and Eve transgressed in the Garden of Eden. Once sin entered the world, all who have been born begin from day one to grow like wood—twisted, crooked, knotty, hard, and often difficult to work with. Even the most notable among us are flawed in one way or another. Consider, for example, the following short list of other well-known names from the Bible who had crooked turns connected to their reputations.

the lawgiver Moses—murdered an Egyptian
the prophet Jeremiah—had a harsh personality
the psalmist David—committed adultery with Bathsheba
the apostle Peter—denied knowing the Lord
the apostle Paul—persecuted Christians

I certainly don't revel in the flaws of these famous saints of the Bible, but the fact that God saw potential in them, even with their imperfections, is most encouraging. I feel this way because I too cannot boast of a life without knots and twists. God's determination to use us is not thwarted by our flaws! He is fully capable and willing to work around them. He certainly made something useful out of the individuals from the Bible whom I just mentioned. Look at the list again…

Moses—the exodus leader
Jeremiah—the heartbroken prophet
David—king over all of Israel
Peter—early church leader
Paul—apostle, missionary, teacher

The records show that these folks from the Scriptures, along with Abraham, have at least one thing in common. They were imperfect people who became perfect examples of the Master Bowyer's willingness to choose and use flawed individuals. Thankfully, the human demonstrations of His willingness to use crooked bows are not confined to people found in the pages of the Bible. There are living and breathing examples among us in our times. And interestingly enough, I learned about one of these individuals as a result of another gift delivered one day to my home. The Barrow longbow had come by truck, but I found this unforgettable treasure in my mailbox.

The sender was a gentleman named Kenny Johnson. Inside his package were two cassette tapes. One was the delightful and moving music of Kenny and his wife, Donna. The other tape was his personal testimony. As I listened to him speaking on the cassette, I was struck with the sincerity in Kenny's voice as he shared the story of his life journey and how he became a gospel songwriter.

From the recording, I learned that just three months before he was born, his dad abandoned his mother and their houseful of kids. Amazingly, on the very day of Kenny's birth, his brother, the eldest of nine children, became a Christian, and shortly thereafter began taking his mother and his siblings to church. Eventually, Eva Lee Posey Johnson (his mother's full name) found the source of her strength to be rooted in her faith in Jesus, and she became a mother who was determined to raise her children in the admonition of the Lord.

That faith would be tested sorely through the years by the haunting sorrow of an absent husband and father, as well as the daunting challenge of providing food and shelter for her kids. Perhaps one of the toughest moments for Eva Lee came the day she heard that one of her sons had been killed while serving his country in the US Army. Yet her resolve didn't wane, and she held the family together. Today, as Kenny puts it, she watches all her remaining children from the "balcony of heaven" as they continue on and lead full and healthy lives.

Needless to say, when the tape was finished, I was melted butter. But of all that I heard, I remember being especially moved by a specific part of Kenny's story that involved a handmade item his mother had crafted. I was so moved, in fact, that I documented this part of his account in a song lyric.

The Pocket

Daddy left in January
And I was born in April
I was down the line, the last of nine
And I'll be forever grateful
For the way that Mama stayed with us
And said our names to Jesus
Oh, but she was sad
She missed our dad
And wondered why he'd ever leave us

We didn't have a dime
But we were rich
And Mom was good at sewing

She took a bag of old cut-up rags
And before it started snowing
She made a quilt to keep us warm
And I slept underneath it
But in the seams was dad's old blue jeans
Among all the other pieces

Then one night I'll not forget
In that quilt I found a pocket
I remember what my Mama said
When I put my hand inside it
She said, "The night your daddy said goodbye
He left everything behind him
Now where your hand is
He once had his."
She left the room crying

How many nights I cried myself to sleep
Underneath that cover
With my hand where his had been
Back when he loved our mother
But sometimes that memory floods my soul
If I tried I couldn't stop it
Now that old quilt is gone
But I live on
With my hand inside that pocket
Yes, my daddy's gone
But I live on
With my hand inside that pocket[5]

Today, Kenny and his wife, Donna, have devoted their lives as musicians and singers to encourage others to put their faith in the Lord. Kenny writes all their songs, and the quality and effectiveness of his lyrics are proof of at least two undeniable facts. One, his ministry through music is evidence that his mother was richly rewarded for her resolve to pass the legacy of trusting God's grace and mercy down to her children. It is an honor she definitely deserves.

The other fact confirmed by Kenny's life is that God truly is willing and able to use imperfect people to accomplish His perfect will. That truth could be clearly heard in a most memorable statement Kenny made on the cassette he sent to me, and it is especially relevant to the picture found in the Barrows longbow. Kenny humbly said, "My dad being gone may have left me a little warped, but I'm not weird. The Lord still uses me, and I'm truly grateful for it."

The following is a portion of one of Kenny's lyrics. It is more proof that God really does shoot straight with crooked bows!

Playing Baseball with Jesus

Jesus doesn't count the strikes
He just lets me swing away
For surely He knew there would come a time
I would be too broken to pray
He pitches the ball with nail-scarred hands
Over and over again
He doesn't want to see me lose
He wants to see me win

At the crack of the bat
I head for the base
Trying to score a run
But I'm a big boy now
And life's game is not always fun

Then comes the words, "Batter up!"
Booming from the throne
And I just smile when I realize
God's not trying to get me out
He's just trying to get me home[6]

12

Don't Unpack Your Bags

Watching the long line of whitetails file into the field was sort of like watching the members of a congregation enter a church. One by one, right after daylight, they walked into their clover-laden sanctuary. It was another October sunrise service for the members of the First Herd of Giles County. Little did they know that an outsider was hidden among the decoration of foliage that formed the perimeter of their four-acre chapel. He was watching every move they were making as they bowed their heads to partake of the offering of nutrition on the floor of the field.

Among the members were at least a dozen mature females and several youngsters. They were grazing together near the center of the sanctuary. A few yards away were three adolescent, short-antlered males that fed intentionally close to the main group. Not too far from them was another gent who looked a little older. Though his beams had more mass and he was obviously the most advanced in age, he seemed a bit too young to be considered a patriarch. Still, there was a certain vigor in his demeanor that indicated he was at least in some leadership capacity. In keeping with the church metaphor, he could be referred to as the pastor.

While the members milled around and enjoyed their fellowship meal of clover and other tender grasses at their feet, the largest of the males, the pastor, started acting a little nervous. He stood motionless and peered toward the door through which he and the congregation had entered their haven. Because that kind of tentative behavior in a male whitetail usually indicates that he has detected the presence of an approaching intimidator, there was no guessing at what troubled him. Sure enough, arriving typically and intentionally late to the morning meeting was the self-appointed leader of the group.

With his head high and sporting a massive throne of antlers, his neck stiff and swelled, he walked into the sanctuary a few yards and stopped. He looked toward the assembly of females first, and then his eyes went to the few young men that were standing around looking at him and acting noticeably edgy. Just behind them was the pastor. He too had his gaze fixed worriedly on the latecomer.

After standing there for about thirty or forty motionless seconds, the sizeable, seasoned whitetail looked once more at the ladies and then began majestically strolling toward the men. There was a threatening air in the way he walked. After he took only a few steps toward them, all the young guys scattered to other parts of the chapel, leaving only the pastor to deal with the heavy "elder."

Suddenly the old man lowered his head and darted toward the young buck, and a confrontation of major proportions erupted. The battering noise of their intermingling head gear filled the cathedral. While it was music to the hunter's ears, the pastor was probably not feeling so fond of the aggressive hits he was taking to his body and his ego.

For what seemed like three or four minutes the two males fought, going in circles as they did, throwing dirt and grass with their hooves as they dug in and lunged toward each other, only to separate and do it again. It was obvious that the blows were not equal in their effectiveness. The elder's body was heavier, and he seemed much more skilled at throwing his weight around. The tattered, younger male was beginning to weaken in the fray.

The hunter sat in his secret perch, stunned but quietly engrossed in the battle he was watching. However, what happened next made him cringe with horror and sympathy. With a force that is unimaginable, the old antlered member of the congregation buried two of his lengthy tines into the young fellow's neck and jaw area. There was an audible moan as the seriously wounded fighter struggled to detach himself from his aggressor.

Bleeding and battered, the poor young pastor stumbled, gathered what wits he had remaining, and limped off toward the back door of the church. All alone he disappeared into the morning mist, probably to lie down and die.

The brute elder panted slightly as he stood and watched his victim make an exit from his presence. Feeling quite sure there would be no other challengers, especially among the very young boys who had just witnessed the power he wielded, the elder strolled triumphantly toward the ladies. It was their turn to be nervous.

Most deer hunters, if they spend enough time in the stand, will eventually observe this kind of battle. In the world of the whitetail (and many other antlered beasts), what took place between the "pastor" and "the elder" is normal behavior. A big buck's nature is to gain dominance over the younger, smaller bucks in a herd. The reward for his aggressive antics is that he gets to be first in line to pass on his strong genes. But as common a sight as these antler wars can be, there is still a certain sorrow a hunter feels for the younger guy that gets his whitetail whooped by the brute of the bunch, especially if the beating is fatal or at least results in a seriously injured sense of dignity.

Whenever I think of the gravely wounded buck that was referred to as "the pastor," I am prone to think of another pastor of the human kind whose story has some similarities. He too has a firsthand understanding of the hurt that can be rendered by an older buck who seeks to gain dominance in a congregation. And though the turf wars are a fully natural aspect of deer behavior, what happened to our pastor friend is not supposed to take place among people who lead in the church of the living God. In support of this young preacher, I wrote an adaptation of his story into a song. The lyric was born during a dinner that Annie and I had with him and his wife.

James and Sherry (not their real names) were nearly in tears as they held each other's hands and told us their dilemma. They had moved from a rather large city to a small town in a neighboring state because they both were absolutely sure God had led them to do so. The pastorate held great promise for growth, and the town was a ripe field waiting to be harvested for the Lord. So with their four small children in tow, they packed up and made the move.

They arrived at their new church and enjoyed being immediately embraced by their new friends and spiritual family. As a man who was relatively young in his calling, the husband was grateful and excited to have the honor of leading such a well-established congregation. He stepped confidently into the pulpit, and all was going well…until one day just three months into his new pastorate, when something dreadful happened. The dark spirit of an "elder" showed up.

The trouble started when the young preacher addressed a subject in his sermon that, until he arrived at the church, had been taboo. Though the truth in his Sunday morning message was delivered carefully and gently, it was without question a definite challenge to the congregation to think and pray about it. However, when Monday morning came, word had swept through the church office that "the elder" was on his way to meet with the pastor, and he wasn't happy. The problem for the preacher was that the man who would be confronting him was entrenched in the church as an influential figure. In fact, he was the very one who had managed to keep the previous pastors in check about the socially controversial issue that the new preacher had addressed the day before. His influence in the small community enhanced the level of intimidation he was known to use inside the walls of the church.

The young pastor stood at his office window watching the parking lot, waiting like a nervous young buck for the dominant buck to enter the field. He knew a battle for position was about to ensue.

The meeting didn't last long, and the pastor managed to hold his ground regarding his message about the biblical stance on the issue. He apologized that his sermon had offended the elder and strongly suggested they bring their dispute before the entire leadership as soon as possible. The elder was not agreeable and left the meeting abruptly.

Though their encounter spanned just a few minutes, the effects lingered on into the weeks ahead. Rumors about the pastor using church funds for questionable personal purposes floated around, along with other chatter about suspicious behavior that he was allegedly concealing. There wasn't a shred of truth about the gossip, but the damage was being done. Though the pastor could not be certain, he was justified in his assumptions about the source of the rumors that were being spread. Wisely, however, he made no formal accusations.

As Annie and I shared a meal with the preacher and his wife, our hearts were broken as the couple confided in us about the severity of the emotional wounds they were feeling due to the false tales that were being told. Without revealing names or intricate details about the staff wars that were being fought between Sundays, it was obvious from their tortured expressions that they were worried about how much longer they could endure the beating they were taking. Their words also revealed that they had serious doubts about their longevity in the town, even though their presence had been so brief.

We were impressed with the amount of discretion each of them showed in regard to not naming names. It was obvious that the reason they came to us was not to return evil for evil but to get some neutral advice from someone who was not only older but who was also detached from the church and could offer an objective view.

As they wiped their eyes, Annie and I realized they were desperately hungry to hear some encouragement. That's when my very astute wife cut to the very core of the matter. She looked at the emotionally tired couple and began talking, addressing most of her comments to the pastor.

"I don't know who the person is who has shown such opposition and who may very well have started the rumors, but it seems to me that what you're dealing with here is a 'Diotrophes.' You probably already know about his legacy in 3 John. Let me simply remind you that he was the one who, according to verse 9, loved 'to be first' among the brethren, and refused to accept what John had to say."

Annie went to our office, got her New American Standard Bible, came back to the dining room, and laid it on the table. "I want to get it right, so I'll read it. This is what John wrote about Diotrophes. I think you'll agree that the spirit of this text sounds familiar. John said, 'For this reason, if I come, I will call attention to his deeds which he does, unjustly accusing us with wicked words; and not satisfied with this, he himself does not receive the brethren, either, and he forbids those who desire to do so and puts them out of the church.'"

Our guests' faces made it quite clear that the scenario in the Scriptures did indeed sound all too familiar. They both looked at each other and nodded their heads in unison, agreeing that "the elder" seemed to fit the mold of Diotrophes. The once energetic but now subdued preacher spoke up.

"What would you suggest we do, Annie? We really love the area, our kids love it, and we really did feel called to the place we are. What should we do?"

I know to be quiet when my Bible-scholarly wife is given the opportunity to respond to a question so loaded with a need to be answered. She grinned and responded as she often does when the Scriptures are opened. She said, "Read on!"

Addressing the pastor at our table specifically, Annie said, "Verse 11 will guide you about what to do. It says, 'Beloved, do not imitate what is evil, but what is good. The one who does good is of God; the one who does evil has not seen God.'"

Annie started turning backward in the pages of her Bible as she said, "Pastor, your response to this situation is to do good. It may be tempting to lash back with words, but that would be imitating what is evil. You must keep in mind that the one who is causing you so much trouble and dividing the leadership is likely a person who has not seen God. In other words, the bottom line is that he may not be a true believer. I can say that because the fruit of the actions is obviously evil. The fruit is certainly not good. And just to offer you this insight, you can count on the very good likelihood that the evil that drives him has moral implications because in the original language of the passage, the usage of the phrase 'does evil' ultimately has to do with morality issues. Your sermon that triggered your adversary's ire may have addressed the exact moral issue that plagues him or at least affects someone he is very close to, someone he may prefer to defend. Who knows? But for whatever reason, you're dealing here with a doer of evil, not a doer of good."

Making sure her Bible was turned to Matthew 13, Annie looked again at the couple and continued. "Folks, the bad news is, as much as you may want to do it, you can't toss this guy out of the church. He's a tare, and, according to the passage here in Matthew 13:24-30, you are required to let the tares grow with the wheat and to trust God with the separating and burning of the tares. The hazard of inheriting a field of wheat is that with it you get the tares that were intentionally planted there by the devil himself long before you arrived. And if you pull up the tares, you will probably uproot some of the innocent, precious stalks of wheat in the church. That's a disaster you want to avoid. Only God can do the kind of separating that does not result in harm being done to His precious ones."

The preacher pursed his lips and sighed deeply as he responded. "I can't tell you how many nights I've lain awake just staring into the darkness, rehearsing what I'd like to say to this fellow as well as those he has convinced to side with him. And I'll admit the words aren't pretty, nor is the spirit I'd like to deliver them with. I know you're right, Annie, to remind me that I can't fight evil with evil. It's not the way of our Savior. But quite honestly, I don't think I have any more cheeks to turn."

Annie closed her Bible, leaned forward, and in a caring, gentle, somewhat motherly tone she said, "It is obvious to me that you are a man who wants to do good and not evil. The fact that you have shown us your wounded heart without uncovering the name of the one who hurt you is proof to me that you are a man of integrity. You are to be commended for following the biblical order to overcome evil with good. It's an absolute shame that the worst storms some preachers face too often start right in the pews of the church. It should not be so. There are souls sinking deeper into the muddy mire of hopelessness while these kinds of conflicts distract the soul winners. It simply is wrong."

The young shepherd and his wife nodded their heads in agreement. What came next from Annie's heart was the wisdom that sparked the idea to write a ballad to highlight the plight of the preacher who sat at our table, as well as the many others who have unfortunate stories just like his.

Annie continued, "You haven't been at the church too long, and the conflict you have encountered is not of God. Just keep in mind that the troublemaker may attempt to control the pulpit, but he will not rule heaven. Even if it doesn't happen until the end of the age, God will see to it that the tare will someday be separated from the wheat and be burned up. May He have mercy on the man's soul and save him from such a fate. But until then, I urge you, pastor, to not stop doing good. Good will win. And whatever you do, don't back down from sharing the truth of God's Word in your sermons. You know as well as I do that it is the only thing that will free the people. But I have to warn you, until this conflict is resolved, if you plan to keep preaching the truth, don't unpack your bags!"

The young pastor smiled as if Annie's words had lit the fuse of his determination to dig in and do battle. I mentally began writing. I eventually wrote the following ballad to help him keep the fuse burning.

Don't Unpack Your Bags

The new preacher walked up on the porch
Knocked on that old screen door
Waited until the light came on
Said, "Good evening, ma'am, I'm Pastor John
I just came by to say hello
Take a minute and let you know
I just moved here to your fine town
And I start next Sunday morning"

She stepped out in the evening air
Sat down in an old oak chair
Said, "Young man, you seem so nice
But could I give you my advice
Preachers have come to that church for years
They've come with smiles, they leave with tears
One by one like a sad parade
And I offer you this warnin'…

"Touch a feather to their ear
Tell them what they wanna hear
Give 'em milk, don't give 'em meat
Make it short and make it sweet
If you wanna stay around
That's what you'll have to do
But don't unpack your bags, young man,
If you plan to preach the truth"

She said, "I don't go to that church no more
There's something dark behind those doors
First time they rang that steeple bell
They must have heard it down in hell
'Cause they sent their minions to that place
And they hide behind the human faces
Of those who would trade your soul and mine

For just a taste of power.
So you better…

"Touch a feather to their ear
Tell them what they wanna hear
Give 'em milk, don't give 'em meat
Make it short and make it sweet
If you wanna stay around
That's what you'll have to do
But don't unpack your bags, young man,
If you plan to preach the truth"

She said, "Now you may wonder how I know
It's 'cause a preacher came here years ago
I loved the way he shined the light
On what was wrong and what was right
We fell in love and we planned to walk that aisle
But they tore him down and stole his smile
He carried that pain to an early grave
It's been hard to be forgiving.
So you better…

"Touch a feather to their ear
Tell them what they wanna hear
Give 'em milk, don't give 'em meat
Make it short and make it sweet
If you like this little town
That's what you'll have to do
But don't unpack your bags, young man,
If you plan to preach the truth"[7]

13

Patterned

Not more than two miles from my residence is a neighbor's forty-acre piece of beautiful Tennessee property that I am privileged to hunt. Though not vast in size, it has all the ingredients a deer and turkey hunter could hope for to cook up an adrenaline pie. There are plenty of thickets where deer can bed, some big oaks that can yield an impressive annual rain of mast in the form of acorns, a substantial stand of cedar trees ideal for roosting birds, and a creek bed that courses through the entire farm. It also has a long and lovely three-acre field with a hardy crop of clover, a plant highly favored by the farm's unusual number of furred and feathered critters.

With its bounty of herds and birds and its short distance from the end of my driveway, I candidly admit that the temptation to frequent the farm reaches embarrassing proportions. And during a recent autumn, it did just that due to some unavoidable circumstances.

As the fall season progressed, so did my busy work schedule. My itinerary prohibited me from investing a lot of interstate highway time to travel to hunting grounds that I enjoy in other counties across our state. In addition to that restriction, I was unable to enjoy the occasional daylight-to-dark vigils in the deer stand that I absolutely love. All this left me feeling rather deprived (excuse me while I wipe the tears!). It was as though I had a severe itch, and I knew my neighbor's property was one place I could go to scratch it.

It would be almost a shame to admit how many mornings and evenings I hunted that farm during the season. The closeness of it allowed me to be there just before daylight, head home around 8:30 (if no "connections" were made), work all day as fast as I could, and be back in the stand around two hours before sunset. I am glad to report that my obsessive response to the opportunity at least bore some redemptive fruit. Specifically, it was something that happened during a series of evening hunts that birthed a revelation that has had a profound impact on how I view my spiritual life.

Before I reveal the discovery, I concede that the overly regular schedule I was enjoying may seem too excessive to some folks. Yet to others (mostly hunters, I'm sure) it might be enviable. You must understand that Annie and I were empty nesters, we had no grandkids at that time, and my sweet wife graciously tolerated my routine since I was usually home in the morning about the time the coffee was brewing (at least the second pot). So before you cast me off as an insensitive jerk, keep in mind that conditions were just right for me to keep such an unusual hunting regimen. I am aware that it would not be a routine that a majority could enjoy. I was truly blessed.

If you are a serious deer hunter, you are likely wondering about another serious concern as you read this—"overhunting" a place. Frequenting a farm too much can contaminate it and cause the critters to abandon an area if care is not given to let a place rest from the presence of hunters. It was for that reason that I placed three stands in different areas of the property that covered all the points of deer movement.

I had a lock-on/climbing-stick combo placed back in the timber at the edge of a thicket. There I could monitor the deer that came from nearby corn and soybean fields to bed in the mornings or be there when they got up in the evenings to head back to the same food sources.

Along the creek bed, I had several shooting lanes cleared around a tall, straight, soft-bark tree that I used for my portable climber-type stand. The deer had dug a deep trail into the banks of the stream where they often crossed. There was nothing like being suspended high above the ground to secretly watch a parade of white-tails as they came through.

I truly looked forward to using each of the trio of stands, but the time constraints I faced made it necessary to favor the location at the edge of the field. I also knew I was ignoring my self-imposed policy of avoiding overuse of a stand, but in this case, there were a couple of advantages to breaking the rule.

One reason was that the clover in the field was a major attractant, making the possibility of at least seeing deer much higher. Thus the needle on the anticipation meter was always higher whenever I was in the ladder stand.

Another reason to favor the field edge was convenience. Because the busyness of the day's chores would often push me far into the afternoon, it was simply more advantageous to squeeze the maximum amount of work out of the day and then hurry to the farm. Upon arrival, I could jump out of the truck, quickly change into my camo clothes at the tailgate, grab my bow, and walk the short distance to the stand. When the weather was warm, as it usually is in Tennessee during most of our bow-only season, a brief trek to the tree meant there would be very little odor-producing sweat on my skin that could alert the sensitive olfactory system of the deer. Because of this, I felt reasonably sure I could slip in and out of that spot without permanently jeopardizing the presence of the critters.

But the best of all reasons to use the field edge stand had as much to do with emotional therapy as the thrill of the hunt. In a flash I could go from the hectic madness of dealing with mind-numbing technology to nearly total quiet within mere minutes. That was my favorite part of the deal.

As I mentioned, it was during my afternoon sits in the ladder stand that I noticed it. Evening after evening, while I scanned the area for whitetail deer, I would catch a glimpse of movement in the grass way down the field. Almost without fail, right around 5:15, the resident wild turkeys would show up. As if they had Timex watches on their wings and knew the time of day, their heads would appear at nearly the same time each evening, bobbing back and forth, moving right to left in the meadow. One by one, until there were sometimes two dozen or more, they would meander out of the timber on the south side of the field, head to the north side, and enter the woods, going toward the stand of tall, mature cedars. Then around 6:00, when all the birds were congregated inside the shadowy cover of the woods, I would hear the vigorous flapping of wings accompanied by the distinct fly-up cackle that turkeys voice when they go to bed. (I'm glad humans weren't designed to do that. Then again, maybe some do. I don't know!) It was always a delightful show to watch and hear on those evenings when I could be there to enjoy it.

One midday early in the archery deer season, I took a break from laboring in the office and walked out to the highway to check our mailbox. As I slowly walked back toward our house, I shuffled through the stack of letters, bills, and other mail. Suddenly I saw it. I stopped dead in my tracks and stared at the glorious piece of mail I held in my hands. It was from the Tennessee Wildlife Resources Agency. I knew what it was. It had arrived just as I had hoped. The envelope contained my fall-season, either-sex, computer-drawn turkey permits. I was a winner! My heart leaped with 12-gauge joy.

As I tightly clutched the permits between my thumb and twitching trigger finger, my mind raced to the scene at the ladder stand where I sat and waited for deer. I could see the line of turkeys filing across the field of my mind. And I could see myself slowly pulling up the sleeve of my camo shirt to check the timepiece on my arm that read, once again, 5:15 or sometimes 5:30.

I could hardly wait to get to the phone and call my friend Lindsey Williams, who had also entered the same drawing. Sure enough, the mailman had delivered the same good news to his box. I knew we were only a few short weeks away from one of the most memorable moments two friends (who enjoy shopping for a Thanksgiving turkey while wearing full camo) could ever share.

By the time the first day of turkey season came, I had enjoyed several more opportunities to observe the ticking of the "turkey time clock" while waiting on whitetails. One doe was in the freezer, by the way, but the commotion created by arrowing and tracking a deer seemed to have done no damage to the regularity of the turkey parade. The only thing that did change was the hour of their appearance. Due to the closing of daylight saving time, their schedule was moved up by sixty minutes.

I called Lindsey to make sure he would be joining me on the first evening of opening day that was posted on our permits. He was fully on go, and on the evening before the fall turkey season began, he phoned me and asked, "What time should I be at your place tomorrow afternoon?" With a confidence that was founded on much research, I responded, "If you're here at 2:45, we'll have us a bird somewhere between 3:45 and 4:30."

Because archery season had been in full swing for several weeks, Lindsey and I agreed that it felt a little strange to put our bows on the shelf and dust off the shotguns that had been cased since the ending of spring gobbler season. But with an elevated sense of excitement, the kind that can keep a fellow up the night before a hunt and make it hard to concentrate on a "real job" during the day, we climbed into my pickup around 2:50 and drove the short distance to the farm.

On the way, I verbally rehearsed with Lindsey what I was sure would happen that afternoon and how we would best prepare for the harvest. I said, "We'll set up on the north side of the field back in the woods a bit just at the edge of the cedars. Be sure to listen hard at about 3:40. Listen for light clucking and purring. Right after you hear the first call, get set 'cause it won't be long until you'll begin to see the birds as they cross the field and enter the woods."

I was getting all keyed up just saying it, but I continued, "Make sure you have your gun up on your knee at around 3:40 to keep the movement to a minimum. There will be dozens of incredibly talented eyes to bust us. Lay your finger on the safety and enjoy the moment!"

Lindsey smiled graciously as he listened to me ramble the instructions he already knew how to follow. He was kind enough to let me say it all out loud because he knew I enjoyed saying it. After I finished, he responded with a sort of chuckle in his voice, "You're pretty sure about this hunt, aren't you?"

I grinned with confidence. "Oh, yeah! I know their pattern, and I don't think it's likely to change today."

We took our places in the woods around 3:15. Facing in opposite directions about thirty yards apart, we sat quietly waiting in the heavy shadows of the cedars. I checked my watch...3:30. My ears were tuned in to every sound. The chirps of cardinals, the distinct and annoying screech of the blue jay, and the distant sound of the flow of traffic on I-24 reverberated in my head. I was listening hard. Then I heard it.

The first soft cluck was muffled by the foliage still on the trees, but I knew that sound. And I knew well that it came from across the field we were facing. My heart rate shot to humming-bird levels as I slowly pushed the "call" button on the two-way radio clipped to my shirt. "Lindsey, did you hear that?"

"Yep," came his reply. I could tell by his breathy whisper that his respiratory pace had also quickened.

Though I certainly didn't need to say it to him, it just felt good to announce, "This is it, they're here. Sounds like they're coming by you first. Get ready!"

I slowly moved my hand away from the radio and back to my trigger and waited, confident that I would soon hear the report of my friend's shotgun. And, as though the birds' beaks were tied to a string right where Lindsey was sitting and someone was pulling on it, the woods began to fill up with turkeys of various sizes. There was no need for him to move his gun barrel. All he had to do was wait for supper to walk into his sight path.

My entire body jumped at the sound of the blast from Lindsey's 12-gauge. Turkeys flew and ran in all directions, cackling as they dispersed. The only muscle I moved was my index finger as I slowly clicked off the safety and felt for the trigger. I knew there'd be birds running by me.

Boom! Another sudden explosion filled the woods and then quickly settled to the sound of flapping of wings and cackles as the flock took flight. I called Lindsey on the radio and said, "Let's sit quiet and let them recongregate and head to the backside of the farm."

Satisfied that we were alone at last with our tasty successes, Lindsey and I stood up, pulled our facemasks down, and looked through the woods at each other with an unmistakable "high five" expression. We gathered our gear and our turkeys, headed to the truck, and were back at my house before dark had fallen. It was a hunt we still like to talk about.

It would be several days after that memorable afternoon that I would finally glean an important insight from the experience. It sometimes happens sooner, but in this case, I'll admit that I was far too caught up in the moment of the pursuit to be cognizant of the spiritual truth that was available in the "on-time turkeys."

About a week after Lindsey and I tagged our two birds, I went back to the same farm in pursuit of deer. As I waited again in the field-edge ladder stand, I was thinking about the turkeys that had provided such an unforgettable hunt and wondered if they would show up once again as usual. Amazingly, that evening the same flock of birds, minus two members, appeared in the meadow around 3:30.

While I witnessed their unwavering commitment to their routine, I couldn't help but look ahead with anticipation to the next year's spring gobbler season. As the birds slowly filed across the meadow, I quietly spoke to the feathered congregation that was gathering in the cedars. "Still singin' the same old tune, are ya? You better be singing a new song come March of next year!"

Ding! I heard the "that sounds familiar" bell, and I realized I had just partially quoted a passage from the Old Testament. I couldn't remember the specific chapter or verse, but I knew the text was in the Psalms. I checked my Bible concordance to find the exact location when I got home after dark, and it was Psalm 96:1: "Sing to the LORD a new song."

As I sat quietly on the deer stand that evening, I became increasingly excited about the connection between the birds' repetitive behavior and the biblical admonition. It was as clear as the bright Tennessee sky I hunted under, but the more I thought about it, the more I realized how sobering it was.

Very simply, the mistake the turkeys had made was allowing themselves to be patterned. As woods-wise as that species of fowl can be, and as difficult as it is to defeat the unbelievably effective ability of their eyes, I had found a weakness in the turkeys' lifestyle. Their devotion to their routine was the breech in their wall of defense.

Had they occasionally altered their point of entry into the cedars or chosen to roost in alternate areas of the territory, I wouldn't have been able to set an ambush for them. Perhaps they had grown overly confident in their routine. After all, they had probably followed it all summer and had no reason to think they couldn't do so into the autumn months. For whatever reason, they were at ease with their evening ritual, unaware that the bitter result would be sweet history for the hunters.

People can be very similar to the "clockwork turkeys." We can find a way (doctrine) that can be right and then follow that trail (liturgy and devotions) daily with amazing consistency. The repetition, however, can lead to a feeling of comfort in doing things only in a certain way (traditions), and eventually we begin to put our trust in the trail. The result is the very thing that can make even the smartest among us quite vulnerable. A pattern develops. And very often it's the pattern that is being observed by the enemy of our souls, Satan, who "prowls around like a roaring lion, seeking someone to devour" (1 Peter 5:8).

With this picture in my mind, I had to ask myself some probing questions about my spiritual life. *What are the good and right things I try to do regularly in my attempt to pursue holiness?* The answers were obvious. Studying the Scripture, praying, fellowshipping with the saints, giving, and witnessing are some list-toppers. *As beneficial and as necessary to the health of the spirit of the believer as these disciplines are, can they ever be used by the enemy against me?* The answer was surprising.

Yes! It can happen when a person's rigid adherence to these worthwhile actions is based on the errant belief that rituals equal righteousness. This deadly assumption was a mistake the Scribes and Pharisees made.

In Jesus's day, the Scribes and the Pharisees were influential interpreters of the Jewish law that had been handed down from the time of Moses. Their interpretation and strict observance of these rules had become more authoritative and binding than the Mosaic law itself. And they were quick to require others to follow their customs.

For example, in Mark 7:5 the Scribes and Pharisees confronted Jesus when they saw His disciples violating their tedious premeal rituals, such as washing cups, pitchers, copper vessels, and couches. And they particularly noted that the disciples did not wash their hands in that special way. They asked Jesus, "Why do your disciples not walk according to the tradition of the elders, but eat bread with unwashed hands?"

Quoting Isaiah, Jesus countered the Scribes and Pharisees' religious spirit and said in verse 6, "This people honors Me with their lips, but their heart is far away from Me. But in vain do they worship Me, teaching as doctrines the precepts [traditions] of men." And in verse 9 Jesus further rebukes the Scribes and Pharisees: "You are experts at setting aside the commandment of God in order to keep your tradition." Jesus knew they placed far too much emphasis on minor details, such as tithing the tiny mint leaves they grew in their gardens, while at the same time ignoring the weightier provisions of the law, including "justice and mercy and faithfulness" (Matthew 23:23).

Essentially the Scribes and Pharisees put their faith in following their rules and not in God. The word "Pharisee" means "separated." Their burning desire was to separate themselves from those who did not observe the laws of ritual purity and tithing and other matters they considered very important. Jesus did not say these matters should have been ignored; rather, He detested the Scribes' and Pharisees' condescending, arrogant attitude toward others. It was for that reason that Christ bravely spoke against them when He said in Matthew 23:28, "So you, too, outwardly appear righteous to men, but inwardly you are full of hypocrisy and lawlessness."

The devil does not want us to ever be free from a dependence on performing rituals as a test of holiness. He knows well that his bullet of self-righteousness will never be fired if God's people were liberated from patterns that we have allowed to become objects of worship. Satan tries to convince us that if we alter our routines, God will not be present or pleased. The devil wants us to operate out of a sense of guilt when we falter in our rituals. Ultimately, Satan would prefer to see devotion as our god rather than God as the object of our devotion.

Let me share a personal example of how I faced this hellish trickery. When my children were very young, Annie and I began fasting and praying for them. We chose to commit each Wednesday to doing this. Though fasting is an incredibly wonderful regimen and has yielded significant results in our children's lives, there were some Wednesdays when I simply could not follow through.

For example, I might go several weeks without missing a Wednesday, but then visitors would show up or a business luncheon with a publisher or music businessperson might be scheduled on a Wednesday, and the day would be a loss in terms of fasting. When this happened, there would be a very real sense of guilt and regret that nagged at my heart: *Well, you've failed your children. Shame on you. Your kids are going to suffer because you let them down this week. And God is disappointed with you. Is your love for Him and the children He gave you not strong enough for you to tell those folks that you cannot be with them on Wednesday?*

I learned early on that these accusations were not from God. They were the devil's attempt to make me put my trust in the process and not in the Lord. I had to resist the feelings of regret and shame regarding missed Wednesdays. I had to learn to be flexible and trust that God's grace extended well beyond my occasional faltering when it came to the regimen I wanted to follow.

I challenge us to become what Jesus was during the time He physically walked on the earth. He was not a sinner, but He was definitely a "religious rule breaker." He not only verbally squared off with the Scribes and Pharisees but also openly associated with sinners like Zacchaeus (Luke 19). He spoke kindly to women (John 4). He also made strange and shocking statements, such as "Whoever wishes to be first among you shall be your slave" (Matthew 20:26). His willingness to break from the traditions of man and their ritualistic mindset of the times made it difficult to pigeonhole the Savior. It certainly frustrated the religious leaders of the day, and they became His greatest enemies.

If you dodge the bullet of self-righteousness by forsaking a "vain repetition" you have held in too high esteem, you may encounter a new enemy. It could very well be someone near you who possesses the accusing spirit of the Scribes and Pharisees. But let his or her unmerited judgment be a cause for joy because it will be a sign that you have successfully dethroned the god of ritualism.

There's one other important consideration when it comes to avoiding the danger of being patterned. Perhaps for some men, the most challenging part of forsaking the god of a treasured ritual is to be willing to accept something that a lot of guys, myself included, try to avoid like an irritated skunk. That dreadful thing is *change*.

I'm convinced that men are more like God than women because we can be "the same yesterday, today, and forever." Many of us simply do not like to change. But without a willingness to break the rules, we run the risk of walking into the sight path of the enemy's gun barrel. It may be hard to embrace the challenge of change, but our spiritual longevity could be at stake. When I struggle with resisting change, all I need to do is recall the sudden report of Lindsey's 12-gauge on the afternoon of the memorable turkey hunt. The echo of the blast reminds me that an easy target makes an easy kill. I don't want to be an easy mark for the hunter from hell.

Did you know you are under surveillance? Perhaps you've never considered that your steps are being watched and that your precious routines are of major interest to the enemy of your soul. One thing is certain: If you keep entering the woods of your spiritual life every day in exactly the same place because you believe therein is righteousness, sooner or later your feathers are gonna fly.

They watch my steps,
as they have waited to take my life.

PSALM 56:6

14

Turtle on a Fence Post

I dismounted my ladder stand around ten on a warm, late-September morning and headed home. As I walked the fencerow that would lead me back to my pickup, I nearly stepped on one of God's most interesting creatures. It was a turtle. It's head and short legs were protruding when I saw it, but when it saw me, it instantly pulled all its appendages inside the shell and closed the hatch doors.

I was standing next to a wooden fence post that supported tightly strung barbed wire, and I leaned my bow against the lower of the four strands. Then I gently gathered up the turtle and held it at eye level to make sure the hard shell was completely closed. After determining the creature was well tucked away, I carefully set it on the flat top of the post. I wanted to see a real live version of a word picture my son had painted in my mind only a few weeks earlier.

Nathan is a full-grown man now, standing well above me at nearly six feet four. It's hard to believe he was once the little guy whose legs barely reached the edge of the couch as we sat together and belly laughed at Bugs Bunny and Daffy Duck. And it's especially hard to believe that the adolescent I gave my tired and overused musical instruments and recording equipment to years ago has now built a business of making and producing music. In fact, Nathan produced most of the recordings Annie and I offer today.

One day as Annie and I shared a lunch with our son, he began thanking us for all the hand-me-down items he recalled getting at home. Repeating a quip he'd heard someone say, he smiled and humbly said, "At the time I didn't know what you meant when you said you'd rather give me tools than toys, but I understand it now." He also added, "I know that what I'm able to do today as a vocation, I wouldn't be doing if you and a lot of other folks had not provided the way." Then he said the words I thought of when I found the turtle: "To be honest, I feel like a turtle on a fence post." We asked him to explain what he meant. His insight was heartwarming.

"There's only one way a turtle can get on a fence post—someone has to help it get up there. There's no way he can do it by himself. And that's the way I feel. I am where I am in life today because of the help of others, and it's a long list of names. I'd have to have a lot of paper and ink if I started writing down all the people who have helped make it possible for me to do something I enjoy so much full-time. I don't have time to mention all the names I've thought of, but suffice it to say that I'm well aware that I needed the help. I will be forever grateful for all who have given it."

We were curious to hear some of the names, so we asked him to humor us and give us at least a few on his list. He didn't start with the two of us. Instead he said the name we wanted to hear most. "Of course," he began, "at the top of the list would be the Lord Jesus. I'm not being patronizing and proper in the presence of my Christian parents by saying His name. I put Him first with all sincerity. But I will say that after Him, you're next," and he looked at the two of us. We were never so happy for being in second place.

Then for several minutes he brought up very familiar family members such as his wife, Stephanie, his sister, Heidi, and his grandparents, PJ and Lillian Chapman and N.R. and Sylvia Williamson. Then there were uncles and aunts, some cousins, and even a second cousin or two. He also included several of our older friends, some of his younger friends, church family, publishers, music teachers, high school and college teachers, roommates in college…and the names kept coming. We were astounded at the number of individuals who were on the tip of his tongue. He said, "I'm sure I've missed some, but it's amazing to think that it took all those folks to lift one young turtle."

Nathan's obvious appreciation inspired us to consider our own list of those who have lifted us up and set us on the fence post of opportunity. We too would start with recognizing God's boundless gifts to us. We would be ungrateful fools to overlook Him. After acknowledging the Lord, we would mention our parents, who placed so much of their lives into ours. Then, without question, our children would be next on the list simply because they invested so many years with us dealing with the rigors of the road. They traveled with us from colic to college and literally have done as much as anyone to help us fulfill the calling we sensed on our lives as itinerate musicians. Then we would add our siblings, friends, church associates, business partners...and on and on the list would grow. I do believe that Annie and I could fill a massive book with all the names and what each one contributed to these two turtles on fence posts. The higher the stack of names, the deeper the gratitude would be for all of them.

While I know I may risk offending someone by highlighting one specific person who would be on our list, I'd like to do so just to make a single important point. (If you're a deer hunter, you know "points" are important!) That point is that very often we may lift someone up onto a fence post without even knowing it's happening at the time. It may not be until much later, even years later, that our name is added to someone's list of significant influencers. Such is the case for the one I personally want to mention. The huge difference this person made in my life didn't dawn on me until I was well into my career as a worker with words.

This individual may very well be the oldest living member on the list. And keep in mind, though she has affected both Annie's life and mine, her first influence was particularly on me. Her impact happened back when I was a twelfth grader in high school. Her name is Mrs. Margaret Withrow.

In the 1960s, the name "Mrs. Withrow" generated a lot of sober respect in the minds of the students at Point Pleasant High School. If the new year came and a student was handed a list of the teachers they would be required to sit under that year, and if her name was on it, there was only one thing to do. The student would bow his head and ask for the rapture of the saints to happen during the prayer. That's what I did, but the rapture didn't happen. Consequently, I would have to remain on earth and attend Mrs. Withrow's class.

I accepted my fate that my senior English course would be taught by the teacher who had a reputation for cracking the academic whip. I braced myself for failure. However, before the first bell sounded, I decided to take one more look at the class assignment form I had received just to make sure I had read it correctly. What I discovered was some gloriously wonderful news. I noticed that it was not English that I would be taking from Mrs. Withrow. Instead, the assignment sheet said "Creative Writing." I didn't really know what it meant exactly, but at least it didn't say "English." I was ecstatic.

Well, it didn't take but about ten minutes in the first day of class to realize my grade average was still in jeopardy. Mrs. Withrow was standing up front using words I didn't know existed. As the next few days went on, I tried to hang on to her instructions, but the fingers of learning were slipping off the cliff of hope. What's worse, the words she wrote on the chalkboard, which I assumed meant something in some language somewhere, were the very words she was asking us to use in sentences. And when we completed the sentences and strung them together, they were supposed to make sense. I was about to go ahead and let go of the rock of education I was clinging to when something happened that changed my mind.

Just before the bell rang, signaling that we could run out into the halls and scream in frustration, Mrs. Withrow said to the class, "Tomorrow, I want all of you to come with a poem. Be prepared to read it to the class. You're dismissed."

A poem, I thought as I gathered up my books and headed to the door. *Wow... now, that sounds interesting. Four, maybe eight lines ought to do it. This should be easy. Cool!*

As I was prone to do, I totally forgot about my homework until about 11:00 that night. In a panic I started wracking my tired brain for a theme for what I hoped would be the shortest poem on the planet. As I perused my thoughts, I remembered a *Reader's Digest* article I had read just a few days earlier. It was about an American soldier fighting in the Vietnam War. He had received a copy of the Bible from his mother and put it into his shirt pocket the day it came in the mail. Within a short time, his division came under fire, and the soldier was thrown to the ground by the impact of a bullet. He discovered that the bullet had hit him in his shirt pocket, and the Bible that his mother had sent stopped the projectile from piercing his chest. He opened the Bible to dig the bullet out and found that the tip of the slug stopped at the book of Psalms. The passage the tip of the bullet was pointing to was Psalm 91:7: "A thousand shall fall at thy side, and ten thousand at thy right hand; but it shall not come nigh thee" (KJV).

I decided to try to capture this story in a poem. Little did I know that it would be one of the most enjoyable sixty-minute homework sessions I would ever know. When the last word was written, I was thrilled that the poem had grown to twenty-four lines. It was a piece I called "Psalm 91:7."

That night, as I closed my spiral notebook and started to head to bed, an idea came to me that kept me up for another hour or two. I was a greenhorn guitar player at the time and knew a few chords. I thought to myself, *I wonder if Mrs. Withrow would let me sing this poem tomorrow instead of reading it?*

I uncased the Gibson J-45 and began strumming, looking for a melody. For some reason the music theme for the TV show *Gilligan's Island* kept running through my head. I figured, *Why not? It's easy and quick.* So that was the chord pattern I based the song on, and before long I had myself a real live, singable song.

I'll never forget how nervous I was when it came my turn to present my poem in the classroom the next day. My knees knocked like a badly tuned car engine as I approached the front. I strapped on my Gibson, and about halfway through the song I realized that everyone in the room was actually listening.

When I finished, Mrs. Withrow promptly stood up, marched to the front, pinched my shirt sleeve in her fingers, and said as she pulled on me to follow her, "Come with me, Steve."

"Where are we going?"

"Just bring your poem and your guitar and come with me," she demanded.

I thought maybe I had transgressed some school policy and was headed to the principal's office to receive my sentence. I was sure I was about to join the rest of the punished souls who paid their debt by cleaning the bathrooms after school. Little did I know that instead of taking me to see Principal Chambers, Mrs. Withrow was taking me to Mrs. Jackson's senior English class.

Unannounced, we barged into the room, and Mrs. Withrow said, "Mrs. Jackson, whatever you're doing, could you stop for a minute and listen to something?"

"Certainly, Mrs. Withrow. What do you have for us?"

I was escorted to the center front of the room and told, "Now sing, young man." So I sang the song again.

After I finished I was taken back to my Creative Writing classroom, and the rest is a blur. The only other thing I remember was something Mrs. Withrow said after we got back to the classroom. She took the piece of paper my verses were on and wrote across the top, "51...out of a possible 50!"

I couldn't believe my eyes. What she said to me as she stood at my desk has stayed with me through all my years. "Steve, you need to pursue the art of song-writing. I believe you have a knack for it. I gave you that score to show you how serious I am about this suggestion."

In that moment, Mrs. Withrow had picked up a fragile, helpless little turtle and set it on the fence post of a vision. I don't think I would have gotten there if she had not been so kind to me that day. And the amazing thing is, there was no way she could know the long-term impact her encouragement had on my life. She was just doing her job as a teacher.

The next time you're out deer hunting or wandering around in the great out-doors, if you find a turtle, I hope you'll pick it up and think of two things. One, may you take the time to list all who have helped you do what you do, and two, the next time you get an opportunity to help someone in some way, may you remember that someday your name might show up on his or her list.

Psalm 91:7

A soldier o'er in Vietnam
Got a package clear from home
In it a Bible marked, "Love, your Mom...
Read it wherever you roam"

Well he placed it in his khaki shirt
Just in front of his trembling heart
Then all of the sudden he hit the dirt
A bullet had hit him hard

He lay there on the ground a while
Just wondering what to do
Not a doc within a mile
He figured he was through

Then all of a sudden a smile appeared
As he raised his precious head
The bullet through the Bible had pierced
And he knew that he was far from dead

He took the little black book out
And the bullet stopped at page one eleven
He began to read aloud
Psalm 91:7

"A thousand shall fall at thy knee
And ten thousand at thy right hand
But it shall not come nigh to thee
Till you reach that promised land"

Then a praise swelled up within his heart
As tears came in his eyes
From my mother's prayers I'll never part
Till we meet there in the skies[8]

15

First-Time Caller

If you were to ask me or any other serious deer hunter to tell one of our favorite hunting memories, you should be warned that our story might require more of your time than you want to give. Plus, we would struggle with choosing just one memory. They are a little like our children in that we love them all and think each one is incredible. So what's my favorite story? I told a brief version of the account in my devotional book *With God on a Deer Hunt*, but I have looked forward to revealing the memorable details of this hunt for quite some time.

The old logging road on the 400-acre farm I was hunting ran straight along a ridgeline for quite a distance and then made a wide, sweeping turn through the woods. On one side of the road was a steep slope that dropped off the ridge down to a water source. I placed my climbing stand on the opposite side, about sixty yards off the road in the open timber. I often watched deer climb out of the ravine and onto the logging road, which was lined with huge white oak trees. Usually they would feed along the 100 yards or so where the acorns had dropped onto the road, and then they'd make a right turn into the woods and walk through the area where I was set up. They favored that route because if they followed the ridgeline, it led them downhill into a bottom where a heavy thicket provided plenty of cover for them to bed down for the day.

When 10:00 a.m. arrived, I had not seen a sign of fur. I was about to start my dismount from the tree when movement caught my eye to the left. Suddenly I saw one lone, antlered deer step onto the logging road and casually begin enjoying a midmorning feast of freshly fallen acorns. Thankful that I had no deadlines to meet and that I could stay put for the excitement, I slowly stood to my feet and prepared for a possible close-up encounter of what looked to be a nice Tennessee buck.

Though it probably took only a few minutes for the deer to meander to the place on the logging road where they usually turned right and walked by my tree stand placement, it seemed like an hour. Finally the buck was within twenty yards of the trail, and my pulse was at a level that would test even the strongest heart.

Though he was at least forty-five yards away, I had no trouble seeing the deer's form through the mature stand of timber. However, what I couldn't see was inside the animal's mind. There was no way I could have predicted that he would choose to ignore the trail that followed the ridge where I sat and instead would walk right on by. I couldn't believe it! My disappointed heart sank through my nervous gut. All I could do was watch him follow the wide sweep of the road that would lead him to the backside of the farm. But then I remembered something I had with me that I thought might save the day. The only problem was I felt a little doubtful about my ability to put it into action.

I had never used a grunt call in all my years of whitetail hunting. I purchased the one I had with me some time before that day and had practiced at home with the instructional cassette tape that came with the device, but I had not put it to the test in the woods. I knew my calling ability was questionable at best. I figured it was time to give it a try.

I searched for the small metal zipper tab on my jacket. I quietly pulled down the zipper, slid my hand inside, and felt around for the tube that hung around my neck at the end of a short lanyard. When I found it, I put my fingers around it and paused for a couple of seconds to process my thoughts.

To start with, I was dealing with the doubts I had about actually trying to talk to a deer for the first time. After all, the whitetail and I are different. Someone said about God and man that we're different not in degree, but in kind. The same is true for man and deer. Though we're each made of flesh and blood and both of us have an instinct for survival, for the most part we are two totally and completely different creatures that were not designed for vocally communicating with each other. Yet in my hand I held a potential link between my mind and his. However, I knew if I produced the wrong sound, the buck's quick departure would be likely.

Though I felt a little anxious about proceeding, any reservations I was feeling were quickly cast aside because the buck was getting away! In the few seconds I spent arguing with myself, he had walked on around the bend of the road, turned left, and entered the timber. Now he was about to casually stroll out of sight. My window of opportunity was closing! I had nothing to lose but a bucketful of ego, so I mentally rehearsed the sound I had heard on the demo tape and put the call to my mouth.

Though he was out of range for my arrow, I didn't think he was out of earshot for the sound of the call. With the open end of the tube pointed toward the buck, I gently forced some air through the mouthpiece of the call. The best way to describe the short, guttural sound the device made was that it resembled a man's post-meal burp. It's not a lovely sound—at least to the nonhunter's ear. But to me the grunt sounded like sweet music.

I was surprised at how much the call favored the recorded demonstrations I had listened to. I was duly impressed with the sound I had made, but I was much more excited by what I saw immediately after sounding the call. The walking deer stopped dead in his tracks and looked my way. Though I had no idea what I had just said to him, I was hoping his interpretation of my call was, "I'm one of you. Come back here!"

As if he had thought it through and decided his ears were playing tricks on him, he started to walk away again. When he did, I quickly put the call to my mouth once more and blew just a little bit louder. He stopped again and slightly turned his head toward me. I couldn't see his face clearly, but I imagined it had an expression that might have said, "That sure did sound like another deer. Nah…it couldn't be." And then he walked on again.

When he took a couple of more steps, I realized one more try would probably be the last hurrah for my first attempt to communicate with a deer. With that possibility in mind, I cast aside all inhibition, put the call to my lips, and gave it a louder, longer, and more confident burst of air. I still wasn't sure what the call would say to the buck, but what I wanted him to hear this time was, "I'm here to steal your girlfriend, Bubba!"

The call must have sounded like some sort of threat, and the thrill of what happened next made me nearly fall out of my stand. He stopped and abruptly turned his head precisely in my direction and gave an aggressive-looking stare. Though I was sure he couldn't see me among the foliage, he appeared to know exactly where the source of the sound was located. Thankfully the slight breeze was coming from him to me, so I knew if he decided to check me out, the conditions were in my favor.

For about three or four seconds that seemed like minutes, he looked back toward me, and then suddenly he wheeled around on his back hooves and began walking toward my stand. My legs shook with excitement as I replaced the tube in my jacket and zipped it up to make sure that if I got a shot, the string wouldn't catch on it.

When he crossed back over the logging road and entered the section of the woods where I was, he was on a brisk, deliberate pace. As he walked, his head went side to side like radar, obviously looking to find the challenging intruder. He didn't look downward to the ground as he came, so I knew I would have to wait for the moment his line of sight was blocked by a huge oak that stood between us about twenty yards out. I calculated that the angle he would walk as he passed the tree would provide about two seconds for me to get to full draw. It would be my only chance to be undetected by his very keen eyes.

When he reached the oak, I put every ounce of strength I could muster into getting to full draw. My overly excited arm muscles trembled pitifully as I pulled back on the taut string. Thankfully the arrow did not jump out of the two-pronged rest. Finally the peep sight was at my eye, and I quickly found fur in the opening.

He had to cover about ten more yards before stepping into range of my bow. I fought the sweat that trickled into my right eye. Knowing very well that I couldn't complete a shot with blurred vision, I had to do something fast. While still at full draw with my hand at my jaw, I quickly abandoned the attempt to blink the sweat away, raised my hand to eye level and carefully raked my gloved thumb across my eyelash to absorb the salty water. It worked! Once again I could see clearly as I found the deer for the second time in the peep sight.

As the buck came closer, I assumed he would walk right on by me. Thankfully, however, he suddenly came to an abrupt halt and stood broadside a mere twelve yards from my stand. Somehow his incredible sense of hearing and his amazing ability to calculate the distance from his eardrums to the sound source seemed to make him aware of exactly how far to walk. While he paused, I put my fifteen-yard sight pin on the lower area of his vitals and slowly put pressure on the release trigger. The bow recoiled in my hands as the arrow began its short flight.

The slap of the bow limbs as they collapsed probably sounded like the blast of a gunshot in the quiet of the timber, but I didn't hear it. I also didn't hear the buck dig into the thick blanket of dried leaves as he made his explosive departure. All I knew in that instant was that the many things that must go right for a dream to become reality in the deer hunter's woods had done just that. I had arrowed a nice Tennessee buck, and it was the first time I had managed to talk an animal into coming to me. The fatally wounded buck ran only twenty yards, staggered, and within mere seconds was transferred from nature's care to the responsibility of Grissom's Meats, my favorite local wild game processor, who would receive him later that morning.

I stood there amazed that a little bit of breath passing through a plastic tube over a thin reed would yield such a result. Using my extremely limited whitetail vocabulary, I had spoken a language that a creature so vastly different from me had understood, believed, and accepted. My call had spanned the huge communication gap between animal and man.

To this day, what happened that morning several years ago remains one of my most unforgettable and treasured experiences in the woods because it represents such a monumental accomplishment for me as a deer hunter. But there is another reason I am so fond of the memory of this hunt. It's a picture of something that happened to me back in 1974—a life-changing event.

As the mid-1970s approached, I was, so to speak, alone in the woods of life. At that time I had wandered aimlessly into my twenties, doubtful of my purpose for existing. I had no direction and no vision for my future. As a young man coming out of the late '60s and entering the early '70s, my thinking had been deeply influenced by the social tone of the times. My generation found identity in having no identity. It was a time when nothing was wrong and everything was right. The rebellion against the establishment and our parents' conservative ways was signaled by several things.

For example, we let our "freak flags fly." That phrase was a line from a popular song of the times that meant, "No, you can't make us cut our hair." We kept as few clothes as possible, mostly denim and flannel, and for the most part only what we could carry on our backs. And by all means, it was never cool to use a lot of soap—just a little dab would do us. When it came to personal hygiene, we believed in being as "natural" as possible. The problem in those days with being natural is the same problem it is now...natural stinks! There were plenty of products available on the market to do battle against natural odors, but it just didn't seem cool to use them.

My choice to partake in a lifestyle that I knew was considered unacceptable by those I loved and liked left me feeling uncomfortably disconnected from both family and friends. They certainly didn't disown me, but they did seem reserved when I was around them. I couldn't see it then, but I now realize that my family's troubled expressions when they saw me in my "hippieness" were not of fear, but of cautious pity. Sadly, I interpreted their desire to keep their distance as a form of rejection. Today I know they were struggling to know what to say to someone whom they so deeply loved but who had so drastically changed. Their most serious concern was that I had traded the narrow way of the Christian faith for the destructive, dark, and broad path of sin.

My longtime church friends were also visibly hesitant to embrace my errant state of heart. They scattered when I came around. The folks in my small hometown were simply not as open to my far-out mindset as I thought they should be. But the disconnect I sensed because of the suspicious reactions of those who were once so close was not the worst of the feelings I faced in those times. I was in great turmoil in my spirit because I felt dangerously alienated from God. And it was that troubling realization that prevented me from fully enjoying the pleasures that were so easily accessible in the lifestyle of "loose living" I had chosen.

There is a name for the unsettled, uneasy feeling that gripped me whenever I dabbled in sin. Christians call it "conviction." This term has its roots in the story of the woman who was caught in the act of adultery. Jesus rescued her from being stoned by her accusers by challenging them with the well-known words, "He who is without sin among you, let him be the first to throw a stone at her" (John 8:7). Verse nine in the New King James Version of the Bible reveals what happened next: "Then those who heard it, being convicted by their conscience, went out one by one."

With that scriptural account as the backdrop, "conviction" is often used by Christians to describe an awareness that rises up in an individual when they are in a spiritually unredeemed condition. They have "fallen under conviction." The term can sound strange to those who have never heard it used in such a way, but it is a very good description of the feeling of guilt that can gnaw at the soul. That's exactly what was happening in me.

The best comparison I can think of is that the conviction was like a blazing fire in my spirit that would not go out. It was a persistent fever, so to speak, that was warning me that something inside my soul was wrong. As hard as I tried, I could not dowse that intense fire of dread I felt in my heart. My desperate attempts to enjoy my waywardness simply didn't work.

There had been enough seed of the Scriptures sown in my heart by my parents as I grew up to produce the fruit of an understanding between right and wrong. While I walked the broad road, there was an abiding fear of what eternity held for me if I died as a sinner. Try as I did, I could not make the uneasiness go away. What I didn't know was that the Divine Hunter, God Himself, was nearby. He saw me wandering, lost and lonely, feeling alienated from family and friends, and walking farther away from Him each day. He lovingly called out to me.

Amazingly, God's call came from a place I least expected. Instead of coming from outside my heart, His call came from within the undying flames of fear that I had of being separated from Him. No, His voice was not audible. It came in the form of a very keen and quiet awareness in my heart that I desperately needed to turn around and go to Him. That inner call is explained in John 6:44 when Jesus said, "No one can come to Me unless the Father who sent Me draws him." God was indeed calling out to my heart.

In a way, the fire of conviction God spoke to my heart reminds me of what happened to Moses on the backside of the wilderness as recorded in the book of Exodus.

> Now Moses was pasturing the flock of Jethro his father-in-law, the priest of Midian; and he led the flock to the west side of the wilderness and came to Horeb, the mountain of God. The angel of the LORD appeared to him in a blazing fire from the midst of a bush; and he looked, and behold, the bush was burning with fire, yet the bush was not consumed. So Moses said, "I must turn aside now and see this marvelous sight, why the bush is not burned up." When the LORD saw that he turned aside to look, God called to him from the midst of the bush and said, "Moses, Moses!" And he said, "Here I am." Then He said, "Do not come near here; remove your sandals from your feet, for the place on which you are standing is holy ground." He said also, "I am the God of your father, the God of Abraham, the God of Isaac, and the God of Jacob." Then Moses hid his face, for he was afraid to look at God (3:1-7).

Notice that it was when Moses said "I must turn aside now and see this marvelous sight" that God spoke audibly to him. The stunned shepherd surely was amazed and awed as God's voice came from *within* the burning bush saying, "Moses, Moses!" He could only answer with a trembling, "Here I am."

I can remember in early 1974 coming to grips with the fact that the fire of guilt in my spiritual bosom was not going to be extinguished. As frustrating as it was to sense the flames wouldn't diminish, I didn't know enough to be thankful that the Holy Spirit of God was calling me to turn to Christ. I readily admit that I was irritated that the heat of guilt would not let me relax and enjoy the pleasures of sin. When I tried to disregard the fire, it burned hotter. All my attempts to kill the flames only fueled them. I tried dowsing the fire with mind-altering substances and unwholesome entertainment, and I surrounded myself with friends who shared my resistance to following God. Yet the conviction raged on.

Finally, in March of that year, I responded to God's call. To put it in hunter's terms, like the buck I called in with my grunt call, I stopped, wheeled around, and then headed back to God, who was calling me in with the Holy Spirit of His Son, Jesus Christ. It was a decision I will never regret and one that many others cherish in their thankful hearts.

How about you? Have the persistent flames of conviction been burning inside you? Perhaps you have been keenly aware that you need God. Maybe you have tried in many ways to suppress the feelings, yet they simply will not go away. Have your unsuccessful attempts to drown the flames of conviction left you feeling bewildered and troubled? If so, I have great news—God is calling you in!

The troubling unrest you feel is described in 2 Corinthians 7:10 as a "godly sorrow [that] produces repentance." It is the source I used for the following lyric that I hope will encourage you to embrace the conviction as your ally.

Blessed Sorrow

Like a fever on the brow
That tells of pain that looms within
A godly sorrow in the soul
Warns the wayward heart of sin

Oh, blessed sorrow
Sacred flame
Kindled by transgression
Oh, blessed sorrow
Fire of shame
Leads me to confession
Leads me to salvation

Oh, what a gift, this burning dread
That calls the sin sick to the cross
And there the healer loves and forgives
And keeps the soul from suffering loss

Oh, blessed sorrow
Sacred flame

> Kindled by transgression
> Oh, blessed sorrow
> Fire of shame
> Leads me to confession
> Leads me to salvation[9]

As you consider God's call, you can be especially glad that His intentions for drawing any of us to Himself are quite different from the reason I enticed the deer to come to me. I called the buck in for the sole purpose of taking its life. God calls us to Himself to give us eternal life! The very familiar passage in John 3:16-17 reveals His purpose for extending the invitation for us to come to Him: "For God so loved the world that He gave His only begotten Son, that whoever believes in Him shall not perish, but have eternal life. For God did not send the Son into the world to judge the world, but that the world might be saved through Him." And the apostle Peter comforts all who are being called by the Holy Spirit of God: "[The Lord] is patient toward you, not wishing for any to perish but for all to come to repentance" (2 Peter 3:9).

God wants to *give* you life, not take it from you. John 10:10 says of those who go to God through Christ, "The thief comes only to steal and kill and destroy; I came that they might have life, and have it abundantly." Furthermore, Jesus said, "I am the way, and the truth, and the life; no one comes to the Father but through Me" (John 14:6). If you are aware that God is calling to you from the midst of the guilt that burns in your spirit, don't walk away from Him. If you do, you may never know the calm that comes only through knowing you are at peace with God. The source of that divine comfort is explained in the apostle Paul's writing to the Romans:

> Therefore, having been justified by faith, we have peace with God through our Lord Jesus Christ...and we exult in hope of the glory of God...
>
> And hope does not disappoint, because the love of God has been poured out within our hearts through the Holy Spirit who was given to us. For while we were still helpless, at the right time Christ died for the ungodly...God demonstrates His own love toward us, in that while we were yet sinners, Christ died for us. Much more then, having now

been justified by His blood, we shall be saved from the wrath of God through Him (Romans 5:1,5-6,8-9).

Knowing you are at peace with God comes through accepting the invitation to embrace His only begotten Son. That call, my friend, is well worth heeding.

Today, if you would hear His voice,
do not harden your hearts.

PSALM 95:7-8

16

"I Saw It on My Own!"

Tim had just turned thirteen years old when his mother, Cathy, called me a couple of weeks before gun season opened for deer in our area. Annie and I had known the family for four years or so, and Cathy was aware that I was an avid hunter.

"Mr. Steve," she said, using the uniquely Southern greeting she always did, "could I ask a huge favor of you?"

"Sure, Cathy, fire away."

Her tone was apologetic as she spoke. "Tim has been bugging us about letting him go hunting. He's been through the state-required hunter's safety course, but his dad and I are so busy with work and raising these kids that neither one of us can take him to the woods. I was wondering if you'd be willing to let him tag along with you sometime this year."

The moment I heard Cathy's request, the rush of excitement made me smile. One opportunity a mature deer hunter won't pass up is helping newbies fill their tags for the first time. There's a satisfying feeling that comes with seeing new hunters' eyes widen at the sight of an incoming deer and hearing their breathing get heavier as the creature comes within range. It's a thrill to watch their hands shake as they try desperately to calm their nerves enough to hold their guns steady so they can take accurate shots.

Perhaps the reason we elders enjoy observing the flustered behaviors of new hunters is that it brings back sweet memories of first tasting the adrenaline pie served up in the hunter's woods. We never tire of remembering those unforgettable moments, and the chance to relive them through a youngster is probably a main reason we are "Johnny on the spot" when it comes to letting a newbie go with us.

I didn't hesitate to answer Cathy's request. "Absolutely! I'd be happy to take your young Nimrod to a deer stand. I have a place I think might yield some good results for him. I'll call you back with some dates."

Before we ended our phone conversation, Cathy told me that Tim was reading everything he could get his hands on about deer hunting. Plus his dad had purchased a few videos for him to watch so he could learn some "tricks of the trail."

I could only imagine how tough it was for Tim to be so wildly stimulated by the hunting magazine articles and films of hunters bagging one big buck after another. I figured by the time the next two weeks passed, he'd be pawing at the ground, ready to run to my chosen deer hunting area. I was right!

The first chance I had to take Tim hunting for a few hours was on the afternoon of a school day. His parents agreed to let him leave school early so we could be in the woods by 2:00. When I pulled into the driveway of his home to pick him up just after 1:00, he was standing on the porch wearing his newly purchased camo pants, shirt, and hat. He had his .243 rifle cased and ready to load into the truck. I've never seen a young man more eager to head to the woods than "Mr. Tim."

As we drove to the farm where we'd spend the rest of the day, I offered some insights I was sure would be useful for a new hunter. Tim was very attentive.

"Your mama told me you've been reading up on deer hunting," I said. "Sounds like you haven't missed a page of the magazines you have. It was smart of you to realize you should learn all you can about hunting. You can never get too much information when it comes to things you need to know to outwit a whitetail. They definitely have the advantage."

As though the dam had broken that held back all the tips about deer hunting I'd gathered during the previous forty years, I rambled on and on. Tim didn't seem to mind as I discussed whitetail traits, including how their ears, eyes, and noses are a hundred times better than humans' and how they seem to have a sixth sense when it comes to detecting danger.

For the next twenty minutes, Tim couldn't get a word in as I deposited more of my hard-earned hunting and woods knowledge into his memory banks. The last thing I told him before we arrived at the farm was a tip about one of the toughest challenges he'd face that day. I put it in that category because it was the biggest challenge for me when I was a teenager on a deer stand.

"Tim, we'll be sitting on the ground this evening instead of in a tree stand. For that reason, we can't move around a lot. In fact, any movement we make must be very, *very* slow. The eyes of a deer will catch the slightest unusual motion. I won't be able to raise my arm to point to where a deer is. If I see one and you don't, I'll whisper to help you spot it, but that'll be about all I can do."

The way Tim leaned forward in his seat told me he was chomping at the bit to experience everything I'd talked about. As I parked the truck, I had one more thing to say before we opened the doors and headed out.

"I'll remind you about this again after we settle in where we'll be hunting, but if I see a deer and you don't, I'll *whisper* its location to you. When you whisper back, don't turn your head. Even that tiny movement might get us busted. Got it?"

"Yes, sir, Mr. Steve!"

Fifteen minutes later I was scraping the leaves away on the ground to make a quiet place for us to sit under a wide oak tree. The old oak stood along a fencerow at the edge of a good-sized rectangular field. It was about seventy-five yards to the opposite side, where I fully expected the deer to enter for their evening meal. Facing the field with our backs leaning against the huge trunk, I quietly gave Tim a heads-up about what might happen.

"As you can see, over on the other side is a hill that drops down into this field we're watching. That hillside is a favorite place for deer to bed during the day. When they get up to feed later this afternoon, they'll browse inside the woods on acorns until about thirty minutes or so before dark. Then, if I'm right, they'll leave the woods and walk into the open field. That's when you might get a chance to take one of them."

Tim shivered with anticipation. He was so excited, I wasn't sure if he was going to be able to sit still. I thought maybe a little more coaching would help calm him a little.

"It's pretty quiet this evening since the wind is down. That's in our favor for two reasons. First, the wind will not carry our human scent to the other side of the field. Second, because the leaves are so dry, we might be able to hear them coming off the hill. You'll love that part. The sound of moving deer is music to a hunter's ears. But keep in mind that if we hear some leaves crunching, it might not be deer. It could be squirrels. They make a different sound. I'll point out the difference if we hear both."

I paused and took a long breath. I decided to resist the urge to tell Mr. Tim everything else I knew and save some for later. "Now it's time to just watch and listen."

I was quite impressed with how still Tim sat and eyed the area. Just like I'd requested, when he moved his head to look up and down the field he did it very slowly. His knees had been raised for about twenty minutes, the heels of his boots tucked up next to his behind. It was a position that even a flexible teenager can't endure for a long period of time.

"Mr. Steve," he whispered, "may I put my legs on the ground?"

"Yes, but let me check around us first."

As I visually scanned the area, I whispered, "Here's a tip. When you're hunting on the ground, it's always good to be as sure as you can that nothing is watching before you make major body adjustments. And clearing away the dry leaves around where you're sitting or standing is also good 'cause when you move, you won't make noise." Satisfied no deer were watching, I nodded at Tim and whispered, "Go ahead."

Tim got comfortable, and for the next forty-five minutes, we quietly watched, listened, and occasionally talked in low tones about some of the articles he'd read in hunting magazines and what he'd seen in some videos.

"What's one of the favorite things you read or saw?" I asked.

Tim slowly turned his face toward me and grinned. He told me about a story written by a hunter who traveled to the West by himself to hunt elk. Tim was intrigued by the idea of going it alone into the backcountry with just a bow, a backpack, a one-man tent, and a week's worth of supplies. "Someday I want to do what that guy did!"

I returned a wide grin as Tim whispered more details of his fantasy. I could hear my own heart in his words. When I was about fourteen, I had dreamed about the same thing as I read about other hunters' adventures in magazines such as *Fur-Fish-Game* and *Outdoor Life*. It was sheer joy to hear the echo of that yearning in Tim's voice. I was ready to tell Tim about my longtime dream of a one-man elk hunt when I noticed some movement on the other side of the field. Slowly I glanced at my watch and then looked at my hunting partner.

"Tim, the magic hour of 4:30 has arrived, and I think the deer have too. Look straight across the field and find that large cedar that's shaped like an upside-down teardrop. See it?"

"The really dark-green tree?" Tim was suddenly so excited his voice went in and out of a whisper.

"Yes, that's the one. Now, to the right of it is a much shorter cedar. Between the big one and the small one, there's a fence post. See it?"

"Yes, sir."

"There's a deer standing on the other side of that post. See it?"

"No, sir."

Tim's legs were flat on the ground, which meant he would have no rest for his gun if he needed to take good solid aim and shoot.

"While the deer is still back in the woods, slowly raise your knees so you can rest your gun on one of them for a shot. I'll watch the deer. If it looks nervous, I'll tell you to stop."

Tim followed my instructions and moved slowly. When he was finally in position, I turned his attention back to finding the deer that was still standing beyond the fence.

"Do you see the deer yet?"

"No, sir. Is he still where he was?" Tim didn't turn his head toward me to answer. He was doing great.

"Yes. It hasn't moved. It might be a doe. Whatever it is, it's almost like it's waiting until it gets a little closer to evening before coming out into the field. Deer are smart that way. That's why they live long enough to get big. Do you see it yet?"

"No, sir."

I'd forgotten about color identification! "Tim, did you notice that the fence post is a really light-gray color?"

"Uh-huh."

"Okay, now notice that the color of the woods *beyond* the post is between a light and dark brown."

"Yes, sir."

"That splotch of color in the middle is the fur of a deer. It's standing broadside with its head to the left. If you follow that splotch to the top, you'll make out the shape of the back. It has a slight curve in it, sort of like a horse's back does."

"Oh! I see it! I see it! Oh, man, I can see it! How did you find that?"

The question was sweet to hear. So were the footsteps of more deer coming down the hillside as I quietly explained to Tim how to pick out the well-camouflaged deer.

"That area beyond that fence post was a dark hole a few minutes ago. When I saw that it had filled with color, it got my attention."

I seized the moment and offered another tip. "When I first get to where I'm going to hunt, I study the area very carefully. I memorize as many of the shapes and tones of color as I can. Then if something changes, it's easier for me to recognize it. Many times I've spotted deer that way. Now, keep watching and see if you can spot more deer coming down the hill. Can you hear them?"

"Not yet," Tim said, sounding concerned.

"Listen for soft crunches. Deer usually walk steadily, so their pace doesn't sound flighty. Squirrels scamper across the leaves, but deer steps are regular and sound sort of humanlike."

Tim turned his head slightly to listen closely for walking deer. His whisper was a bit louder when he spoke. "I do hear them now! Oh…I think I see another deer! It's beyond the next fence post, to the right of the one we've been looking at. Yes! I see it. I found it all by myself! Do you see it?"

"I do! It's brown like the other one. I can make out the shape of the head, and its ears appear to be tall. Looks like a doe to me."

I could hear Tim's feeling of satisfaction in the way he whispered, "Wow! I can't believe I found it on my own just the way you did the first one. This is so cool."

It took fifteen long minutes before five deer walked out into the field. And as the sun was setting, I was teaching a youngster how to field dress his deer. The ninety-five-pound doe was a real trophy—as good to both of us as a twelve-point buck would have been.

Besides the joy of helping a newbie get his first kill and the celebration that followed, there's one other thrilling memory I especially enjoy recalling about the hunt. It was a great moment when I heard him say, "I found it all by myself!" As far as I'm concerned, it was the highest compliment he could have given me. His words reminded me of what Jesus said to the woman at the well. The event is highlighted in the book of John, chapter 4.

When this woman encountered Jesus just outside her town at Jacob's well, she learned that she'd met the One who would introduce her to the water that would forever quench her spiritual thirst. She also learned that He found her acceptable even though He knew she was a Samaritan (most Jews of that time detested Samaritans) and was aware of all that she'd done. She was so moved by Him that she went back to town and told the men about Jesus. Then she said, "Come, see a man who told me all the things that I have done" (John 4:29).

Because of her words, the men responded and went to hear Jesus. What they said to her after listening to Jesus was the highest compliment that can be paid to anyone who, like the Samaritan woman, is a witness or evangelist for Christ. They said to her, "It is no longer because of what you said that we believe, for we have heard for ourselves and know that this One is indeed the Savior of the world" (verse 42).

Hearing Tim, my hunting student, say that he saw the deer on his own was indeed a huge thrill for me. But it's miniscule compared to the immense joy the Samaritan woman must have felt when she helped the people of her town recognize for themselves the Savior of the world. Without a doubt, their saying, "We have heard for ourselves and know" was the highest honor she could imagine! And it's an honor that is available to all of us who have seen and acknowledged who Jesus is through eyes of faith and are willing to introduce Him to others.

My prayer is not for them alone. I pray also for those
who will believe in me through their message.

JOHN 17:20 NIV

17

Tangled Web

Deer hunting in early archery season in our neck of the timber means being in the woods while the insects are still active. Consequently, I've had lots of creepy-crawly things appear in my stand area that get my attention. When many of them show up, like harmless black ants or grasshoppers, I simply ignore them. But on occasion, one of my least favored of all multilegged creatures invades my space—the spider.

The scientific name of the pest is "Araneae." In my opinion, the name sounds much too innocent. I wonder if the science community got together and talked about how hated spiders can be and decided that if it had a moniker no one could pronounce, people would be less afraid of them. Somewhere along the way, however, the more general name "arachnid" was applied to the spider. My guess is that it was coined by a little lady named Muffet who decided the spider needed a name that carried more weight on the fright side of the scale.

While Araneae and arachnid are okay titles for spiders that crawl on trees or across the ground, I have my own pseudoscientific name for the little intruders when they are suddenly caught crawling across my clothes. I call them *iiiyyyeee getofffmmmeee.*

I've discovered the cursed little creatures on my person more times than I care to remember. I don't hesitate for one single second to abandon my self-imposed policy about sitting still in a deer stand. Without giving it one millisecond of thought, I go into self-defense mode. The intruder will either find itself airborne with a fast-flying flick of my finger or, more likely, crushed flat by the gloved hand of human hatred.

As much as I dislike spiders, I've managed to glean some redeemable insights from them that I've written about in other books. For example, in my book *A Look at Life from a Deer Stand Devotional*, I highlighted two characteristics of a spider that are noteworthy. One is that its tiny size gives it an advantage not available to larger creatures. Because of its smallness, it can take up residence even in a palace and enjoy the food of kings. "What an inspiring picture this can be of how insignificance can be an advantage if used wisely. For example, think of how many employees who started as backroom janitor types that fed on the knowledge of a company's operation and ended up either owning that business or creating an improved version of it."[10]

Another interesting yet thought-provoking characteristic of the spider is its web. As amazingly intricate and beautiful as a fully woven web can be, its microthin, sticky strands have a rather sinister purpose. They are designed to trap other bugs so the spider can kill and eat them (or save them for a later feast).

Though a web is an extremely effective weapon for the spider, I'm personally glad that the types found in Tennessee can capture nothing much larger than a fly. It was this limitation of the spider's web that led me down the path of imagination one morning while deer hunting. As I watched yet another spider build its trap, I wondered, *What if humans really were able to weave a web like the Spiderman character does?*

When the question crossed my mind, I followed it up with another thought: *Now I know who got the idea for the Spiderman character. It had to be a hunter because only people like us have enough time to sit and think of insane ideas like this!*

I proceeded to visualize a hunter in skintight camo instead of the red outfit that Spiderman wears. The hunter's superpowers gave him the ability to build a web across a deer trail, a web big and strong enough to capture a trophy buck that was leaving a field and walking into a thicket. Then I went completely off the deep end and jumped to spring turkey season. I imagined a mature gobbler hanging in a web, flopping around trying to free itself.

I spent more time than I should have thinking about some of the hunter's other advantages of being able to weave a web. Thoughts like how much cash we would save by not having to buy guns and bullets, bows and arrows. Trespassers and poachers who came onto private land that we owned or leased could be dealt with very quietly (except for their screaming). We could go to the woods early in the morning, make a web, go home and watch a golf tournament or a football game on TV, and then go back that evening to gather up the meat. What a deal!

As wild as the thought of humans being able to weave webs might be, the truth is that we really can—and do. How do I know? I've seen it done! Though the strands aren't like the ones Spiderman creates, they are just as real and a lot stickier than we expect. And the webs are extremely effective—but not for trapping food from the animal or insect kingdom. Instead, the web I'm referring to is the kind that traps the hearts and lives of humans. Here's a song lyric that explains one situation I witnessed.

The Tangled Web

Quiet room
Late night
Spend some time searching that site
Unaware that they're being led
Into a tangled web

Picture book
Familiar face
From another time and another place
Send the words—they might be read
It's a tangled web

New sparks from a flame that's old
Warm feelings where love has gone cold

Every line in the message makes another thread
To catch a heart
It's a tangled web

Quick reply,
"How do you do…"
"You're looking good."
"So do you!"
"It's been too long—can we connect?"
It's a tangled web

Make up a reason
To take a trip
Secret place and a hello kiss
Stealing love
From someone else's bed
It's a tangled web

New sparks from a flame that's old
Warm feelings where love has gone cold
Every line in the message makes another thread
To catch a heart
It's a tangled web.

Now what they do
Leaves them blind
Can't see the broken hearts left behind
Someday there's gonna be regrets
It's a tangled web[11]

This lyrical account unfortunately reflects a very real situation. Annie and I were quite shocked when we heard that a friend I'll call Joyce had used social media to connect with an old boyfriend from high school who lived far away. After a few weeks of communicating online, she drove many hours to meet her former beau halfway between their two towns. A couple of months later, she announced to her husband of nearly forty years that she was leaving him to be with her old flame. At the same time, the man on the other end of the cyber connection broke the news to his wife that he was leaving her for his high school sweetheart.

When Joyce sent her first message to her old friend, it was probably innocent curiosity. His reply could have been equally harmless. However, at some point, perhaps at the second, third, or fourth exchange, something happened that turned their innocuous online visits into a desire to get together and kindle a forbidden romance.

On the surface, Joyce and her husband seemed to be getting along just fine. There was no hint of unhappiness or dissatisfaction with each other, and Joyce gave no signs of unrest in her marriage. Of course, we don't know what went on behind their closed doors.

Whatever the reason was for Joyce's decision to leave her husband and family, Annie and I are sure of a valuable lesson. When people allow themselves to entertain wayward thoughts, those thoughts can weave a surprisingly sticky and powerfully effective trap for them and others.

To guard our own marriage and help others, Annie and I discussed what Joyce could have done to avoid such a disastrous outcome. Naturally, the first thing we thought of was how dangerous the internet can be. We know that the World Wide Web is a very useful tool that can serve humanity in positive ways, but in this case, it served as a dark dungeon where a web of destruction was woven. Joyce could have immediately unfriended her old flame the moment she felt an errant emotion about him or he sent a message that suggested anything questionable. Of course, the man could have done the same thing.

Because the world of social media technology has inherent dangers, I urge all users—men and women—to make it a matter of utmost importance to be on guard against the threads of verbiage that are covered with the lethal glue of lust or potential attraction. As you connect with friends from the past or present, don't forget these lines in the lyric: "Every line in the message makes another thread to catch a heart / It's a tangled web." May those words echo in your head and in your heart the moment you detect something illicit in a message, whether it came to you or you from you.

There are other things you can do if you are tempted to continue connecting with someone on the web who shows a questionable interest in you. A friend of ours did these things when an online exchange with an old friend heated up. He simply broke it off with the person, pulled out of that particular website's world, and changed his email address. And he never again checked the other person's site. His decision to disconnect from the website was a choice to keep his relationship with his wife and children strong. He has never regretted getting off that online grid.

Avoiding the particular social media website where the encounter took place and changing email addresses are commonsense suggestions. The problem is that common sense is hard to come by these days. It is mind boggling to consider that people who appear so sensible one day can be so insanely obsessed with the fantasy of forbidden love the next. But it happens because the spider of temptation weaves such masterful traps.

If you're a hunter and spend time in the woods, sooner or later you're going to see an Araneae at work. When you do, it's okay to admire its amazing weaving skills. It still astounds me. But when you see the web, let it remind you to be careful when you're on the internet. Spiritually, emotionally, and even physically, your life depends on your willingness to not get caught in the web of temptation.

He who dwells in the shelter of the Most High will abide in the shadow of the Almighty. I will say to the LORD, *"My refuge and my fortress, My God, in whom I trust!" For it is He who delivers you from the snare of the trapper and from the deadly pestilence.*

PSALM 91:1-3

18

He Cares

Billy's cell phone buzzed in the middle of a lunch meeting with his fellow production managers at the furniture factory where he worked. As he kept talking, he pulled the phone out of his shirt pocket to see whose name was in the window. It was his wife calling from their home.

"Sorry, guys. I gotta take this call." He left the table and clicked the answer button. "Hey, babe. What's up?"

Cindy's voice sounded a little strained. "Your mom called, and she's worried about your dad."

Billy heard his wife's worry in her voice. "What's up with Dad? Everything okay?"

"Well, your dad went hunting this morning and promised he'd be back home before 11:00, but he's not back yet."

Billy felt a wave of relief. He tried to pass the reassurance on to his wife. "Dad's probably tracking a wounded deer. We hunters can get so focused on a blood trail that we forget important stuff like calling and letting people know what's going on."

Cindy didn't want to counter with what she had to say next, but she did so as calmly as she could. She knew it would likely prompt her husband to drop what he was doing and go to the farm where his dad was hunting.

"Billy, your mom said your dad called her about 8:30 this morning from the woods and reported he wasn't feeling well. He told her he'd climbed out of his tree stand, the one on the backside of the property, and was going to walk back to the truck and head home. She hasn't heard from him since. It's now past noon. That's why she's worried."

Billy couldn't speak for a few moments as he processed what he'd heard.

"That doesn't sound good. I think I'd better wrap up my meeting here and head to the farm. Call me if you hear from Mom."

Cindy ended the call and said a prayer for her father-in-law. As she looked out of their kitchen window toward the east where her worried husband would be going, she said a prayer for him as well.

Billy went back to the lunch table and announced that the meeting would have to end and told them why. His friend Keith insisted on going along, and Billy took him up on the offer. With his imagination running wild with worry about what might have happened to his dad, Billy knew the twenty-minute drive they were going to make would seem like twenty hours.

Keith held on as Billy sped around the turns that took them out of the factory property and onto the main highway. Once they reached the edge of town and less traffic, he hoped he could help his friend by distracting him with some conversation.

"Tell me about your dad, Billy. How long has he been a hunter?"

It took a few seconds for Billy to answer, but he finally did.

"Dad's been a hunter since he was a kid. My grandpa—his dad—introduced him to squirrel hunting when he was about six. When he was only eight, he got his first deer. That's mighty young to start hunting, but there weren't a ton of regulations regarding kids at that time. Hunting got into his blood. I don't know anyone who loves the challenge of a hunt more than my dad."

Keith noticed that it seemed to help his friend to talk, so he probed a little more.

"How old were you when your dad took you hunting for the first time?"

Billy half smiled. "Much to my mother's protests, Dad took me with him to a deer stand when I was four years old. I remember it vividly. I can still smell the coffee in the thermos he opened while we were sitting in the old wooden tree stand together. I wanted to take a drink, but he wouldn't let me. He had a little bottle of orange juice for me…and a Snickers bar. Dad tried to keep the news from Mom about what he gave me for breakfast, but leave it up to a kid to tell everything."

With five more miles to go on the main highway before turning onto the narrow gravel road that led to the farm, Keith kept the conversation going.

"Isn't your boy about four years old now?"

"Yes, he is. And I figure I can't break tradition. I plan to take him hunting with me this fall. I bought a pop-up blind just so BJ can move around when he wants to. Cindy's not crazy about the idea, but she understands. She voiced her worry, but she also believes it will be good for us to be in the woods together. My dad can't wait to be there the first time BJ goes. It'll be tight in the tent, but that's what family and hunting is all about—being tight."

The conversation ended when Billy turned onto the gravel road. White dust billowed behind his pickup as he hurried toward the blue metal gate where he'd park. Keith saw that his friend's expression had turned serious as he pulled up along the fence next to his dad's pickup and turned the engine off. He pointed toward an opening in the distance between two patches of woods.

"We're going to walk across this field and go through that opening in the trees. The stand Dad went to this morning is a ten or twelve minute walk beyond that point. As we go, keep scanning the area all around us…just in case."

A chill hit Keith from the way Billy paused before he said "just in case." Keith tried to lighten the moment.

"Sounds like your dad knows what he's doing out here. I suspect he's just fine."

"You're right. What I'm hoping is that you and I are going to be helping a sixty-five-year-old hunter drag a monster deer back to the gate. But we'll head to the stand first to make sure he's not there."

Billy didn't take the time to unlock the gate and walk through it. Instead, he quickly climbed over it, and Keith followed. Moving quickly, they topped the last rise before reaching a spot where they could see the stand. Billy stopped and took out his cell phone. After touching the speed dial number for his dad, he put the phone on speaker. The two of them listened as his dad's phone rang several times before going to voice mail.

"Hey, this is William. I'm probably hunting and can't answer. Leave a number, and I'll call you back."

Keith smiled. "He is a diehard hunter, isn't he?"

Billy didn't answer as he touched the off button on his phone. He resumed their brisk pace as he put it back in his pocket. "Dad usually puts his phone on silent when he's hunting, but it was worth a try."

Billy looked toward the hill where the tree stand was located. He spotted the familiar platform made of treated lumber and saw that it was empty. He visually followed the two-by-four steps down the tree to the ground. Because of the camo clothing his dad was wearing, at first Billy missed the form of a man sitting at the base of the tree. Realizing something seemed odd, he kept looking. When he finally realized what he was seeing, his face turned pale.

"Dad!" Billy's yell reverberated powerfully through the woods. He didn't get an answer, and he yelled louder as he sped up his pace. "Dad!"

Still seeing no movement, he broke into a hard run. Keith fell in behind him, and the two of them jumped over and around the natural debris on the floor of the woods. After a fast descent into a ravine and an even faster climb up the other side, they reached the flat where the tree stand was located. Billy stopped when he got about ten yards from his dad.

His rifle lying on the ground at his side, his father was sitting with his back against the tree. His head was bowed as if he were praying or sleeping.

Though William's hat covered most of his face, Keith could see enough of his skin to notice it was an eerie gray color. His soul ached when he glanced over at Billy and saw the look on his friend's face. Billy had noticed it too. Keith watched as the weeping son slowly covered the remaining yards and knelt in front of his dad.

Billy didn't touch him. Instead, he leaned down low enough to look up at his face. "Dad? Are you okay? Are you asleep?" he asked softly. "Can you hear me?" After waiting a few seconds, Billy put his hand on his dad's shoulder and gently shook it. There was no reaction from his dad.

Keith knelt next to Billy but didn't say a word. Both men's eyes were glistening with tears as they processed the reality they didn't want to face.

Finally Billy spoke. "I think he's gone, Keith. Dad's gone." After a pause, Billy cried out, "Oh, God, this can't be happening!"

Billy and Keith stood and then sat down on the dry leaves around the tree, Billy next to his dad. Billy kept hoping his dad would lift his head and say something, but it didn't happen. Keith dreaded to say what had to be said.

"Billy?" Keith kept his voice gentle. "We have to notify some folks about this. I say we call 911 and find out who needs to come out here to help."

"You're right, Keith. I know you're right. But let's give Dad a few more minutes. Maybe he'll come around."

Billy knew he was only delaying the inevitable, but he felt compelled to wait.

Keith put his arm around his friend and patted his shoulder. "Take as long as you want, Billy. If it's all right with you, I believe I can find my way back to the gate. I'll call for help and wait for the people there."

"Thanks, man. When they come to where we're parked, call me so I know you're coming. I'll be right here. Give me five minutes before you call anyone so I can call Mom and my wife."

When the sound of Keith's footsteps faded beyond the rise, Billy sat next to his dad and wept. The dread he had in his heart about calling his mother and Cindy was almost more than he could bear. Finally he gathered the nerve to do it, knowing it would be the worst call his mother could imagine.

He cried harder as he called his mom and broke the news. There was another flood of tears when he spoke to Cindy. When he was through with the calls, he felt weary under the burden of sorrow. Weak and broken, he leaned against the tree his dad was leaning against. He was shoulder to shoulder with his father. Billy looked up at the afternoon deep-blue sky and felt hot tears run down his cheeks and jaw as he whispered toward the heavens.

"God, how am I gonna get through this? How's Mom gonna get through it? What about my boy, who loves his grandpa? What's he gonna do? And Cindy? Oh, God, please have mercy on us."

Billy didn't say another word or ask God another question for several minutes. He put his head back against the tree trunk. He couldn't look at his dad's lifeless body even with his peripheral vision without sobbing, so he kept his eyes closed and waited for Keith to return with help. He searched his mind for something that might ease the pain of despair.

Not being heavily into music, he never expected a song to come to mind at such a time and offer needed consolation. He was surprised when he remembered an old hymn that had given his dad great comfort when his only brother passed away. The two men had been very close. Billy remembered his dad playing the song over and over. He could almost hear his dad's voice as he sang along with the quartet. Though Billy's voice felt weak and shaky, he sang as much of the song as he could remember:

> Does Jesus care when I've said "goodbye"
> To the dearest on earth to me
> And my sad heart aches, till it nearly breaks
> Is it aught to Him? Does He see?
>
> Oh yes, He cares, I know He cares
> His heart is touched with my grief
> When the days are weary, the long nights dreary
> I know my Savior cares.[12]

Billy sang through the only verse he could remember and the chorus a few times. Each time, the river of tears grew deeper, yet the pain of sorrow seemed to ease a bit. He knew the sting of finding his dad at the base of one of his favorite deer stands would likely never go away completely, but he also realized this melody was one he would hum when the waves of sorrow rose.

Billy's parents had made advance plans regarding what to do when one of them died. They'd agreed to be cremated, and each of them chose where their ashes were to be placed. The locations were included in the instructions in their wills. When Billy and his mother opened the envelope, they read William's last request: "Put my ashes at the base of the tree on the backside of our farm. Scatter them there

148

and let them fertilize that mighty oak. I want it to stay strong so Billy and BJ can use the stand that's in it."

As instructed, William's ashes were scattered around the last tree he'd climbed and the one he'd designated as his final resting place. On the trunk of the tree is Billy's handiwork. Using his dad's favorite hunting knife, he carefully carved into the bark two words from the song that meant so much to his dad and now to him: "He cares."

Humble yourselves under the mighty hand of God . . . casting
all your care upon Him, for He cares for you.

1 PETER 5:7 NKJV

19

Bear Attack

When Les and his sixteen-year-old son, Brent, pulled out of the driveway in the fully loaded family Suburban and headed toward the main road, they waved goodbye to Kathy, standing alone on the front porch of the house. As Les's wife and Brent's mother, she tried hard not to let her worry show. Her husband and teenaged son were going to be venturing into the rugged Montana mountains armed only with bows and arrows while pursuing black bears. Concern for their safety clawed her heart, but there was an abiding hope that something more might be obtained in the wild than just bear—especially for Brent.

The previous two years had been tough for the boy. Though gifted as a learner, his frail frame and quiet demeanor opened him to ridicule from some of the students. A few bullies focused on him, casting cutting and hurtful comments his way frequently. The hurt chewed through his tender spirit like bear's teeth. And the more emotional blood he shed because of the word wounds, the more the predators circled, taking quick nips while awaiting opportunities for vicious bites. On more than one occasion Brent came home emotionally battered and bruised.

This academic year wasn't going any better. By early October, Kathy could see the stress in her son's face and the despair in his eyes. He'd endured just about all he could. Attempts to solve the issues via the authorities at the school weren't yielding results, and in fact, often created more problems.

Even though Brent might encounter danger in the Montana mountains, it was a different kind. Kathy knew he needed a break from the emotional harassment at school. And since Les had been wanting some concentrated hunting time with Brent for quite a while, this seemed like a great opportunity to give Brent much-needed down time and a supportive time with his dad.

Kathy turned and walked back into the house. As she closed the door she whispered, "God, Les is so excited that he's going hunting with Brent. Please give them a great trip and a life-changing journey. Bring them back to me safely, and if You will, bring them back changed for the better—both of them."

Twenty-two hours and what seemed like a half-ton of fast food later, Les and Brent could see the towering mountains of Montana through the windshield of the Suburban. As they crept closer to their destination, Brent felt excitement and nervousness building up regarding the hunt. Whether it was because of the awesome size of the mountains or the fact they were going to hunt predators, he was feeling a bit anxious. It was also his first trip to the land of dark timber and his maiden voyage into the woods as a bow hunter.

Earlier that summer, his dad had finally convinced Brent to put aside his favorite book for a couple of hours and go to Phillips' Archery Shop with him for an evening of friendly competition. For Les, it wasn't just a time to enjoy the company of other archers gathered to engage in a little ongoing rivalry. The event also offered a surefire way to ensure that his muscles stayed tuned for the movements bow shots require during hunting season.

Brent had quietly sat on a bench behind the firing line and watched the participants. As he focused on his dad, a figure appeared before him with a half-dozen field-tipped arrows in one hand and a compound bow in the other.

"I'm Ed Phillips, the owner of this place. You're Les's son, right?"

"Yes, sir." Brent's brief answer was delivered with a reserved and awkward tone, but it didn't sway Mr. Phillips from his quest.

"Well, while your pop is trying to outshoot his buddies, how about trying your hand at this archery thing tonight, young man? We have one open lane, and I have a bow for you that should work great. It has a peep sight and a first-class setup. What do you say? Want to give it a fling?"

Brent hesitated for a moment and then stood up. "Sure. Why not?"

Les couldn't believe his eyes when he happened to look down the shooting lane and saw his normally reserved son accepting the challenge to nock his first arrow. As he waited to return to the firing line, he watched his son receive a quick-shot technique tutorial from Mr. Phillips. His heart raced with excitement that his prayer for Brent to discover an interest in shooting the bow might be answered. His hopes were high, and he held his breath as Brent stepped to the line and came to full draw. It seemed like forever before he let the first arrow fly.

The aluminum shaft flew straight, and the arrow sounded a familiar *fwap* as it hit the paper target mounted to several layers of fiberboard fifteen yards from the shooting line. Amazingly, Brent's first shot had pierced the target inside the thin ring that surrounded the ten spot. Les was thrilled to see where the arrow hit, but that sight was no comparison to what he saw when his eyes shifted back to the shooting line. There was his only son, uncharacteristically smiling from ear to ear as he received congratulatory pats on his back from Mr. Phillips. Maybe a bow hunter was being born this night!

Brent looked down the shooting lanes toward his father and their eyes connected. Les saw a huge grin, a yes nod, and an excited expression that said, "Now I know why you like this place, Dad!" That assumption was confirmed when Brent gave his dad a thumbs-up. He then put his hand out toward Mr. Phillips for another arrow.

Brent's second shot hit just left of the first one and above the bull's eye about five inches—but well inside the outer edges of the eleven-by-fourteen paper target. As Brent nocked another arrow, it was all Les could do to hold back tears of joy. He felt a wellspring of thankfulness that Mr. Phillips had issued an archery invitation to Brent.

"Hey, Les!"

Les looked toward Mr. Phillips.

"Hang your bow on a nail and come over here!"

Mr. Phillips didn't have to say it twice. Les walked toward lane 1, his heart pounding with excitement. He was witnessing the birth of a new archery buddy *and* a new era in his relationship with Brent.

"Les, I don't think I've ever seen a young man with a more instinctive leaning for the archery shot than your boy has. His form seems to be as natural to him as breathing." Mr. Phillips turned to Brent and challenged good-naturedly. "Show your pop what you can do, young man."

With a surprising air of confidence, Brent snapped the bright-orange arrow nock onto the string, placed his index finger above the nock and his middle and ring fingers below it, carefully pulled the string back toward the right corner of his lip, took aim, and released it. The arrow flew true and smacked the paper between the other two.

"Hot dog!" Les exclaimed.

Some of the other archers had paused to watch, and they clapped at Brent's success. Les beamed.

During the summer, Les was elated when Brent took the state's bow hunter's safety course. After more practice, Brent had accepted his dad's invitation to go to Montana to hunt bear in the fall. Now they were on their way. As Les drove along in the westbound lane of the interstate, enjoying reliving the steps that had led up to this moment, his thoughts were suddenly interrupted.

"How much farther, Dad?"

Les heard two distinct emotions in Brent's question. He could tell his son was excited about the hunt that would start the next morning, but he also sounded a little tentative with the reality that they were only a night's sleep away from it.

"We're about an hour from the hotel. We'll check in, get some supper, and go over the topography maps again. You'll love this territory we're going into. I've been there three times. You're in good hands with me, buddy. We'll be fine. And we'll never be more than a hundred yards apart during the hunt." Les hoped his confidence would settle his son's apprehension. He decided to add an extra measure of encouragement to help that cause.

"Brent, I've watched you destroy the ten spot many times at the range over the summer with your bow. And the 3-D targets are worn out in the heart areas from your shots. Like Mr. Phillips said, you're a natural with the bow. You can count on that ability plus the skills you've developed to serve you well out here. I believe if you get a chance to take a shot, you'll do just fine."

"Thanks, Dad. I guess I am a little nervous…and excited!"

"Hey, son, if hunting wasn't a rush and didn't test our nerves, why would we bother to go into the woods? You're ready! And even better, since you've got all your schoolwork done already, we can put our minds in bear gear and concentrate on the hunt."

Brent's smile was more carefree as the tires of the Suburban hummed closer and closer to their destination.

Les silently lifted a short prayer to heaven: "Lord, please bless my son with an opportunity for a bear—and a steady hand to take advantage of it!"

The sunrise the next morning was spectacular. After a two-hour climb, the men were enjoying it from the mountain. Perched on a huge rock that jutted out from the hillside, father and son waited patiently for enough light to search the nearby meadows using their binoculars. They sat quietly, enjoying the view for twenty minutes, and then Brent broke the silence.

"This is awesome, Dad! I had no idea what kind of view we'd have from up here. This is different from our state. I think we should call Mom and have her pack up everything. Let's move here!"

Les chuckled, putting the rubber rims of the binoculars up to his eyes. "I fully agree, son. But it would be best if you made the call. Your mama might accept the idea from you quicker than she would from me."

Both guys searched the high country.

"Well, son, I'm not seeing any bears, so let's hike up a little higher. There's another spot where we can do some glassing, and I've seen bears from there before."

An hour later, Les removed his pack and sat down behind a huge tree that had fallen. He rested his elbows on it for a steady look through his binoculars. Brent followed suit, and the two of them swept the open areas.

"Hey, Dad. What's that in the meadow on the far right? A cow?"

Les pulled his binoculars away from his face to see which direction Brent was looking, and then he put the glasses to his eyes and searched that area.

"Whoa! That's not a cow. That, my good buddy, is a bear. Good eye. You've just found us a beast, and from its size it's probably a male—a boar! He's huge!"

Brent felt a surge of satisfaction that he'd spotted the first bear on their trip. "What now?"

"We get our packs on our backs and go after him! That's 'what now.' This is great stuff for our first day out, especially since we only have three days to hunt. It'll be a tough hike, but I suspect that meadow is full of something that bear likes to eat. If we don't waste time, we hopefully will get there before he pays his tab and leaves."

An hour later, sweat poured off the two hunters as they gasped for air and hurriedly dug the toes of their boots into the steep terrain. The ascent to where the bear was thought to be wasn't an easy one, but they managed to make it relatively quickly. As they approached the meadow, Les gave a signal to stop, hunker down, and listen.

"Brent, if the bear is still here, we're probably about three hundred yards from him. I want you to stay right here. I'm going to move closer to the edge of this meadow and take a peek. Keep your eyes on me. I'll wave when it's a good time for you to come closer. Bears don't see all that well, but when you come to me, stay low and be as quiet as you can. Their ears and noses are really sharp. Right now the wind is in our favor, but it could shift anytime. If it does, we'll have to back out and go around to the other side. Keep your eyes on me, okay?"

Brent nodded, swallowed hard, and settled down on his knees to wait. He watched his dad duck-walk toward the open area ahead of them. The lay of the land didn't allow Les to get a full view of the area until he was a little higher. In fact, he would reach the edge of the field before he'd be able to get a clear look.

With his bow tethered to a sling and draped over his back, Les crawled on all fours toward a Volkswagen Beetle–sized rock. Before he stood up to take a look over the rock, he motioned for Brent to make his way up the hill. A few minutes later, the two of them squatted side by side as Les quietly coached his son on what to do next.

"I'm going up to that rock about thirty yards from here to see if I can see the bear. If he's there, I'll motion you to come over. Go ahead and nock an arrow in case he's close. Be quiet and stay low as you come up."

Brent could hear the unbridled excitement in his dad's voice and felt it's infectious effect. His heart was beating as fast as a hummingbird's. He was shocked at how much he was loving the challenge. He quietly cheered his father on toward the boulder.

When Les reached the rock, he slowly stepped up on a low mound, stretching to peek over the top of the boulder.

Just as he peered over the top of the rock, he realized the swirling breeze had shifted, possibly carrying his scent to the monstrous critter that hopefully was on the other side.

Suddenly, only nine yards away, the bear stood on his hind legs and aggressively growled, staring straight at Les!

Man and beast were in a standoff. Knowing a bear can charge at thirty miles an hour, Les quickly backed down and turned toward Brent. With respectful fear in his eyes, Les desperately motioned for Brent to move back to safety.

Les backed downhill quickly, watching for the bear. The hunter didn't see the stump until his right foot was caught, and he tumbled backward. Just then the bear came around the rock. Alert, sniffing, and growling, it moved toward him.

The older man quickly wrestled with the pepper spray can attached to his belt, frantically trying to unclip it as he heard the crunching of leaves and snapping of branches announcing the bear's approach. Knowing he was easy prey for the startled and unhappy beast, Les rose up on his knees and waved his arms while yelling at the top of his lungs, "Get out of here! Yaaaaa yaaaaa! Get out of here!"

The bear halted seven yards from Les and stood upright again. The huge body appeared to be twenty feet tall from Les's on-the-ground perspective. Not good. In the next few seconds, Les was amazed at how many thoughts went through his head. *Will Brent get away safely? Kathy's not going to want to get this news. God, have mercy on me... and Brent!*

Suddenly he heard the telltale sound of collapsing bow limbs off to his left. As though in slow motion, he saw a flash of white and neon-green fletching sink deep into the bear's ribs in the lung area. Instantly the monster dropped to all fours and ran off, moaning in pain. Les couldn't believe his eyes. He shot a glance back toward Brent and saw he was scrambling to remove another arrow from his bow-mounted quiver and nock it onto the string.

Les looked in the direction the bear had escaped to make sure he hadn't decided to come back for another round. The beast was nowhere in sight. After about twenty long seconds of reassuring himself he was safe, Les sat down, emotionally exhausted. He watched as Brent approached quickly, his mechanical release still attached to the string of his bow. He stood over him like a protective soldier guarding a wounded comrade.

"Son!" Les heaved a huge sigh. "Brent, thank you! Thank you! I can't believe what just happened! What a nightmare!"

"Well, Dad, if you're dreaming, I wish you'd wake me up. I'm shaking all over—and I'm not sure I'll ever stop."

"Brent, do you realize what you just did for me? You saved my life! And probably yours too. How did you have the nerve and presence of mind to get to full draw just now?"

Brent, still in his ready-to-shoot-again stance, looked in the direction the bear had run and answered, "I really don't know, Dad. But I wasn't about to let that bear have you for lunch. I did what I had to do."

With legs that were weak, Les forced himself to his feet and assured his son that the bear wouldn't be returning. Then he said, "Boy, it's time for a bear hug—the human kind!"

As father and son embraced, Les placed his open hand on the back of Brent's head and pulled it to his shoulder. He held him tightly in heartfelt thanks, embarrassed to reveal the tears streaming down his face. Crying wasn't something Les was used to doing in front of anyone, especially another male—even if it was his son.

Brent's heart filled with gratitude that he'd been able to keep his focus and accomplish the task set so suddenly before him. His eyes also filled with tears as the two men shared the most emotional moment they'd ever had together.

After a full minute of a tight, arm-in-arm embrace, Les pulled back and put his hands on the shoulders of his wet-eyed son.

"Son, I've hunted since I was a kid, well before I was your age. I was ten when I started going to the woods with my Uncle Travis. I've seen a lot of unbelievable accomplishments by hunters in my time, and I've been in the woods with the best of them. From that fourteen-point elk your grandpa has hanging on his wall to the Dall sheep Uncle Travis bagged when we hunted in the dangerous and slippery high country of Alaska, I've witnessed amazing things. But what you did today tops them all. You showed the most poise in the face of grave danger I've ever seen."

Brent looked at the ground, an embarrassed but hearty smile on his face as he took in his dad's heartfelt praise. This was his first experience with the not-so-common sensation that overtakes a man when he hears another man talking from the deep region of his heart. He enjoyed the affirmation and approval in his dad's words. He raised his head to hear more.

"Brent, I don't know how you did it. Today you reached way down inside and found the courage and calm to save my life. I have a feeling you didn't know you had those qualities, and I pray you'll remember where they came from. When I could almost smell that bear's breath and count his teeth, thoughts passed through my head that were things a man thinks about just before he goes to meet his Maker. I was scared for me but also for you and your mom. When I heard the smack of bow limbs, my fear was interrupted. And then I heard the thud of your broadhead finding the bear and saw the fletching sticking in the bear's side. Your shot was right on the money! I was delivered from death. Son, God used you today in a mighty way."

Les noticed that Brent's eyes were wide as he took in every word. He looked like a lost traveler who had just been saved and was getting nourishment for the first time in days.

"There are a lot of giants in the world that are not any different from that bear," Les continued. "They're sort of like Goliath—you know, the giant young David killed. They want to take you down and devour you and the people you love. Today you've discovered you can defeat them. You have the courage and strength inside you, Brent. You proved it to me and to you. On this Sunday morning, right here on this great cathedral mountain, God showed you He is with you. He knew you were ready and worthy to be tested! And I'm sure glad you passed!"

Les was gently squeezing his son's shoulders and felt them relax. He knew his words were finding his son's heart.

"Son, I'm not sure if this is the best time to mention this, but I'm going to go ahead while the windows of our hearts are wide open. I know you've been badgered by bullies at school. I feel sorry for them now because they don't know who they'll be facing next Wednesday when you get back. The truth is, those kids are pitiful, and they've obviously never had anyone show them how to treat people and why they should be considerate. They need help. It might be tempting for you to use your newfound confidence to take some revenge, but that's not what those boys need. I urge you to be brave enough to love them and pray for them."

Brent's lips went straight and his jaw muscles tightened, but gradually his face relaxed and understanding shone in his eyes as his dad's logic took hold.

"And I'm sure you're not the only target of their insults. The best way to deal with this situation is to respond quietly but firmly, pray for them, and if you see someone being attacked by them, stand beside that person and bolster his or her courage. Your friendship with their other victims could very well make those cowardly predators run."

"I'll be honest with you, Dad. And this isn't easy to say. I've rehearsed all kinds of insults to use to get back at those guys, but none of them ever seemed strong enough. About a month ago, I started thinking hitting back would be better. Then I realized they'd gang up on me and I'd lose again. The next step seemed obvious. I should use some kind of weapon. Bullets would certainly work better than words.

In my mind I imagined firing as many rounds as the times they've hurt or embarrassed me."

Les's eyes were wide and his mouth tight as he studied his son. He removed one hand from Brent's shoulder and waited for more information.

"Dad, that's not going to happen. I promise. Not after today. This trip has changed me. Thank you for bringing me with you. I don't like being hurt…and I sure didn't like the thought of hurting anyone, because I know how it feels. But I didn't know what else I could do. Now I have an inkling. I'm telling you now, on this Sunday morning, on this great mountain, that those guys are never going to hurt me again. I won't let them do it anymore. I'm going to try what you said about responding firmly, praying, and putting up a united front with other kids being bullied. For the first time in a long time, I can't wait to get back to school!"

Les put his open hand on the side of his son's head and gently said, "I'm proud of you, Brent. You're da man, and I mean that from the bottom of my heart! And if you ever get frustrated and hurt to the point where you think about resorting to violence, come to me. I won't judge you negatively, and we'll work together on what you can do about it. Okay?"

"Okay, Dad. Thanks. I appreciate that."

"Now we need to get back to business. That bear is out there, probably mortally wounded. We need to find it."

As the two men hefted their packs onto their backs, Brent's chest swelled with the assurance that he was greatly loved by his dad. He smiled as he realized how great he felt…and it seemed to go to the very core of his being. Self-doubt had been erased in the last twenty minutes. His steps felt surer, his hearing seemed keener, the air on his exposed skin felt crisper, and his eyesight seemed to pick up more of his surroundings. Confidence flooded his heart and soul. He felt terrific.

Less than ten minutes later, the invigorated hunters found Brent's momentous kill collapsed next to a downed tree. After making sure the animal was dead, they attached the carcass and hide tags and spent the next few hours field dressing the bear and removing the cape. They talked and laughed as they labored over the beast, and by early afternoon they were making their way down the mountain, packing the heavy hide and two game bags full of meat. They stopped often to rest and relive their morning's adventure. Each time the story was rehashed, more details came to light, making the telling even more dynamic and dramatic.

When they reached the Suburban and loaded the meat and hide into the over-sized coolers they'd tied to the hitch-mounted tray, Les proposed a change of plans.

"Brent, I don't know about you, but I'm not sure I can wait until Tuesday to tell your mom about your adventure…and I'd sure rather show her your trophy instead of just telling her about it on the phone. Why don't we go straight to the checking station, report this kill, and then head east? We can get some of the trip under our belts this evening, find a hotel, and then finish it tomorrow."

"Are you sure, Dad? You haven't filled your bear tag…but I'm sure looking forward to telling Mom and my friends about this hunt!"

"Yep. I'm tuckered out with all the excitement. And your mama's probably worried about us. You've bagged enough bear meat to last us a while. And most of all, I want to see your mother's face when she sees this cape and hears what you've done. The sooner that happens, the better."

"Okay, Dad! Let's head home. Do you think we should let Mom know we're coming home early?"

"We'll call her when we get up tomorrow to complete the drive. We'll give her ample notice, but I'm not going to tell her the details of why we decided to head home so soon. I'll let you do that when we get home. Deal?"

Brent smiled. "Deal!"

Kathy heard the Suburban roar into the driveway just before sundown on Monday evening and ran out to meet her men. As they hugged and said their hellos, she noticed Brent's excited smile and Les's big grin. "You guys look like the cat that swallowed the canary," she said. "What's up with you two? And don't try to hide anything from me. You know that's not possible!"

Les cleared his throat and gestured for Kathy to join him and Brent at the rear of the Suburban. The two guys lifted the two coolers off the metal hitch tray, opened the one that contained the cape, and took it out. As they unfolded it, Brent was sure his mom's eyes were bigger than fried eggs as she realized the size of the pelt and saw the head.

"My word, Les and Brent! That thing is huge! Who got this beast?"

Les grinned and glanced at his son. "That's the look we gave up two days of hunting and drove all those hours for, buddy! Was it worth it?"

Brent, an ear-to-ear smile distorting his face, answered, "Sure is!" He turned to his mom. "I got this one, Mom!"

For the next half hour, Kathy stood next to the vehicle and listened as her son and husband talked about their dramatic hunt. They interrupted each other to fill in details, and when they got it all out, Kathy asked them to repeat their tale. She was speechless and kept shaking her head in awe and relief as the story unfolded again.

Finally the story was told and retold, and the men returned the hide to one cooler and toted the meat-filled one into the garage for butchering and packaging later that night. They would take the hide to show Mr. Phillips and then have it tanned and mounted by a local taxidermist.

As Les and Brent unloaded the Suburban and put away their gear and supplies, Kathy noticed a difference in her son. His quick, sure steps and squared shoulders revealed a new confidence and self-assurance. Even the tone and pitch of his voice seemed stronger. And best of all, he was sticking close to his dad as they worked side by side in companionable silence. Suddenly the prayer she'd said right after they'd left for their hunting trip echoed in her mind: *Bring them back to me safely, and if You will, bring them back changed for the better...both of them.* Gratefully, she acknowledged God's answer. She knew Brent had turned a corner and would be okay.

That night, after their son was settled in his room for a night of deserved and peaceful rest, Kathy went to the garage to help Les wrap up his chores. As her husband cleaned his hands, she said, "Les, I'm thrilled you and Brent could share the hunting experience you had. But if I'd known what your trip was going to entail,

I would've done my best to keep you both here. I'm so glad God was watching over both of you!"

Les rolled his eyes a bit and smiled slightly, debating whether to share that if he'd known what was going to happen, maybe he'd have stayed home without a fight.

Kathy shifted from one foot to the other, a movement she always made when she wanted to continue talking without interruption.

"Of all that you and Brent told me regarding that bear, the one thing I haven't heard about is how this experience has drawn you two together. I can see there's a new bond between you. Brent followed you around this evening like a real buddy. The change is obvious to me, and I wanted to make sure you noticed it too."

Les nodded his head in humble agreement.

"And, sweetheart, there's something even more astounding that took place while you and Brent were in Montana. I saw it as plain as can be this evening."

"What's that, Kathy?"

Kathy moved in and put her arms around her husband's waist. She softly and confidently said, "Les, you took a boy to the mountains…and brought home a man."

Les looked toward Brent's bedroom and then lowered his gaze to his wife. With moist eyes and a gravelly voice, he whispered, "I guess so, honey. I suppose we both changed…for the better. Thanks for letting us go."

20

Pete's Prayer

Pete's breathy whisper was as soft as he could possibly make it and still be heard by his friend next to him. "Don't move a muscle, Lenny. There's a huge gobbler coming down the edge of the field to my left. He's gonna walk right in front of us. When his eyes go behind that big tree, that's when you can get your gun up to your knee."

Lenny felt the torturous ache in his rear end from sitting so long and quietly. He complained quietly to Pete, "I can't stay in this position much longer."

"You can wait," Pete prodded. "The tom is almost behind the tree. Wait... wait...now! Move your gun up!"

Lenny quickly raised his weapon and lowered his cheek to the stock. He took careful aim to the right of the tree. His breathing quickened, and his pulse raced. The world around him disappeared except for his gun, the tree, and the huge tom that would appear any second.

There he is! Lenny squeezed the trigger and couldn't resist adding his vocal 20-gauge shotgun blast imitation the second his gun fired. A projectile of saliva flew from the back of his throat and hit his teeth before dribbling down his chin.

Pete instantly reacted to Lenny's shot. "You got 'im!"

As the boys turned toward each other to do a high five, reality abruptly butted in. They froze as they realized two hundred or so saints at Wells Grove Church were staring at them. The silence was deafening. Even the people sitting up front and in the choir loft were staring at them, mouths agape.

Shocked, the pastor stopped his sermon midsentence.

Only the subdued swooshing sound of material sliding against oak pews filled the hall as the congregation members shifted their bodies to look back and forth between the pastor and the two boys.

The two youthful hunters felt their faces getting warm from the hot glares coming their way. Pete froze, not moving an inch as he took in what was happening as far as eye movement alone would allow. Lenny, still crouched in shooting position with both feet up on the pew, realized he couldn't feel his body. Seconds passed like hours.

Lenny finally looked up, white faced, and stared at Pete.

Fully aware that the turkey that had wandered into their fourth-row fantasy hunt was not the only creature that would be suffering that morning, Pete quickly tried to think of a way to survive the incident. He mentally hurried through possible ways to ward off pastoral and parental execution. Amid his racing thoughts, he noticed Lenny was still holding his mother's umbrella on his knee like it was a shotgun. Very slowly he placed his hand on the flowered, hook-handled, shiny, makeshift 20-gauge and lowered it to the pew.

Pete lifted his head and looked over the benches to the front of the church. The first face he focused on was his dad's. Standing behind the pulpit, the look on his face resembled someone who had just witnessed a horrible car wreck. As disturbing as it was to see his dad's contorted face, it was nothing compared to the expression he saw when he scanned the choir loft's sea of green robes and found his mother. When his eyes met hers, he instantly recognized the similarities between his mother's choir robe and the cloaks judges wore. Pete realized his days of freedom were probably numbered.

Not bearing to maintain the connection with his mother's eyes, Pete looked down. He'd heard sermons about hellfire and brimstone, and he was sure he was experiencing the first signs of them right now. The fiery darts his mom was shooting at him hit their mark. His insides felt like a churning mass of fear. He blinked and hunched his shoulders.

Convinced his life—and likely his friend's—was about to be stripped of necessities such as bicycles, TV, video games, baseball gloves, and ice cream, Pete desperately aimed a prayer heavenward. Suddenly, as though an angel had hand-delivered the thought, he remembered a sermon his dad had preached not long ago. He closed his eyes and puckered his lips as he tried to remember the details. It was about a grand and joyful, yet-to-happen event.

What was the word Dad used? Something about future happiness Christians would experience. He searched through his memories, and lo and behold, there it was! Armed with the knowledge, Pete instantly enacted the plan he was sure God had given him. He jumped to his feet, reached skyward with both hands, looked straight up, and with the impetus of desperation, let loose a fervent prayer: "Oh, God! Let the *rupture* happen right now!"

Two levels of silence are known to mankind. There's a quiet that is simply a lot lower volume than the noise it has replaced. Though called silence, it is really a "near silence." What might be considered stillness in a large room might include slight hints of noises, such as breathing, an occasional soft clearing of a throat, or perhaps a creaking pew. The deeper level of silence is not often experienced, so when it is, it's rarely forgotten. This is when a complete and pure hush falls over everyone and everything in attendance.

Pete lowered his gaze to see if the plan had worked. He noticed stunned looks on some faces but quizzical looks on others. *Did I get it wrong?* he wondered. He waited. His lungs seemed to be working overtime and sweat was beading on his forehead. No one moved. Pete was sure everyone's hearts had stopped beating, and people must have quit breathing because he couldn't hear a thing. Even the candles seemed to stop flickering.

Gradually he heard the sounds of life creeping in. Then he heard something. *What was that? A giggle? Is someone laughing? What's happening?*

The stunned members of the congregation were slow to react, hesitant to be the first to break the silence. At first, trickles of giggles broke through the cracks in the dam of seriousness, followed by snickers and then outright nasal snorts. Suddenly the concrete wall of poise burst, and a torrent of laughter reverberated through the sanctuary. Knee slapping, floor stomping, pew pounding, as well as some shoulder slapping and gasping from laughing so hard added to the din.

The pastor—Pete's dad—bent over double trying to contain his laughter. He knew there would be no immediate recovery. The only thing to do as the leader was to let the laughter roll on for a while.

After a while the room calmed down a bit, and the sounds of deep sighs of relief, nose blowing, and eye wiping with tissues were heard. At that point, the pastor stood behind the podium with his hand on his chest, as if checking to make sure he wasn't experiencing a cardiac episode. He said, "Folks, in all my years of being in church and around praying believers, I've never seen a prayer answered so quickly. A *rupture* has indeed taken place here, and I can still feel its effects in my aching side."

As it often happens, once laughing starts in a crowd, whatever words follow, even if only slightly funny, rocket up the laughter meter. The volume of chuckles rose again, and the loudest decibel maker stood behind the pulpit. As Pete Senior stepped away from the solid cherrywood podium that usually evoked clerical seriousness, he knew he was helplessly in the throes of a laughter breakdown. Fighting for air, he abruptly glanced over at the choir loft to locate his wife. He couldn't find her right away and momentarily worried whether she was headed to the fourth-row pew to take care of their mischievous son.

Soon he noticed one of the choir members wiping her tears with the sleeve of her robe with one hand and waving at him with the other. When he focused on her, she pointed to the floor at her feet. There, partially hidden behind the backs of the chairs, was his dignified wife. All he could see was the top of her back. From her movements, he guessed she was laughing hard.

Completely unraveled by the sight, Pete Senior made his way back to the podium and placed a palm on each side to brace himself so he wouldn't collapse from the restricted amount of oxygen he was taking in. Then, struggling for composure, he spoke brokenly to his unglued parishioners.

"For a moment there, I couldn't find my wife. I was so afraid she'd been…" He paused to gain some semblance of control and say the next word clearly…"*ruptured!*"

With that statement came one more tidal wave of hooting and hollering. As the laughter rolled over the congregation again, the people who hadn't been feeling well physically and emotionally when they showed up for service suddenly were feeling much better. There were hard-line, crotchety stoics of the church who would never dream of letting people act with such frivolity in the sanctuary, but because they were so surprised by the boy's innocent prayer, they too were caught up in the merriment.

While all this was going on, Pete had slithered back onto the pew next to Lenny. They looked at each other, mouths agape, as they took in the unexpected reaction. Pete smiled a bit, interested and surprised by the way his folks were handling his prayerful outburst. Hope seeped in…his prayer may have succeeded!

Look at Dad, Pete thought. *He's lost it. Since he's laughing so hard, maybe he won't kill me after all. And Mom…where is Mom? Oh, there she is. Good grief—she's on the floor. Is she mad? No…no…I think she's…yes, she's laughing! A minute ago, she looked like she was going to ground me for life. I don't understand why everyone is laughing, but this has to be a good thing. Is this what a rupture is?*

"Hey, Lenny, I have no idea what just happened here, but if I'm right, me an' you ain't in trouble."

"My folks are going crazy," Lenny whispered. "Look at them! I don't think I've ever seen Dad laugh like that—ever. And Mom keeps elbowing him even though she's laughing too."

"Do you know why everyone is laughing? I don't get it. It's probably good for us though. No one looks mad anymore."

Finally order returned. Pete's dad straightened his tie and stood behind the podium. "That was certainly an unexpected development, wasn't it? In the interest of time, I'm going to table the rest of my sermon. We'll talk more about Paul's teachings next week."

Pete's mother settled back into her choir chair and turned her gaze to her nine-year-old son. She gently dabbed at her wet and red cheeks. She wasn't sure whether she should laugh at Pete's hesitant smile or frown at him for disrupting the service. She could tell he wasn't sure why everyone was laughing and smiling at him. He was fidgeting but listening intently.

"Pete…son…you know I love you. And you are my favorite hunting buddy. Obviously you and Lenny let your imaginations get the best of you this morning. We'll discuss this situation later."

He watched his son nod slightly and look at the floor. He could tell Pete was worried about what was going to happen…and rightfully so. Pete Senior decided their yard was going to look exceptionally nice by the end of the month.

"Now, about the rupture…I mean, the rapture, of course. There were two very important principles in Pete's prayer this morning. The first is knowing for certain that in the last days when Jesus calls us to heaven, each of us will be ready. John 14:1-3 says, 'Let not your heart be troubled; you believe in God, believe also in Me. In My Father's house are many mansions; if it were not so, I would have told you. I go to prepare a place for you. And if I go and prepare a place for you, I will come again and receive you to Myself; that where I am, there you may be also.' And in the book of Revelation, chapter 22 and verse 20, John reminds us, 'He who testifies to these things says, "Surely I am coming quickly." Even so, come, Lord Jesus!' Let's live in such a way that we're never afraid and we can look forward to that momentous day."

With a pastoral gentleness, Pete Senior wrapped up. "And in today's service, we've certainly discovered the importance of a good sense of humor. Proverbs 17:22 says, 'A merry heart does good, like medicine.' We adults often forget that during the stress and busyness of our days. This morning we've been reminded of what a gift God has given us when He wired us to enjoy good belly laughs.

"Laughter decreases stress hormones and increases immune cells. It improves blood flow. Science tells us also that endorphins, those unique feel-good chemicals our bodies create, are stimulated by laughing. And shared laughter brings us together, joining our hearts and lives."

Around the sanctuary, heads nodded in agreement, and the music director came forward and led them in a hymn. Pete Senior noticed an increased energy level as people stood for the benediction. He bowed his head and prayed, "God, thank You for how You surprised us at this service with the very welcome gift of laughter. We needed the visit. In fact, some of us feel much better right now than we felt when we came through the doors this morning. Help us share the invigorating medicine of humor with the people we meet this week. In Jesus's name we pray. Amen."

After his prayer, he looked over at the organist and said, "Please play the G note." He turned to the congregation. "You'll know this song the moment we start it."

With a certain graceful perkiness, the lady at the organ raised her right index finger and brought it down confidently on G.

The pastor hummed the note then turned to the congregation and said, "For our benediction, please join me in this familiar chorus by George Willis Cooke:"

> I've got the joy, joy, joy, joy
> Down in my heart (Where?)
> Down in my heart (Where?)
> Down in my heart
> I've got the joy, joy, joy, joy
> Down in my heart (Where?)
> Down in my heart to stay

As 200 voices lifted in festive singing at Wells Grove Church, none of them sang harder or louder than Pete and Lenny. That's what fellows do when their prayers have been answered.

21

I Aim to Please

Don set his gear bag next to the ladder-back wooden rocking chair on his front porch as he sat down. He laced up his leather boots as he listened to the muffled sounds of shouting coming from inside the house next door. "What could they be fussin' about at this early hour of the day?" he wondered aloud.

At quarter past four, Don was up to go hunting with his neighbor Phil. The young man and his wife, Marcy, had moved in two years ago, and on a couple of other occasions the sounds of marital discord had filtered through their walls.

As he finished securing his boot laces, Don noticed the new silence. A couple of minutes later, the aluminum storm door squeaked open and Phil appeared with his bow case and a bag of camo clothes. As he walked toward his truck, parked at the curb, his steps were heavy and his head was hanging down. Except for the hunting gear, he could have been going to a funeral.

"Morning, Phil!" Don called as he walked toward Phil's rig. He intentionally added a bit of cheer to his greeting in hopes his young friend wouldn't realize he'd overheard the less-than-happy start to his day.

Phil mumbled, "Hey, Don. You packed and ready?"

"Yep. Thanks for driving this morning. My son insists he needs the truck today to help his girlfriend haul something. I bet it's a load of hairspray and makeup."

Don's attempt at humor roused only a flustered complaint from Phil as he circled around, opened the truck door, slid the bench seat forward, and stowed the gear behind the seat. He flipped the seat back and climbed in behind the wheel of his huge, eight-cylinder, four-wheel-drive truck.

After Don opened his door and climbed in, Phil replied, "Yeah. Women. When you get 'em figured out, call me."

The two men slammed the truck doors and latched on their seat belts, and Phil turned the key. The big engine roared to life. Phil put the transmission in drive and pulled away from his house, accelerating so quickly that Don's head nearly slammed the window behind him.

Don glanced over at Phil but resisted the temptation to offer fatherly advice about his heavy foot. He searched for something else to say that might slow the street rocket that had just been launched.

"Did you get your bow restrung, Phil?"

"Yep. Picked it up after work yesterday and got it honed in last night at the archery shop. I reckon I was there till nearly nine thirty."

Don was thankful to hear the engine back off some rpms as Phil talked.

"I can't believe that bow came unraveled like it did. And of all the times! That buck was not more than fifteen yards from my stand. I would have had him, Don. Stupid bow."

"How long you been chasin' this buck, good neighbor?"

Phil quickly rubbed his eyes. "I saw that monster in mid-August while clearing out some shooting lanes around my stands. I've only seen him a couple of times since. Now that we're so far into the season without spotting him, and after I educated him about my presence like I did the other day, I'm not sure if I'll ever get another chance. If I don't see him within a few minutes after first light, it probably ain't gonna happen this morning. That means I'll have to come back out here this evening."

Don heard the frustration in Phil's voice. And hearing his advance plans to return for an evening hunt if no string was released this morning was revealing.

At nearly sixty-two, Don had hunted with enough fellows through the years to recognize serious hunting obsessions when he saw them. Some of his friends were deeply passionate about the pursuit of whitetail but could laugh away times when things went right for the deer. However, there were a few of his buddies who took the chase so seriously that they weren't a lot of fun to be around from late September to mid-January. Phil seemed to fall into the latter category, and Don wondered if a little probing might help him understand why…and maybe even help him avoid the unhealthy plunge.

"My friend, that old boy has a hold on you, doesn't he?"

"Yeah, I reckon he does. You don't know how bad I want to plug that critter. And I'll be honest with you, Don. You have no idea how badly Marcy wants me to get it done too."

Don kept his facial muscles relaxed and didn't break into a smile when he realized his prying had generated important information. Phil's subtle admission about Marcy's interest in the hunt implied she might not be all too happy with Phil's hunting strategy.

As the darkness submitted to the first light of another November day, Don and Phil sat in their tree stands, separated by a tall ridge and about 400 yards of hillside timber. They welcomed the coming sun as their eyes slowly adjusted to the change of light.

Phil was replaying the argument he'd had with Marcy that morning.

Don was trying not to imagine the young couple in the throes of the spat he'd heard earlier. He wasn't being too successful. The images conjured up weren't pleasant as he silently reviewed what he thought was their dilemma. *Poor Marcy. If she could look inside Phil's brain right now she'd probably find nothing but bows and arrows, binoculars, range finders, scent bombs, tree stands, camo clothes piled up everywhere, and huge deer running around in small patches of woods. I'm afraid the last thing she'd find is herself. She's dealing with a fellow who is saturated with a level of zeal for the hunt that I've not seen in a while. I wonder where that drive is coming from?*

Don paused for a half minute or so and searched his brain for clues to what could be pushing Phil. Nothing specific came to mind. He went on with his quiet musings as he scanned the ridgeline above him for movement. *There's got to be something deeper going on in Phil's life that's got him at odds with Marcy. For sure, he should never let an aggravation about a malfunctioning piece of equipment and a deer that got away generate the kind of word war they were having this morning. I wish I could put one of those tiny cameras in Phil's mind and work it around until I found the reason...*

Don suddenly interrupted himself when he caught a glimpse of something moving against the narrow patches of gray sky visible between the tree trunks on the ridge. "There it is again," he whispered, sure he was seeing a deer.

He reached for the binoculars that hung on a hook attached to the tree. Talking quietly to himself, he put the glasses to his eyes. "Doggone, that's gotta be the huge deer Phil's been seeing. Look at the size of the body...and that rack! It looks like the rocking chair on my front porch. And unless I miss my guess, he's gonna walk over the ridge on the trail that goes right by Phil's stand." Don grabbed his walkie-talkie and turned it on.

Phil's walkie-talkie vibrated in his pants pocket. He dug for it as his eyes scanned the area. "Yeah, Don. What's up?"

"Phil, I think that monster you've been chasing is about to come wandering by your stand! My estimate is five or ten minutes. I just saw him through the timber near the top of the ridge. If he doesn't get distracted, he's gonna drop down on that trail that runs by your stand!"

Phil's quiet, serious voice answered, "Got it, Don. I'm going dead on the radio. I'll turn it back on in a little bit."

Don put his walkie-talkie back in his pocket and attached his release to his string just in case the buck altered his course. He listened hard for that telltale dry-cornflake crunch in the leaves that would alert him to an approaching buck. Enough time passed that Don realized the buck probably wasn't going to go by his stand. He still felt the jitters that can accompany a possible encounter, even if it was more likely that his neighbor would be the one to have this one. He searched for other deer, watching intently for movement. *If that buck passes under Phil, I sure hope that boy nails it. What a trophy that would be.*

A long fifteen minutes went by before Don suddenly felt his radio tickle his leg. "Tell me about it, Phil. Talk to me!"

Heavy breathing was the response he got. It sounded like Phil had just finished a hundred-yard dash.

"Don, I got into him! I can't believe it. He came within twelve yards and stopped broadside. I was so pumped I thought I'd never get the peep sight on him. I'm telling you, it felt like I was pulling on piano wire. When I released the arrow, he almost went to his knees. Then he shot out of here like a bullet. I know I got him! I can see my arrow, and I think I see blood on the yellow fletching. Don, I did it!"

Phil's enthusiasm arced like an electrical current between them. Don laughed at the thought of what would happen if another hunter got between their tree stands right now. *He'd be fried to a crisp,* he decided.

Don punched the talk button and answered Phil's radio report with a string of well-deserved kudos. Then he asked, "Did you see him go down?"

"No, but I know he's hurt bad. He's gotta be nearby. I'm sure of it."

Don accepted the assessment. "Unless I have something come by me I can't pass up, I'll pack up in about thirty minutes and head your way. Will that plan work for you?"

"Sounds good, Don. It's gonna be a long thirty minutes, as you can guess, but I can hold on. I'll dig out a candy bar and try to calm my racing heart."

When Phil saw Don coming through the woods toward him, he quickly gathered his gear, lowered his bow to the ground with his pull-up string, and descended the tree. The two men smiled broadly and exchanged congratulatory knuckles.

"Which direction did he go?" Don asked.

Phil pointed downhill toward a small ravine and answered confidently, "That way. I visually marked the spot where I last saw him. You ready to do some tracking?"

Don grinned big as he watched Phil walk over and jerk the black-colored carbon arrow out of the dirt where it had been stuck. After quickly scanning the arrow from tip to tip, he snapped it into its place in his quiver and started walking the direction the buck had taken. Don almost had to run to catch up with him.

The two hunters walked about fifteen yards and, in the same instant, saw a thumb-sized spill of red liquid on a leaf.

"Yes! Blood!" Phil shouted.

Concerned about Phil's noise level and hoping he would get the hint, Don responded in a whisper, "That is a good sight. Seeing blood drops is the most emotional part of the hunt for me. The sight makes me nearly weak in the knees because I know for sure that I connected."

"Same here. And it's even more intense knowing what size the buck is that I believe I'll find at the end of this trail."

"Amen, Phil. Amen."

Another fifteen yards or so were covered before Don softly whistled to Phil, who had put about ten lateral yards between them.

Silently mouthing the word "blood," he pointed to the ground.

Phil quickly joined Don to look at a large oak leaf that cradled another splat of crimson. It wasn't quite as big as the first find and contained a little extra coloring that didn't look right. Don carefully picked up the leaf and examined it closely. He handed it to Phil. "Take a look at this. Do you see what I see?"

Though his years as a bow hunter didn't stack up against Don's, Phil had seen enough debris from entrails that he recognized the truth. His shot had been a little further back in the buck's body than he'd thought.

"Can I see that arrow you used, Phil?"

"Sure." Phil got out the arrow and handed it to Don.

Don put the arrow to his nose and whiffed it from tip to tip. The look on his face told Phil the bad news.

"I guess in my rush to get started finding this buck I got a little ahead of myself back there. I should have done the smell test too. I may have a trophy of a lifetime that isn't dead yet, and in fact is probably really sick…sort of like I'm feeling right now."

"Well, let's not jump to conclusions, Phil. He may be more hurt than you think. There's not a heavy amount of stomach content on this arrow, which means you may have barely sliced the front wall of the belly. Let's hope that's the case. Besides, we've got the rest of the day ahead of us. We can take our time and slip along slowly so we don't spook him. We'll look for more blood."

Phil respectfully protested. "Naw. I appreciate your offer, but we both know we can't go on with this search, Don. We gotta back out and let this old boy lie down somewhere and expire. If we go any farther, we risk pushing him out of the county and out of our hunting area. I hate to admit it, but we…or I…have to come back early afternoon or this evening."

Don wanted to do some more tracking to find more blood and offer comfort to his despairing partner. However, he knew the right decision was to leave the area and return later. "Phil, I have a suggestion."

"What's that, Don?"

"I say we go get some breakfast at my house and call for some help. I've heard you say your dad is really good at finding a wounded deer. Why not ask him to come out with us?"

Unexpected silence followed his idea…and seemed to last forever.

Phil stared toward the area where he last saw the buck. Without saying a word, he stuck his arrow into the ground next to the place where they found the last bloody leaf, turned, and walked in the opposite direction with his head down.

That's how he looked this morning when he left his house, Don noted. He followed his young partner on the twenty-minute walk back to the truck and thought about Phil's reaction to his suggestion. Suddenly the pieces of the puzzle started falling into place. *Mentioning his dad triggered the sudden silence.* He walked and thought about it more. Don suspected the argument he'd heard filtering from his neighbor's house that morning was probably not so much about Phil and Marcy and hunting as about Phil and his dad and hunting. With that assumption on his mind, Don trailed Phil out of the woods and prayed for words that might break through the barrier of his young friend's feelings.

The warmth of the cab of the truck felt good as they drove away and headed to the paved road. Phil finally broke his long silence.

"I suppose it would be good to give Dad a call and see if he can help us find this deer. He is without a doubt one of the best trackers around. He was always quick to make sure I knew it too."

"I assumed your dad taught you everything he knows about hunting, tracking, and such. Is that right?" Don could see that Phil bristled a little at the question.

"Oh yes sir-eee. He tried to teach me all that stuff, but like everything else he got me into, the harder I tried to do it right, the more I seemed to do it wrong—at least in his opinion. Hunting is the one thing I discovered I really can do, but so far nothing I've killed to this day has ever been big enough for him. The nice nine-point I got three years ago probably weighed in at 190 pounds, and the rack had a good seventeen- or eighteen-inch spread on it. What did Dad say about it when I got it back to the house? 'One more point and you'd have yourself a real trophy, Phil.' It was the same when it came to baseball, golf, workin' on cars, and even marrying Marcy. Nothing is ever good enough for that man. I aim to please him, but so far I haven't hit the target."

Don was surprised at Phil's openness, but he appreciated the candor. His confession about the failed attempts to gain his dad's favor revealed the painful fact that the buck they'd left behind today hadn't been the only wounded critter in the woods. And Don knew what he could do to help. As they drove back to town, he quietly worked on his plan.

As they turned onto their street, Don spoke. "Since Marcy is at work, why don't you come on in to my house. I'll see if I can sweet-talk Becky into frying us up some eggs. And you can call your dad from our place and see if he's available."

"Okay," Phil said. But when they pulled up to the curb, he announced he would make the call from his house first.

Don gently objected, and Phil conceded.

When they entered Don's house, Phil removed his boots at the door and greeted Becky. He went to the phone and called his dad. The conversation lasted only a minute or two.

"Did he say he would help us, Phil?" Don asked when Phil came to the table.

"Yes. He said he'd meet us about a quarter to noon at the barn where we park. He said he'd have no trouble finding the deer."

"Great. Now let's have some chow while we wait."

When Phil pulled up and parked his truck by the barn, his dad was leaning against his vehicle's passenger side door with his arms crossed.

"Howdy, boys."

"Hey, Dad." Phil's voice sounded strained. "This is my neighbor, Don. Don, this is my dad, Frank."

Don extended his hand. "Nice to meet you, Frank. This is one fine son you've got here. And he's quite a hunter too. I saw the brute he arrowed before he got to Phil's stand. Saw him through my binocs. I knew if that critter went by your son there'd be some major adrenalin pumping on the other side of the hill from me. I didn't get an accurate count, but best I can tell he has to be at least a twelve-point. And I'm guessing probably well over 200 pounds. I believe I was as nervous as Phil was about the shot, and I'm pumped about finding this deer. Glad you're here to help. Phil tells me you're really good at tracking."

Frank pushed himself away from the truck door with his hands.

"Well, if that buck didn't go down right away, the shot must have been off. Guess we better get to finding it."

Don quietly noted, as did Phil, that no mention was made of the thrill of simply getting the string back on such a mature deer. Frank didn't ask to hear the exciting details about the shot to give his son the opening to share his enthusiasm. No word of encouragement was offered that would help carry the obvious burden of anxiety over a search for a gut-shot deer.

As the trio left the trucks and headed up the hillside toward Phil's tree stand, Don led the charge, Frank was in the middle, and Phil was noticeably well behind. After 300 yards or so, Don turned and looked over his shoulder to check on the father and son. Once again he could read Phil's thoughts by the way he walked. His chin was almost resting on his chest as he plodded along. With Frank in the picture, Don wondered whether the heavy worry on his young friend's shoulders was caused by the dread of not finding the deer... or the fear of finding it.

As they stood near the tree Phil was in that morning, Don spoke up. "This is where the deal went down this morning, Frank. We marked the first find of blood with some toilet paper about fifteen yards from here."

The three walked to the spot where the white tissue hung on a small knee-high sapling. Phil added a little more detail about their previous search.

"Um...there's another tissue...um...right over there by my arrow—the one that did the damage."

Frank walked over and pulled the arrow out of the ground. He looked it over carefully and then put it to his nose. "Yep, there are digestion juices on this shaft. It's not much though. I have my doubts about this one."

Don felt the sting of Frank's skepticism and had no doubt that to Phil it felt like a gunshot to his gut.

As the three of them stood over the second blood spot, Frank laid out his plan.

"You two spread out about ten yards on each side of me. We're going to go down this hill really slow. If someone besides me finds blood, don't yell out...just softly whistle. I'll come and mark that spot, and then we'll continue. Now, let's take our time and be as quiet as we can."

Hardly two steps were taken when Phil said, "Stop. I can't believe it. I forgot my bow. We can't continue this search until I get my compound! If we find that deer and he's got some life left in him, I might need to close the deal with another arrow."

Phil's dad cocked his jaw sideways and bit his lower lip. He didn't have to utter a word to reveal how disgusted he was at his son's incompetence. He stared into the woods in the direction the buck had been going.

"I have young legs," Phil asserted. "I can be back in twenty minutes or so. I'm really sorry, guys!"

Don's heart leaped with the opportunity that was suddenly his to claim...if he dared step between Phil and his dad. Don chimed in with some third-party assistance. "We have plenty of daylight left, Phil. We'll wait for you right here."

Like a rabbit leaving its hiding place at the sound of an approaching beagle, Phil bounded off toward his truck. Frank and Don looked anywhere but at each other since they didn't know each other well. Both of them looked through their binoculars, hoping to see a furry body somewhere on the ground.

"How many kids do you have, Frank?" Don finally said, cutting through the silence.

"One boy and one girl. Phil and Deanna. When they were about five and three I thought about having their names changed to Plenty and Quit."

Don chuckled politely, not sure if Frank was being serious or not. "That's a good one, Frank," Don said, choosing to be positive. He waited for a thanks but heard only a proverbial cricket as they continued to endure the long moments of silence.

During the painful lull in their almost wordless wait, Don decided to take a risk. He quietly and quickly coached himself before speaking. *I don't know this man very well. But we're both grown-ups, and whether he can take it or not, I'm going to take the chance and see if I can do something to turn things around for this father and son. I mean, Why not? I should just go for it. I have nothing to lose.*

Feeling amply self-inspired, Don spoke in the friendliest voice he could muster. "Frank, I know we just met, and I only know you through what Phil has told me about you. I've sensed the tension between the two of you. And Phil shared something with me this morning after we abandoned the search that you might want to know. I know I'd want to hear it if I were Phil's father. It wasn't much in terms of information, but his words told me volumes about something he desperately needs. So I thought you'd want to know about it. Do you want to hear it?"

Frank's expression barely changed, and only a slight compression of his lips and tightening of his jaw muscles revealed he'd heard.

"Do I have a choice?" he finally stated quietly.

"Of course you do," Don responded. "But I think Phil would benefit greatly if you'd hear me out."

"All right. Take your best shot."

"Um…to get straight to the point, Phil needs something from you that he's yet to receive. When we called off the search this morning and got to the truck to head to my place for breakfast, we started talking about how you got him into hunting. In the course of our brief conversation, he opened up about how much he'd like to make you proud of him. To quote him, Phil said, 'nothing ever seems to be good enough for that man. I aim to please him, but so far I haven't hit the target.'"

Frank stared hard at Don and then looked toward the direction of his truck. "That boy knows I love him. I don't know why he would tell you something like that. Seems like he'd come to me with that kind of stuff."

"Well, Frank, I have no doubt Phil knows you love him. But the problem is that he doesn't feel it. Let me explain it this way. My granddad told me one day that he had a twenty-dollar bill in his pocket for me. He didn't give it to me right away, and I followed that man everywhere all day long, just waiting for him to let me hold that twenty in my hands. You see, Frank, it was one thing to know that twenty was mine; it was a completely different thing to touch it and feel it. That's a little like Phil right now. He knows you love him, but he needs to feel it. And the way you can touch him with it is with your words, your expressions, and even your body."

"That's a good analogy, Don. The twenty-dollar bill description is a good one." Frank looked down at the ground. "I…I g-guess it doesn't take a r-rocket scientist to see there's a bit of a divide b-between Phil and me. Fact is, it's been there q-quite a while, and to be honest, in the p-past few months I've been trying to figure out what to do about it. B-but I'm just not good at these kinds of things. I've seen Phil's head and shoulders droop when I've talked hard at him. I h-hate it when that happens. I keep hoping he'll b-buck up and get over it. That's what I had to do with my dad. I just had to g-get over it."

"Did you get over it, Frank? Or did you just pass your pain on to Phil?"

"Ouch, Don. That hurt. Are you a shrink or something?"

"No, Frank. I'm just like you—a dad who cares about his son."

Frank gathered up a wad of leaves and fresh, moist dirt. He wiped the dried blood off Phil's arrow. "Okay, Don, since you're on a roll, what do you suggest I do about Phil?"

"Well…" Don hesitated. "I guess first you can pray we…"

"I'm not much at prayin'," Frank cut in. "You can do that for us."

"We can work on that later if you'd like, Frank. But for now, we need to find that buck that's around here somewhere. Hopefully it's dead so it's not suffering anymore. I think the reason Phil has worked so hard at getting a shot at this huge buck we're tracking has everything to do with what we're talking about right now. He's been so consumed by it that I believe it's even affecting his marriage.

"When we do find it, why not grab Phil by the shoulders and give him an 'atta boy' encouragement? Then you can look at me and tell me how amazed and delighted you are that your son could get the string back on such a monster deer. And tell him you want to hear the replay of the details of the hunt, starting from the minute the sun rose this morning.

"And when you do all that, watch his face closely. You'll see a young man who just got the biggest trophy of his life! And it's not the deer, Frank. It's your approval and belief in him. That's what he really wants, Frank. Let him know that when it comes to a father having a son, Phil's the best thing that ever happened to you."

Frank stuck the now very clean arrow back into the ground. After several seconds passed, he pursed his lips and then nodded yes.

Within a couple of minutes, Phil appeared. "I…(gasp)…told you…(gasp)…I'd be quick. Nineteen minutes!"

"That was pretty quick," Frank replied.

Phil stood upright, smiled at his dad, and then shot a surprised glance at Don.

"No time to waste, Phil. You can catch your breath as we track this beast," Don stated.

It took almost thirty minutes for the three men to cover 200 yards. Frank managed to find several small drops of blood on the way. Each time he did, they regrouped, marked the trail with bright white tissue, and continued. As they gathered around another find of blood that was half the size of a dime, Frank looked back through the woods and got a visual on the line of escape from the tissue markings.

"Looks like he's headed toward the creek, boys. I think it's safe to say there's a reason he's headed toward the water. He must be really hurt. And since we're not but fifty yards from it, Phil, why don't you go on ahead to the creek and take a look around while Don and I follow the trail. And son, you might want to make sure you step away from the line this deer seems to be following so the blood trail doesn't get ruined."

"Good idea, Dad. I'll be right back." Turning to go, Phil wondered if his ears were playing tricks on him. *Dad actually sounded nice.*

Phil walked twenty-five yards to the left of the tissue line and headed toward the creek.

Less than a minute later, Don and Frank heard the loud yell of a happy hunter.

"Oh, my word! Here he is. Ya'll get down here!"

Don and Frank dashed to the creek. Don nearly fell into the water as he burst out of the woods and slid to a stop at the creek bank. Frank didn't even stop. Like a schoolboy at a swimming hole, he shot between Phil and Don and landed feet first next to the huge buck.

Standing in the calf-deep stream, Frank excitedly said, "Would you look at this thing? Son, get in here with me and take it in! He's a twelve with a double-drop tine. Son!"

Bewildered and elated, Phil looked at Don for a second before frog-leaping into the creek next to his dad. Water splashed over Frank's clothes as he grabbed Phil around the neck with his long arm and said, "Boy, you did it! This one's gotta go on the wall. Wait 'til your mama sees this monster. I can't wait to show my friends pictures of this bruiser."

Phil was speechless.

"Don, can you believe this?" Frank continued. "What nerve it must have taken to get an arrow into this deer. I believe the excitement would have had me messing my britches if it had been me."

Frank slapped his son on his back and added, "I want to hear the tale of this kill—every detail from the time you got up this morning until this moment. Will you share that at suppertime at the house?"

Phil's grin was huge. He reached down and grabbed the massive rack and raised it out of the water.

Don got Frank's attention. When their eyes met, Don drew a circle around his face then pointed to Phil.

Frank nodded and then looked at Phil's face. The sight of his son crying and laughing in the same instant was all he needed to see to know he'd helped his son receive a greater trophy than the one that floated in the creek. As the realization of it washed over him, Frank's eyes watered up, and he began to laugh as well.

Don sat on the creek bank and watched a father and son begin a new journey together. As the two of them examined the heavy buck and decided how to get it back to the truck, Don was grateful he was present when a son finally aimed to please and found his dad's heart.

22

Old Ironsights

Merle couldn't believe how noisy he was being. The dry leaves crunched loudly under his boots as he hiked on a Pennsylvania hillside. He tried to lessen the commotion of his entry into the woods, but nature was winning the decibel war. With each step announcing his presence to every deer in the area, he acknowledged the good possibility that his morning hunt might turn out to be a nice, quiet, therapeutic sit. Normally the likelihood of no action would bother him, but on this day, another matter was preying on his mind. Some time to think was exactly what he needed. The problem had to do with the longtime friend cradled tightly in his arms.

In the low light of predawn, he reached the familiar old red oak where he'd stood vigil so many times since his early teen years. He unfolded his collapsible stool and placed it as close as he could to the wide trunk. Making sure it was steady, he turned around and sat down. He loosened his grip on the .32 Winchester Special and laid it across his lap as he leaned back against the tree. After catching his breath from the thirty-minute trek up the hill, Merle sighed deeply. He looked up through the leafless branches silhouetted against the sky that had turned blue-gray and prayerfully whispered, "God, You know how much I love this place. I give You my sincere thanks for letting me come to it again." As he said a heartfelt "Amen," Merle's grip tightened on the rifle in almost a stranglehold.

"I'm sorry, Old Ironsights," he said as he relaxed his grip. His mind went back through the years to when he'd reached the ripe young age of fourteen.

Merle remembered walking into the local hardware store in May of that year. Without a background check or answering a single legal question, he'd put a lay-away payment on the counter for the Winchester. As the store owner counted the cash, Merle promised, "Mr. Adams, I'll be back with the rest of it before summer is over."

When early August came, Merle headed back to the hardware store with a stack of bills that were mostly hard-earned, although a few were hard-begged. The dollars that were the toughest to collect were the ones he'd gotten when he sold his favorite bicycle. Though giving up his fat-tire Schwinn wasn't easy, the anticipation of owning the brand-new rifle helped his affection for the old bike fade.

Mr. Adams smiled when he saw the teenager come through the entrance. "I see you've kept your promise. Are you taking the Winchester home with you today?"

"You bet I am, Mr. Adams!" Merle plopped the cash down on the counter, added his high-caliber smile, and said, "Thanks so much for holding it for me. I also need two boxes of shells."

"You're certainly welcome. Do you want me to put a scope on this fine piece, young man?"

"No, sir. I was doing well to come up with the dollars I needed for the gun and the shells."

Mr. Adams responded with the certain tone of experienced salesmanship, "Wouldn't be but another thirty-five dollars for a pretty good three-by-nine. Seeing as how you're a man of your word, I could mount one for you, and you could pay me when you can."

Merle thought about the idea. "That's a mighty tempting offer, Mr. Adams. But I'd better wait. Maybe someday I can add a scope, but for now it's gonna be just me and…"

Merle paused midsentence.

Mr. Adams had lifted the .32 Winchester out of the long, cardboard box. He held it up to the light so it glistened on the wood stock and showed off the metal workmanship. He handed it to his young customer.

"Sounds like you've named this gun already. What did you choose?"

Like a proud papa would name his first child, Merle threw his shoulders back and answered, "Old Ironsights. That's what I'm gonna name him. Saw it in a book I read once, and it's as good a name as any for this beauty."

The cash-and-carry exchange was over in minutes, but the relationship begun that day between Merle and Old Ironsights promised to last a lifetime.

As soon as he got home, Merle began a prehunt ritual that he would repeat often through the years. After putting on his hunting clothes in the utility room at his folks' house, he picked up the Winchester and whispered, "Well, Old Ironsights, let's go huntin'!" It felt good and natural to speak to the gun, to his hunting buddy.

With that, he pushed the squeaky screen door open, and almost before the slinky, rusted spring pulled the door closed, the excited teenager and his friend were almost at the tree line at the base of the hill about fifty yards behind the house.

Eventually the prehunt ritual altered slightly when Merle married Peggy. They bought their own little home close to his family's place, so now he dressed for the hunt in his own house and had to drive a bit to get to his favorite hunting spot.

But this morning had been different. For the first time in fifteen years, Merle's prehunt ritual lacked enthusiasm. This time, when he quietly spoke to his Winchester, there was a noticeable reserve in his voice.

As the late-November sun rose and the woods gradually let in the light, Merle reluctantly faced the reality of what was coming. He uneasily calculated the number of days left before December 25 arrived. "Only twenty-eight days. Time's running out. If I'm going to do this, I'm gonna have to do it really soon."

Merle slid his left glove gently down the length of the Winchester, patted the barrel near the forward sight, and then gently said, "It hasn't been a good year for me business-wise, Ironsights. Actually, it's been a dismal bust. There have been some unexpected things to cover, and what's worse, I don't see the situation gettin' much better in the months to come." With his right hand, Merle patted the honey-colored wooden stock that boasted its share of deep scratches and telltale signs of being well used and loved.

"You know I don't want to do this to you, old buddy, but I've got those three little boys down there at the house who deserve a good Christmas. And the only way I can see gettin' them the things I've picked out for them is if I go through with this. I can't believe I even put the ad in the paper. I feel terrible, but it's the only choice I have. Today might be the end of the line for you and me, old friend."

Merle looked up and checked the surrounding area for movement. Then he looked at Old Ironsights again as tears welled up in his eyes. "You've been a faithful friend. Never gave me a minute's trouble. And boy, do we have some history. But it seems it's time for me to let you go."

Merle felt somewhat foolish when he looked up again, this time to see if anyone happened to be nearby. "Good grief, man, do you realize you're talking to a gun? You're getting teary-eyed over a rifle?"

He hoped no one was close enough to hear his one-sided conversation. An hour passed. While looking for game, Merle debated whether he should cut his hunt short, head on home, and make the call to the man who had responded to his ad. Before he talked himself out of going through with the sale, he decided to gather his things to make the long descent down the hill to his truck.

Just as he stood, he saw a flash of brown about 150 yards through the openness of the timber to his right and below him. He stared and made out a small herd of deer hurrying up the hillside. Merle guessed they were probably escaping the neighboring Johnson boys, who seemed to always be late getting to the woods on a hunting day.

As the four whitetails quick-stepped onto the flat below him, Merle slowly raised the Winchester to his shoulder. If the deer stayed their course, he figured they would come by him at about seventy yards, moving right to left. His opportunity to touch off a shot would come in about twenty seconds.

With the stock plate of the .32 resting solidly on his right shoulder, he tenderly laid his jaw on the cold wood, pulled the hammer back, and lightly rested his finger on the trigger. As he looked down the barrel across the open iron sights, a sudden rush of melancholy washed over him. *Remember how this feels... memorize it!* he thought.

The loud and welcome report of the rifle was music to Merle's ears. But as the small lead bullet sped out of the muzzle, a cannonball of emotions entered his heart, exploding the dam in his soul that was holding back a river of tears.

It was a full minute before he could clearly see the deer lying on the flat below him. He quickly chambered another shell, carefully put the hammer down to the safety position, and took his binoculars from his pack. After wiping his eyes with his sleeve, he focused his field glasses on the deer's side. With no sign of up and down breathing movement, he cradled the Winchester in his arms and walked down the hill to the buck.

Standing over the sizable animal, Merle lifted Old Ironsights to his face, kissed it on the serial number, and said, "An eight-pointer, huh? You're trying to make this decision extra hard on me, aren't you?"

The climb required to hunt at his favorite oak tree was rewarded with a relatively easy drag of the deer downhill to his truck. On the way down, Merle had time to rehearse the conversation he would have with the fellow who had responded to the ad about the Winchester. He knew how much he needed to sell the gun for to buy his three youngsters the gifts he'd chosen. Armed with that number, he audibly practiced holding out for his price. Though he had no plans of coming off the number, he wondered if he had subconsciously set the price so high that no one would make an acceptable offer. But a man had responded to the ad, so Merle knew it was probably a matter of his willingness to negotiate.

The eight-point caused quite a stir at the check-in station. Merle enjoyed the "atta boy" that his friends and neighbors offered. As he climbed into his truck to head home with his trophy, one of the hunters approached Merle.

"Did you get that deer with that .32 you're trying to sell?"

"Sure did. It's a fine rifle. I guess you saw the ad."

"I did. I'd take it off your hands right now if I had the funds. You wouldn't come down on the price, would you?"

Merle's rehearsal regarding his asking price made it easy to respond to the inquiry. "No, sir. I'm not negotiating. I don't want to insult a great gun!"

The stranger understood how deep feelings can go in a fellow's heart for his favorite deer rifle. He smiled at Merle's defense of his price and tipped his ball cap. He hopped into his truck and drove away.

Merle drove home, and after skinning the big buck and hanging it in his back-yard shed, he went into the house to make the phone call he dreaded. His wife, Peggy, could hear his side of the conversation, and from what she could gather, she guessed that within a couple of hours they'd have a visitor. When he hung up, she turned from the stove to look at him.

"Sounds like the buyer didn't balk at your price."

"I'm not sure why he wants my Winchester so much, but he didn't make a single attempt to challenge the price. He lives way over on the other side of the county, so he said he'll be here around three. He asked me to hold the gun until then. I said I would."

Merle sipped his coffee as Peggy continued making breakfast.

"I may be one of a few women who understand your affection for that Win-chester, Merle. My dad had a 12-gauge he was mighty fond of. I know in a hunter's mind, his gun is more than just meticulously crafted wood and steel. For Dad, it was a means for providing food, a protector, and perhaps most important, a con-nection between him and something he felt he was really good at. And he was, as you know. Being one of the best hunters in these parts, Dad took care of that gun nearly as well as he cared for us kids. So, Mr. Merle, I know how hard this is for you. I know what it's taking out of you."

Merle smiled at Peggy but didn't comment.

"The reason you're selling that gun says a ton about you as a dad. I've never known a man who is as good a dad as you are, Merle. You're beyond amazing. Not many serious hunters I know would choose a good Christmas for their sons over their love of the sport. I love you for that, honey. And I'm proud of you." Tears welled up in her eyes as she walked over and gave Merle a hug. "And Merle, if you want to change your mind, it's okay. We can get by. The buyer probably hasn't left home yet."

Merle stood up holding his coffee cup. He walked to the window and looked outside toward the shed where the deer was. He stood there for a while, quietly sipping his brew.

"Peggy, you'll never know how much your words mean to me. I love you. I know the boys will be fine with that whatever happens Christmas morning, but I want this year to be extra special. Mike is old enough now for the pellet gun I want to get him, and Charles has been talking about that radio-building kit he saw at the hardware store since last summer. Thomas has had a picture of that Navy ship model he's dreamed about tacked to the bottom of the bunk bed above him for I don't know how long.

"This doggone economic downturn sure came at a bad time. Maybe I'm letting it mess with my manhood, but I really want to see pure joy on the boys' faces when they open their presents this year. Seeing and feeling their joy will trump any affection I feel for Old Ironsights."

"You're right about the boys," Peggy affirmed. "Christmas morning will be fun for them whatever happens. Besides, we both agree we want to be careful about sending them the wrong message about what Christmas is all about. We don't want them to focus on the gift giving as much as on the gift God gave us in His Son, Jesus. As long as we keep that fact first, the boys will be fine.

"But I can also see the twinkle in your eyes when you think about how excited the boys will be with their presents. I'll say it again, Merle. You're a good man—a very good man."

Eventually three o'clock arrived, and so did the potential buyer. Merle met him on the front porch of their little house and invited him in. He didn't offer small talk; he simply handed him the gun, cleaned and packed in the original cardboard box.

The man pulled out the gun, looked it over carefully, and asked a few questions about its age and if there was anything he should know about it.

Merle offered a couple of tips on how to clean it and what grain of bullet worked best.

The man got up. "I'll take it." He handed Merle an envelope filled with cash and then packed the gun back into the box. He picked up his purchase, shook hands with Merle, said goodbye, and walked out the front door.

Merle watched him get into his truck and back out of the driveway. As a way of saying a respectful farewell to an old friend and a huge piece of his heart, Merle stood on the porch and watched the truck until it disappeared around a bend in the highway.

A few days later, funds in hand, Merle headed to the hardware store.

"Good morning, Merle. Merry Christmas to you and yours."

"And the same to you, Mr. Adams."

"Merle, I saw the ad you placed in the paper a couple of weeks ago. Was that .32 the same gun you bought here when you were a lad?"

"I'm amazed at how many people saw that ad. Yes, it was the same one." Merle sighed. "I'm thinking the entire world gets the paper."

"The price you put on that gun represented quite an appreciation in value."

"Truth is, Mr. Adams, it was a whole lot more valuable to me than the dollar figure I put on it. A fellow across the county wasn't deterred by my asking price. He came over and bought it a few days ago. And now I'm here to bless your business with the appreciation value. I'd better get to it."

With his mind on Christmas morning, Merle searched the store for the items on his list. He felt great as he picked out the presents, and he was really pleased when he had enough cash left to get Peggy the blender she'd drooled over the last time they were in the store together.

Christmas Day arrived. It was a glorious time. Merle's spirits were sailing high when his boys tore past the wrapping paper and found their gifts. The high-pitched squeals of excitement were followed by neck-breaking hugs of youthful thanks. Merle beamed and knew he'd received plenty of rewards for sacrificing his Winchester.

And when Peggy opened the blender, her oohs and aahs warmed his heart. Merle admitted that the morning had yielded even more joy than he imagined. However, though the room was electric with Christmas joy, for a passing moment Merle thought of Old Ironsights and wondered if his beloved gun was out hunting with a stranger. *I sure hope the new guy appreciates what he has.*

The following year, the economy turned around a bit, and Merle's business improved. Merle eventually purchased a new gun and continued to take his boys hunting even as they grew into their teens and into young adulthood.

Time passed as it always does, and soon the three boys were married and on their own. They often converged at the "old home place" to visit. The three boys often showed up together. Peggy was convinced they always smelled the fresh apple pies baking in her oven.

One morning just before Thanksgiving, while Merle was helping a friend with a house repair, the three boys sat at the kitchen table talking to their mom and, of course, eating pie. As they discussed the plans for the upcoming holidays, they also reminisced about Christmases past. All three of them readily agreed that one of their favorite memories centered around the wonderful year the gifts included the pellet gun, radio-building kit, and model ship. They glowed with the warmth of the memories.

"Boys, do you know how that Christmas came about?" Peggy asked.

"What do you mean, Mom?"

"Let me tell you something about your dad. That particular year, times were pretty rough. The business was struggling, and the economy was down. Your dad was worried about Christmas and how he could make it especially memorable for you boys. He loves you so much, and that year he wanted your gifts to be extra special. The only way he could figure out how to get you the gifts you longed for was to sell his hunting rifle."

Peggy continued fleshing out the story, adding the pertinent details. She shared how their dad had saved his money as a teen to buy the rifle and how much he'd loved taking Old Ironsights to the woods. "They were quite a team," Peggy said as she wrapped up the story.

The boys were silent for a long time. Finally Michael, the oldest, said, "That's an amazing story, Mom. I'm glad you told us about Old Ironsights." He looked at his brothers. "We have a wonderful Dad, don't we?"

After the chorus of agreement, Michael continued, "Guys, I have an idea for something for Dad for Christmas. It might take some doing…and maybe even a God-given miracle, but here's what I'm thinking…" As Michael laid out his idea, his two brothers wholeheartedly agreed.

Christmas morning arrived, and in keeping with tradition, the entire family, including spouses, gathered at noon at Merle and Peggy's house. The collective excitement emanating from the three brothers was electric. In fact, the brothers could barely stand the suspense of knowing they'd found their dad a perfect and unique gift.

Michael, Charles, and Thomas finally announced, "Dad and Mom, this year we're going to do Christmas a little bit different. And Dad, you can't stop us. We want to exchange gifts before we eat lunch."

Before Merle could respond, Peggy responded. "That's fine with us, boys. No need to be in a rut. Let's do it."

Wrapping paper and ribbons flew as the family members took turns opening gifts. Per tradition, the youngest person opened a present, then the next youngest, and on up the age ladder. When all the gifts had been opened and it looked like it was time to dig into the delicious food simmering on the stove and in the oven, Michael spoke up.

"Dad, there's one more gift to open. It's a special present to you from us boys. We think you're going to really like it."

Charles got up and walked across the living room to the closet. Opening the door and digging way back inside behind the coats, he finally pulled out a rectangular box wrapped in dark green paper.

"It's heavy, Dad," he said as he handed it to Merle.

Merle smiled and looked at his family. "What have you boys done?" He slipped his fingers under the wrapping paper between two tabs of Scotch tape and tore the paper back. A brown box with a large logo was exposed. He spelled the word out loud: "W-I-N-C-H-E-S-T-E-R."

Merle's eyes filled with tears as he grinned and stripped off the rest of the paper. Suddenly he stopped. He stared at the box, noting it's yellowed color and bent corners. He looked up. "I've seen this box before…" Carefully he lifted the lid and stared at the lone item inside.

"Old Ironsights. It's Old Ironsights! My first rifle!" Merle's grin rivaled the one on his face so many years ago when he'd paid Mr. Adams and took the gun home for the first time.

The grin was repeated on everyone's faces.

"Boys, I can't believe it! How did you know about this? And how did you track Old Ironsights down?"

"It wasn't easy, Dad," Thomas said. "Just before Thanksgiving, Mom told us the story about what you did for us that Christmas so many years ago. We decided we would try to find the buyer and get your gun back. You didn't have a receipt, but Mom finally remembered enough about the man to get us started."

Michael added, "You might like to know that the fellow who bought the gun from you passed on seven or eight years ago. He left Old Ironsights to his son, who was willing to part with it. He drove a hard bargain, but we didn't hesitate. Mom told us what this .32 meant to you…and what it did for us. It would have been a sad Christmas if we didn't bring it back home."

"Did he beat you boys up really bad with his asking price?"

Charles chuckled. "Yep. Our wallets are bruised a little, mainly because of something he said. We stopped trying to negotiate when he said, 'I ain't dickerin' with you boys 'cause it just wouldn't be right to insult a great gun.' He told us his dad taught him that. So we went ahead and bit the economic bullet. We spread out the cost between the three of us so it didn't put any of us in the poorhouse."

Thomas added, "At least he threw in two boxes of shells. They're in the closet on the shelf."

"Boys, you done good—real good. By the look on your dad's face, I'd say the outlay was worth it."

"Yes, ma'am," the three boys replied in unison.

The next morning, the clock on Merle's side of the bed sounded at three thirty. Peggy roused, sat up, rubbed her eyes, and looked at the clock on her side of the bed. Then she looked at Merle.

"I'm sorry you woke up, Peggy," Merle said. "I was hoping you wouldn't."

"It's okay, Merle. No need to explain. I know why you're up so early. Be careful and enjoy the morning with your old friend."

"I love you, honey."

She couldn't see the smile on Merle's face in the darkness, but she knew it was there.

Half an hour later, Merle parked his truck and climbed the hill toward the red oak. Though the ascent took longer and consumed more energy than it used to, he managed it in the predawn. He set up his portable chair, settled it next to the red oak, and sat down, leaning against the tree while cradling his rifle. He looked up to the sky that was showing more light. "Thank You, God, for this place and for letting me come back to it. And thanks for the fine sons You gave me. Can You believe what they did for me? They found Old Ironsights. And God, thank You for all You've done for me too."

He patted the stock of his .32. "Welcome home, Old Ironsights! It's time to get to huntin'!"

23

Making Somethin' Happen

There is a saying that a lot of turkey hunters use when the springtime gobblers are being way too quiet, thus making hunting slow and laborious: "If they ain't talkin', I'm walkin'!" These words are normally muttered with a bit of exasperation and are typically said about a microsecond after the derriere announces that it can't endure sitting on the hard ground any longer.

Usually before this statement is completed, the packing-up process starts. After gathering up the slate calls, strikers, and box calls that were laid out on the ground within easy reach and putting them back in their designated pockets in a waist pack, the eager turkey hunter stands and is on his way to either check out some fields or walk around to do some contact calling.

How do I know so much about the tendency of a turkey hunter to be so impulsive? Simply because I am among their number. More than once I've whispered those words of frustration to myself or to a friend, and within a minute or two the hunting party is on the move.

Deer hunters can be just as impetuous, and I'm numbered among them as well. I've been known to mumble, "If they ain't gruntin', I'm goin' huntin'!" These code words for "If I sit here any longer I'm gonna freeze to death" have been used in the past to get me moving. My standard reaction to a hunt that has gone bland is to exclaim, "It's time to make somethin' happen!" It would be embarrassing to admit how many times that slightly irritated declaration has resulted in my quick descent out of a tree stand. Yes, I have a tendency to succumb to impatience, and it's definitely something I need to work on. But every once in a great while, my "get up and go" yields something good. Such was the case for a deer hunt my son and I enjoyed several years ago.

Nathan was home from college for a Thanksgiving visit. Due to his heavy study schedule, he'd warned us that he could stay only from Wednesday to Saturday morning. That year, Tennessee's firearm deer season was scheduled to start Thanksgiving Day. Though I wanted to go to a nearby farm for a hunt that morning, I did the smart thing and conceded to my wife's wishes that everyone be home when the big noontime meal was served. Consequently, I assumed that with Nathan's short stay we wouldn't get to the woods at all. I quietly but reluctantly resolved myself to that likelihood.

When Friday afternoon arrived, my hopes were resurrected. Nathan approached and asked the question I'd hoped to hear.

"Dad, do you think we could go hunting tomorrow morning before I drive back to school?"

Bingo! "You bet, buddy," I quickly replied. "We can go to Joe's place. I'll put you in the ladder stand at the edge of a soybean field. There's plenty of deer, and there are lots of residual beans on the ground to attract them. With the hunting license you have, you can take either a buck or a doe, so you should be able to fill your tag. We'll go before daylight in the morning. If things go well, you should be on the road back to school by ten o'clock."

Dawn came Saturday morning with Nathan on one end of the 180-acre farm perched in an eighteen-foot-high, metal ladder stand. The stand was placed next to a thicket where deer loved to bed down during the day. I was sitting on a stool at the other end of the property next to a harvested cornfield. I waited for the deer to appear and hoped to hear the report of Nathan's .270. But there were no blasts to be heard. Eventually I was concerned, worried that my son wouldn't get an opportunity to take a shot. After another fifteen minutes of wishful listening, words tumbled out of my mouth. I seemed to have no more control over them than I have over an avalanche on a Colorado mountainside. "It's time to make somethin' happen!"

With that said, I promptly stood up, folded my three-legged stool and tucked it under my arm, shouldered my rifle, and headed to the north side of the farm. When I got to the ladder stand, it was around nine. I looked up at Nathan and asked the obvious question. "See anything at all, Nate?"

His reply was gracious. "No deer, Dad. Just a beautiful sunrise, a few blue jays, and a couple of squirrels. But it's been a great morning. I guess we'd better go to the house so I can get ready to head back to school."

While I sensed his sincere gratitude for the chance to be in a deer stand at least one morning that year, I also detected a bit of disappointment. Feeling some fatherly sorrow for the boy, I offered an opportunity I was sure he'd agree to. "Nate," I whispered as softly as I could, "it's time to make somethin' happen."

There were those words again! This wasn't the first time Nathan had heard me say them while deer hunting. Through the years during hunts, he'd been on the receiving end of several "deer drives" that started with my "Let's make somethin' happen!" exclamation. When I did resort to this tactic, I was always careful and quick to remind him, "Son, this isn't always the best way to hunt, but sometimes you just have to stir 'em up to see some action." I had no idea that I was teaching him a principle that would serve him well later in life.

Nathan knew exactly what I meant by making something happen, and he smiled down at me as I continued. "How about you stay put for about fifteen minutes while I walk down this fencerow and get into the thicket behind you. Since its nine o'clock, some deer may have come in from the other side and bedded down. If there's something in there, maybe I'll push it out and you might get a shot."

"Yeah, I'd be happy to stay here," Nathan replied.

I took off. When I got about two hundred yards down the fence line, I took a hard right. It took me a few minutes to loop around, but I stepped into the thicket and started pressing through the heavy brush and briars toward Nathan's position. When I got about a hundred yards from where he was sitting, I heard the sweet sound of his .270 announcing that I had indeed stirred up a bedding deer. I couldn't have been happier. Three more booms in quick succession occurred as I stood in the middle of the thicket. I had an experienced guess at what was happening, so I added a running commentary as the shots sounded.

Bang! "Oh, yes!"

Bang! "Oh, wow!"

Bang! "Oh no!"

Bang! "Oh well…"

As quickly as I could get through the thorns that clawed viciously at my camo, I returned to the ladder stand where my son waited. He was standing on the ground, and he reloaded as we talked.

"Do you think you got one, Nate?"

"Nah. I don't think I touched him. He was a big-bodied deer, Dad. Nice rack too. I could see the dust flying up around him as I shot, so no, I don't think I touched him."

"Well, we won't leave the farm until we've made sure he's not hurt," I responded.

Then I heard my son say something that has been etched in my mind since that moment. It's a confession we've both laughed about for years in the retelling.

"Dad, I need to tell you something."

"What is it, son?" I was ready for anything from "I think I shot my toe off" to "I'm gonna drop out of college and join the circus." Instead, it was something much more grave.

"Dad, when I took that last shot, I could see your truck in the scope."

I know my face turned pale when I heard his humble admission. I looked toward the truck and immediately tried to give my son the benefit of the doubt.

"That's an awfully long way for a bullet to travel, buddy. But if the old pickup is dead, we'll get it mounted and hang it over the mantel."

We spent the next hour looking for signs of a bleeding deer but found none. When we got to the truck, we checked it over and didn't find any bullet holes in it either. Since it started up right away, we headed home. Nathan did his best to assure me he'd had a great morning even though his tag would go unpunched for the year. I accepted his assessment of the day, and we stored the memory away to enjoy in the years to come.

When he was out of college and married, I discovered my son had found something redeemable in my "It's time to make somethin' happen" attitude that he'd seen and experienced while hunting with me. The advice I'd given him that it wasn't the best way to go about deer hunting was well-received, but so was the other part of my instruction. He'd accepted the reality that sometimes it is necessary to "stir things up." He realized the tactic wasn't just valuable in the woods, but that it could also be effective in the business world. And apply it he did!

Being a musician by trade, I bought Nathan an electric/acoustic guitar as a Christmas gift when he was ten years old. When he opened it, I told him, "Son, your job is to not just learn how to play that guitar, but I want you to learn how to make it talk!" Never did a youngster take a dad's challenge more seriously. He proceeded to spend untold hours learning scales, discovering how to read music charts, and trying to mimic great players, such as Phil Keaggy, Stevie Ray Vaughn, Eric Johnson, and Eric Clapton.

As he was learning to play the guitar, I also passed down some old recording equipment we'd used in our family business of writing songs, recording music, and putting on concerts. When we replaced a recording machine with the latest technology, Nate got the earlier version. Within a short time, he was skilled on the guitar and was developing an in-depth understanding of "signal path" (meaning he was learning how to be a recording engineer). Nathan's skills as a musician and engineer eventually became good enough to enlist him in updating some of the earlier recordings my wife, Annie, and I had released.

After marrying Stephanie, Nathan worked a few jobs that included being a cashier at a bookstore and roofing, but music was his first love when it came to doing something that would earn a wage. He considered entering the business of music by performing, but he wasn't that fond of being center stage. After "sitting on the music stand" for a while and seeing nothing really generate with his musical skills, he decided, "It's time to make somethin' happen!"

Armed with a stack of CDs containing samples of his ability to produce full-blown studio versions of songs featuring his guitar, his bass, his keyboard, his drums, and his engineering prowess, he hit the streets of Nashville. Willing to face rejection, he marched into the offices of publishers on Music Row, handed them a disc, and said something akin to "I can do your songwriter demos fast and cheap, and they'll sound good. Give me a chance, and I'll prove it to you!"

When publishers hear the words "fast," "cheap," and "good," that's music to their ears! As a result of his brave presentations, he landed opportunities to make some music as well as get some dollars going his way. Then one day, the big payoff came for his "make somethin' happen" efforts. An established songwriter Nathan had worked with brought in a fifteen-year-old songwriter to collaborate with. Nathan heard something in their cowrites that made him perk up. He offered to produce a couple of songs for the two writers on a gratis basis, quietly hoping they'd let him continue as their go-to guy for song demos.

The music Nathan produced for that fifteen-year-old songwriter got the attention of the team that surrounded her, and they hired him to work with her on a full CD. Her initial recordings were very well received by country music radio networks and yielded a couple "top of the chart" singles. On the heels of that success, they began work on a second CD. The follow-up recording generated so much commercial success that it was nominated for and won a Grammy Award for album of the year, the music world's equivalent of the Super Bowl, Daytona 500, or World Series.

Nathan has worked with other recognizable artists I could mention, but suffice it to say that he remains plenty busy as a producer as well as a songwriter. Each time I hear his handiwork on the radio or TV, I marvel at what he's accomplished. I'm proud of how his solid work ethic has served him well in the world of music, but I'm even more excited when I hear Nate give God thanks for everything he's achieved.

As I bask in the glowing joy of a son whose industrious spirit has yielded such accomplishments, I also wonder where he'd be today if he hadn't been willing to respond to the urge to get up and hit the streets of Nashville. I know I can't take total credit for his relentless fortitude, but I like to think that just maybe a few of those "let's make somethin' happen" moments we had while deer hunting helped shape his drive for success.

24

The Call

Danny picked up the phone and pushed four of the eleven digits of his dad's long-distance number. Then he stopped. He paused to think again about what he was about to do. After five seconds or so, he pressed the off button and whispered, "What if he says no?"

Danny's passion for chasing whitetails had not been handed down to him from his father, who had never shown any interest in it. For that reason, Danny knew that his dad's response to his proposal could go either way. Hoping to say just the right words to entice him, Danny had rehearsed the invitation many times. As he held the phone and debated whether to complete the call, he went over the idea one more time.

Hey, Dad, a few of my buddies and I are headed to the mountains in a couple of weeks for opening day of rifle season. I wanted to call to see if you'd like to go along. We have plenty of room in the cabin for you. I'll treat you and provide a rifle, ammunition, a buck tag, and all the warm clothes you'll need. And there'll be lots of good food there— enough to feed an army. You won't need to bring a thing but your plans for a good time with us. It'll be more fun than you can imagine. Wanna go?

Feeling hopeful that he would remember every word, Danny dug for courage, pushed all eleven buttons of his dad's phone number and waited anxiously for his dad to answer.

211

"Hello."

"Hey, Dad. Danny here. Wanna go deer huntin' with us on opening day in a couple of weeks?" The combination of intensely wishing that his dream would come true—hearing his dad say yes—and the terrible dread of hearing no instead had wiped Danny's memory clean of his rehearsed words. He couldn't believe how he'd mentally locked up at the crucial moment. The dead silence on the other end of the line was painful to hear. Without the extra enticements of food, a free license, and fun, Danny was sure the long pause would be followed by, "Naw, son, I don't think I want to do that. Hope you have a great time though. Thank you for asking." Then the real answer came.

"You know, son, I've been thinking about going with you to see what it is about this huntin' thing that you like so much. I don't know the first thing about deer hunting, but if you're willing to take a greenhorn along with you, I'm game."

Danny couldn't believe his ears! He was glad his dad couldn't see him do four strong victory pumps with his fist and then look up to heaven and quietly mouth, *Thank You, God! You heard and answered my prayer!*

"Son, other than a good pair of boots, I don't have any of the gear I'll need, so I'll have to borrow some of that camo stuff from you, as well as use one of your rifles, if that's okay. You'll also have to show me how to shoot."

Danny smiled big as he spoke. "I can definitely show you how to use my .30-06. And I have everything you'll need when it comes to warm camo clothes. And by the way, after we hang up I'm going to the store to get your deer license. My treat—and I insist." He'd finally remembered the rest of his rehearsed invitation, so he added an enhanced version. "There's plenty of room in the cabin for you, my buddies and I will supply all the food, and best of all, you're gonna enjoy the guys we'll be with. They're all first-class and very safety conscious, and we'll make sure you get a good spot on the property in terms of where the deer are."

"Thanks, son. You certainly don't have to get my license for me, but I can tell by the tone of your voice that I probably can't change your mind about that. I'll meet you at your house in two weeks. If it's all right with you and Sherrie, I'll bring your mama with me so she can visit with Sherrie and help out with the kids while we're gone. A young mom can always use a break, and your mama is itching for some grandbaby time."

Danny said that was a good plan and thanked his dad for agreeing to come for the trip. After saying goodbye and ending the call, he turned and danced through his house like a little boy who'd just found out he was going to a Major League Baseball game.

The next fourteen days passed way too slow, but Danny busied himself by getting things ready for the first-ever hunting trip to the mountains with his dad.

The day finally came when his dad and mom arrived. After settling his mom in and transferring his dad's gear to his rig, Danny announced it was time to head out. After the goodbyes, Danny and his dad had a good visit as they headed into the mountains. When they rounded the last curve in the dirt road that brought the log cabin into view, Danny's heart was pounding with excitement. The rustic setting looked like a picture in a magazine.

"Whoa!" was all his dad could say as the truck came to a stop and he took in the view. "This place looks incredible! I saw the pictures you sent, of course, but I had no idea how great it would look live. And you were involved in building this cabin? I'm amazed."

Danny's chest swelled a little. "I sure was. My three hunting buddies and I built this place. Don't forget, among the four of us, one is a contractor and one is an electrician. Even though I push a pencil, I learn quickly. I was able to do a lot of nail pounding and some roofing, and I even remembered some of the stuff you taught me about plumbing. I was glad I could contribute. It was pure fun to build this place."

As the two of them sat in the cab of the truck admiring the cabin and surrounding country, the other hunters pulled up in separate trucks. Everyone piled out and introductions were done.

"Hey, guys, this is my dad, Jerry," Danny announced. "Dad, this is Tom, Brandon, and Gregg." After a network of handshakes and a few minutes of friendly chit-chat, the unloading process began. Within thirty minutes, the men had settled in and were enjoying the warm flames in the woodstove.

Feeling anxious to introduce his dad to the bolt-action .30-06 he'd be using,

Danny stood up and spoke. "Hey, guys, I'm gonna take Dad outside and let him get acquainted with my Remington. I'm also going to sight in my .308 to make sure it's dead on. Anybody else need to double-check his weapon?"

All five hunters grabbed their gun cases and headed to the hundred-yard shooting lane that had been cleared in the area behind the cabin. It took only a couple of shots each for Danny, Tom, Brandon, and Gregg to feel satisfied their guns were sighted in. Within a few minutes, it was Jerry's turn to take his place at the homemade shooting table. He seemed a little nervous as Danny showed him how to work the safety.

Jerry noticed how confidently his boy pushed a fully loaded clip into the underside of the rifle and explained the basics of how the gun operated.

"Have a seat here, Dad. Rest the barrel on the sandbags and look through the scope. Do you see the crosshairs?"

Jerry nodded.

"Great. Look down the lane at the paper target. Tell me if everything looks in focus."

"Looks good to me, son. Looks just like the pictures I've seen of looking through scopes at targets. What now?"

Danny again showed his dad how to use the bolt action.

Jerry followed the instructions, and the metallic sound and feel of the cartridge being transferred from the clip into the chamber caught his attention. "Yeah! That sounds rather manly!" he exclaimed.

Danny looked at his friends and grinned. "Cool, isn't it, Dad. Now, to fire this rifle, you make sure the butt is snug against your shoulder, slide the safety button forward, put the crosshairs on the big orange dot on the target, and slowly pull the trigger. The gun will kick back into your shoulder a little as it fires, but nothing you can't handle."

After a few moments of settling in on the target, Jerry pulled the trigger and felt the sudden jolt of the gun against his shoulder. Stunned, he sat silently for about three seconds. He looked up, turned to the guys, focused on Danny, and gave his postshot report. "I thought the sound of the bolt action was manly, but that was nothing compared to pulling the trigger! That's what I call a big-time testosterone moment! But how'd I do? Did I hit the target?"

All three of Danny's friends looked through their binoculars and almost simultaneously said, "Dead deer, Mr. Jerry!"

"You can look through the scope and see where it hit, Dad," Danny encouraged with a wide smile.

Jerry put his eye to the scope and saw that the bullet mark was on the right edge of the two-inch orange dot.

"May I shoot some more?" Jerry's voice revealed his excitement. He wanted to get back to the fun.

"Absolutely, Dad. In fact, I have two boxes of shells for you. You can take thirty-nine more shots if you want. But since it's starting to get dark, I think five or ten more shots will give you the skill you need to be ready to hunt tomorrow."

With the sighting-in process done and a meal of hot pizza under their belts, the five hunters bedded down for the night.

Jerry smiled in the dark as he listened to the group strategize about the next morning. As they talked back and forth, he could hear their excitement. While they were still making their plans, he drifted off to sleep.

It didn't seem but a minute of sleep to all of them when the alarm buzzer woke them the next morning. Following some cereal and coffee, the camo-clad crew headed to the porch to cover some last-minute details as they prepared to part ways for the woods. Danny went first.

"Dad and I will take the buddy stand on the west end of the property. My phone is on in case any of you need help dragging a deer out. Blessings on everyone. We'll see you around noon—or earlier if someone pulls a trigger."

After the other guys shared their general plans, the group finished their prehunt ritual, split up, and disappeared into the predawn darkness.

Danny quietly led his father away from the cabin and down a long, well-trimmed trail that followed a ridgeline. The distance they had to cover was about a quarter of a mile, and the terrain was relatively level. As the small, bluish flashlight beam bounced along the ground in front of Danny's feet, his heart was filled with joy at the sound of his dad following right behind him. He stopped briefly and turned to speak. Before he could say a word, his dad had something to say.

"It's darker than the inside of a coffin out here, Danny. I'm glad you brought a light for me to use."

"We're almost there, Dad, and with plenty of time to spare before legal shooting light. This ridge stand has yielded some really good deer in the past five years we've hunted from this place. I hope we see a buck, but for herd health, some does need to be culled, so whatever comes by first is yours to take."

Jerry flinched a little at the thought of actually killing a doe...or any deer for that matter. It wasn't something he had a hankering to do, but being here in this setting that his son was passionate about was very important to him. He nodded his agreement and said, "Okay. Got it."

Within ten minutes, the two men ascended the ladder of the two-man deer stand and sat down to wait for shooting light.

Danny whispered softly, "If we see something this morning, it will likely come from our right. At night, the deer like to feed in a field about a hundred yards away. They usually come through these woods to get to a thicket on our left. That's their daytime bedding area. So check to your right often, and I'll watch the left side."

"What do I do if I see something, son?"

Danny realized he'd forgotten to cover the steps to take if a deer was spotted approaching the stand area. He thought quickly how to make the tutoring brief. "Basically, don't make any quick moves. Deer have keen eyesight and are very alert and nervous. When you lift your gun to fire, move slow as a snail. And you might get a little excited when the moment of truth comes. I still do, and I've been doing this for a while. That can make holding the gun steady a bit of a challenge."

"What do you mean by 'moment of truth'?" his dad asked.

"That's what hunters call it when the time comes to take the shot. It can mess with your nerves. Some people get shaky when it happens. They look a little like Barney Fife at a bank robbery. But you'll do fine."

Jerry smiled tentatively at the explanation, and then he looked to his right into the semidarkness of the woods. He wondered what he would do when he faced the "moment of truth."

Finally the morning sky turned pale blue. A few minutes later Danny whispered, "Shooting light is here, Dad. Anytime from now till sunset is legal hunting hours. Keep your eyes open. We'll need to be very quiet now."

Jerry could hear tension in his son's whisper, but as he replayed the sound in his mind, he realized that Danny wasn't feeling tension; instead, it was joyous anticipation. Jerry knew very well the huge difference between the two emotions. One had the potential to cause ulcers, and the other could bring a satisfying sense of expectation to a soul, the kind that can heal an ulcer. Suddenly it occurred to him that there might be a whole lot more to deer hunting than just shooting deer. Feeling the same wave of excitement his boy was enjoying, Jerry turned his eyes to the right and watched the woods carefully.

There was only an occasional word whispered between the two of them as they watched for deer. Jerry had feared that the sitting and waiting that is part of the hunting experience would bore him to tears, but when he looked at his watch and saw that an hour had passed seemingly quicker than a minute, he admitted his thoughts to his son. "I can't believe we've been sitting here an hour already," he whispered. "It went by in a flash. I guess it's all the stuff that is here to entertain a fellow. That sunrise was unbelievable as it came through the trees. And I bet I've seen at least a half-dozen bird species. Plus, I had no idea that chipmunks could be so busy—and noisy too. This is great!"

Danny smiled as his dad whispered so favorably about what he'd seen that morning. "It really is amazing what all goes on in the living room of nature. It's almost as busy as a city out here. One of my favorite parts of the hunt is sitting and watching the show. I—"

Danny's eyes suddenly got big. He stopped talking as he looked over his dad's shoulder in the direction of the field. "Dad, there are three deer coming toward us—two bucks and a doe. Slowly turn your head, and I guarantee you'll see 'em."

Jerry's muscles tensed as he slowly moved his face toward the deer. He felt his head jerking a little with the adrenaline that suddenly surged through him. Before he saw the trio of deer, he heard the faint sounds of their steps in the dry leaves. It sounded like a group of people walking through the woods. He knew he couldn't detect the distinctness of the noise the way Danny probably could, but the audio was thrilling to hear.

The deer stopped briefly to browse for some residual acorns under a huge red oak. Danny took the opportunity to coach his dad through the next step of the hunt.

"Dad, as slowly as you can, move the rifle up and look through the scope. At the same time, slowly shift around to your right. Try really hard to not make any noise." Danny's heart was pounding like a symphony kettledrum, and he wondered if his dad was feeling the same rush of emotion.

"Son, I'm shaking like a leaf." Jerry's voice was barely audible.

"That's okay, Dad. It's normal and part of the hunt! Rest your elbows on the railing and take a deep breath. One of the bucks is a nice eight point. He's plenty bigger than the other buck. He's the one you want to get. Let me know when you have him in your scope."

Jerry had to fight the unfamiliar battle with nerves—"buck fever," he decided. He struggled to hold the gun steady on the buck.

Danny listened to his dad's heavy breathing and knew he was experiencing more than just a little piece of the adrenaline pie that comes with deer hunting. In fact, Danny figured his dad was chowing down the whole pie.

"I've got him in my scope! Where do I aim?"

"I'm looking at him through my binoculars too. He's broadside just like you need him to be. Now, move the crosshairs to a spot just barely behind his front shoulder and about eight inches above the underline of his belly. That's your target. Now, push the safety button forward. When you feel your aim is steady, slowly squeeze the trigger. Don't anticipate the kick; instead, let the gun surprise you when it goes off."

Five seconds later, the ladder stand rattled as a shot rang out, and Jerry experienced the kick of the .30-06.

"Jack another shell into the chamber, Dad, and get the scope back to your eye!" Danny encouraged. "You might need to take another shot."

Jerry wrestled with the gun to reload. He peered through the scope again. "I don't see anything. The deer are gone."

Danny kept looking at the area through his binoculars. "Two of them are gone, Dad, but one of them is lying on the other side of that red oak! He's hard to spot, but I can see some white hair on the ground." He lowered his glasses, stood up in the stand, and looked down at his father. "Dad, you're the man today—you just got yourself a really nice eight-point buck!"

"You're kidding!" Jerry looked toward where the buck was supposedly lying. He looked back at his son. "Are you serious?"

"Serious as a heart attack, Dad! He's brown and down. You need a high five and a big hug, but we'd better get on the ground to celebrate. I'm so pumped, I'm about to fall out of this tree stand!"

On the ground, the father and son embraced and then headed toward the red oak. After several minutes of admiring the heavy-beamed, eight-point rack on the buck and retelling the details of how the kill came about, Danny forced out the question he was afraid to ask. "What do you think of this deer huntin' thing, Dad? Is it anything like you imagined?"

Jerry thought for a few seconds. "Son, I have only two things to say in answer to your question. One, when I heard you say those deer were coming in and I turned to take the shot, I thought my heart was going to leap out of my jacket. I haven't been that nervous since I asked your mama to marry me. The second thing I have to say is, When does deer season start next year? You gotta let me come back and do this again!"

Danny's face felt like it would break in half as he grinned at his dad. "You have no idea how welcome you are to join us on this mountain, Dad. I'm so excited and pleased that we…that *you*…have discovered you are a born hunter. The way you handled the challenge of keeping calm enough to take a solid shot was amazing. Only a true deer hunter could pull that off. There's a ton to learn about this huntin' thing, and I would be beyond thrilled to show you everything I know about it."

Jerry smiled. "And I'd be more than thrilled to let you show me. This is a new day for me…for us. One I'm really glad I've lived to see."

Danny took out his cell phone to call his mom and tell her what had just happened. As he touched the numbers on the keypad, he remembered the hesitation he'd felt two weeks earlier about phoning his dad. A shiver went up his spine at the thought that he almost hadn't dialed the numbers and extended the invitation. As the phone rang, he looked across the body of the big buck at his dad, who was still admiring his trophy. Danny silently prayed, *Thank You, God, for helping me make the call. Thank You!*

That's a Call

Hey, Pop, how you been?
I'm coming to see you again
I'm leaving in the morning, gonna drive straight through
By the time the sun goes down, I'll be pulling into town
We'll go to dinner at the diner, just me and you

That's a call he's so glad he made
'Cause heaven knows how much regrets can weigh
Things unsaid, things undone
They pile up till they weigh a ton
On the heart every day
That's a call he's so glad he made

Hey, boss, change of plans
Tonight I'll be driving back in
A day early, but don't worry—I'm gonna close that deal
But there's a place I gotta be, sitting right there in the seats
At the kickoff, yelling my head off
It's my boy's first game

That's a call he's so glad he made
'Cause heaven knows how much regrets can weigh
Things unsaid, things undone
They pile up till they weigh a ton
On the heart every day
That's a call he's so glad he made

The Call

Hello, I know it's getting late
But before you drive back tomorrow
I just need to tell you that I love you
Be careful on the road
I can't wait to hug you when you get back home

That's a call he's so glad he made
'Cause heaven knows how much regrets can weigh
Things unsaid, things undone
They pile up till they weigh a ton
On the heart every day
That's a call he's so glad he made[13]

25

My Rack Hunter

My daughter, Heidi, stopped me in my tracks, put her hand on my forearm, and softly said, "Dad, there it is! Straight ahead...do you see it?" Her voice had an excited tremor. I could hardly believe how quickly she was able to spot the trophy we'd been looking for during our hunt. The area where we were had an endless pattern of colors to test even the keenest of vision, but her eyes were well trained by experience.

She looked around to make sure there were no other hunters in the area and whispered, "That's the same one I saw two days ago. I'm sure of it. I just hope no one else has a bead on it. We gotta move!"

Confident that our long hunt was about to meet with success, I fell in behind my daughter as she began a determined stalk. I knew she was about to explode with excitement and that it wasn't easy for her to resist breaking into a run. After weaving our way through a thick stand of obstacles, we managed to get within shooting distance. That's when I heard the gun go off.

Cha-ching!

It was followed by, "That'll be $89.99 plus tax, please."

The smoke drifted from the barrel of my credit card as Heidi smiled and admired the dress we'd just bagged.

"Now this is the way to hunt, Dad. I find 'em and you shoot 'em for me. And don't you like that it's already cleaned and hangin' up?"

"Yes, Heidi. I wish deer hunting were as tidy as this, but after the two hours we've spent walking around this mall, I can tell you that your kind of hunting is a lot harder."

Heidi threw her trophy over her shoulder, and we headed to the car. We'd just finished another annual tradition that we'd enjoyed through the years—the annual birthday hunt for a dress. The trips to the mall with my expert "rack" hunter grew more expensive as time went by, but the memories with Heidi are worth every dime I'll never see again.

Though Heidi is all girl and enjoys the pursuit of a trophy dress, she also loves the outdoors, especially fishing. In years past, we've wet our lines in waters from the Gulf of Mexico to the Atlantic, from off the coast of Miami to the Pacific Ocean, from off Canada's outer banks to the lakes in Tennessee. Angling is her preference, but thankfully, she appreciates my passion for hunting wild game. One year she went with me on a springtime turkey hunt. It was a hunt that yielded a memory I still enjoy recalling.

We got to the farm where we were going to hunt about two hours after daylight. Normally I like to be in the area where the gobblers are before the sun rises, but knowing that a four o'clock wakeup call would not contribute to Heidi's affection for the hunt, I'd deliberately delayed our arrival to the woods. Furthermore, I knew by the time we got there, the hens would be nearing their midmorning preoccupation with their nests, which would, in turn, make it easier to entice the lovesick toms with my turkey calling. In addition, Heidi wouldn't have to spend a lot of time sitting in one spot since the strategy was to walk around and do some contact calling.

After forty-five minutes or so of checking out a few of the lower fields on the property and then ascending a hill via a logging road, a gobbler finally responded to the sound of my slate call.

"Quick!" I said as I slipped off the logging road and into the woods. "Follow me. We gotta find a spot just off this road, sit down, and get ready. I think that bird might come in."

Heidi could tell I was jazzed by the sound of the gobbler. She seemed to share in my excitement.

"What do I do, Dad?" she asked when we found our spot.

"Just sit next to me and get comfortable. And whatever you do, if I say 'Don't move,' then don't move. The eyesight of a turkey is amazing. They can see everything…they see almost as good as you when you spot a dress from a mile away."

She understood the comparison and smiled as she pulled the mesh camo mask I'd loaned her down over her face. Within a few minutes the gobbler responded again to my call. I guessed it was probably about sixty yards away. The lush, late-April foliage was so thick I couldn't get a visual.

"He's pretty close, Heidi, so don't move."

She cooperated and kept looking in the direction my face was pointed.

As gobblers often do, the bird hung up just out of sight and wouldn't come in. I knew he was out there staging, strutting, and waiting for the hen he'd heard to come to him. Seconds turned to minutes, and before I knew it, ten minutes had gone by. The turkey gobbled occasionally at my quiet yelps, but it was obvious he hadn't advanced any farther toward us.

"We gotta wait this bird out, Heidi. If you don't mind, let's stay right here for a while."

"I'm fine with it, Dad. This is kinda fun!"

Another few minutes and a few stubborn gobblers went by as we sat quietly against the huge oak. I was enjoying this rare opportunity to be on a hunt with Heidi. I smiled at the thought and then found my thoughts drifting from the nearby bird to a time when Heidi was still a baby. I recalled a detail that I decided might explain why she was so good at dress hunting.

When Annie and I had our two children in 1977 and 1980, ultrasound technology was reserved primarily for examinations of preborn babies with medical concerns. For that reason, we didn't know in advance what the sex of our newborns would be. That was fine with me. Though we couldn't plan our nursery colors and choose a specific name in advance of the births, I enjoyed the mystery of boy or girl that grew with each passing month of Annie's pregnancies.

Our firstborn, Nathan, was nearing three years old when we learned we were expecting a second child. He began campaigning for a brother. Annie conceded that another boy would be a good sibling for our son, and she joined Nathan in his prayers for a boy baby. Not me! I longed to have a little girl in our home. I was so hopeful that the newborn would be a daughter that I went to a department store, marched straight to the children's clothing section, and planned to get a dress for my new baby girl. It was my act of faith that God would hear my prayer request.

I wandered up and down the aisles until I finally saw a dress that gave me that "ah-ha!" feeling. It had a velvety black top, a red-plaid skirt, and a matching plaid bow sewn on at the waistline. Without even looking at the price tag, I bought it. I was quite proud of my find, but what I didn't know was that I'd purchased a dress that would fit an eighteen-month-old child. All I knew was that it looked small and really pretty.

When I got home, Annie nearly went into labor from laughing at my uneducated attempt at shopping for a young female.

"This is so sweet," she said, "but do you know how dangerous it is to buy a dress for a female that is three times the size she needs?"

I gave her a puzzled look.

"A purchase like that can send a gal the kind of message that can get a fellow in some deep doo-doo. Just be glad you didn't get me a dress while you were out shopping today!"

I defended myself with my best shot. "It's not about the dress, babe. It's about who I'm hoping will wear it." Annie knew my wishes regarding the little one growing in her belly. She smiled and hugged me before dropping a bomb on me.

"I know how you are about never wanting to waste anything, so I gotta ask. What if our baby is another little boy? Are you gonna make him wear this dress?"

I didn't have a response other than, "Just make sure you have a girl." And with that, I took the dress and hung it in the nursery. And I prayed some more.

As it turned out, on April 15, my hope for adding a daughter to our family was filled. Annie went along with my choice for a name—Heidi Anne. As far as I was concerned, if the goal of mankind was to produce the perfect daughter, there was no need for anyone else on the planet to get pregnant. Heidi was it.

As experienced parents know, it didn't take long at all until Heidi grew into that dress. When we put it on her, Annie and I agreed that it was perfect for her. Heidi looked absolutely stunning in it.

Now, after the passage of many years, I was considering how my innate ability to find just the right dress had somehow been imprinted in her DNA. That means, of course, that I'm solely responsible for her tremendous rack hunting skills!

It seemed that in the flicker of a deer's tail, my little girl went from eighteen months old to sixteen years old! And now she was sitting beside me, waiting for a turkey to strut closer. I looked over at her. *My, how grown-up she seems—and oh, how lovely. She's such a joy in my life…*

Suddenly another ground-rattling shout from the gobbler shook me back to the present and the hunt.

"Heidi," I whispered, moving nothing except my lips, "could you tell if that bird is closer? I think he's decided to come on in."

"I did notice he sounded louder. Don't move, right?"

"Absolutely. Not even a muscle, and if you can, don't even blink if he rounds the bend of this logging road 'cause he'll be within twenty-five yards of us."

I rested my shotgun on my knee. I could feel my heart pounding as I gently placed the tip of my index finger on the safety button. I was happily immersed in a pool of adrenaline. I couldn't wait until the red head of the gobbler appeared.

Just to be sure Heidi was doing okay, I slowly turned my head to check on her. What I saw was one of the main reasons she's such a delight to have in our family. She was adding a little comic relief to this otherwise tense moment. She'd lifted her left hand up to the bottom of her long, brown hair and was pushing up on it slowly but repeatedly. She was mocking the motion that a fancily dressed woman might do just before making a grand entrance into a ballroom. As she did, she looked at me through her mesh face mask.

I could see the mischievous glint in her eyes and the smile on her lips. I was pretty sure what was going on in her mind. *No way am I gonna miss this chance to mess with my daddy's head!* And mess with it, she did. When she saw my eyes widen at her antics, she snickered and whispered, "I gotta look good for the feller that's on his way."

Once again I'd been had by a master jokester. Actually, I should have expected it, but she always manages to surprise me with her well-timed antics, a skill she'd started developing at a young age. There are several more examples I could offer, but one of our family's favorites is when we had a dozen or so kids at our house for Nathan's eleventh birthday party. They had arrived at eleven o'clock, and each one brought a ravenous appetite for the pizza and chocolate cake Annie was planning to serve at lunchtime.

Heidi was about eight, and she knew that the combined level of hunger that our company felt was huge. Armed with that knowledge, she stepped out on the elevated deck at the back of our house around eleven thirty and yelled down to the crowd of hungry youngsters, "Lunch is ready!"

Like a stampede of cattle, the kids ran for the basement door, nearly trampling each other as they entered the house. Once inside, the hungry little mob ran up the stairs and into the kitchen—only to find that not a morsel was ready for consumption. Heidi's eyes gleamed with satisfaction as she announced to the bunch, "Kidding!"

The kitchen filled with starved moans when the kids realized what had happened. As each child lowered his head in disappointment and headed back down the stairs, Heidi pulled her shoulders back and grinned maniacally from ear to ear. In fact, it was exactly the way she was grinning right now as we waited for the gobbler to appear.

I'd like to report that Heidi got to see that bird meet its Maker that day, but as it turned out, the old tom decided to go in another direction. I'm confident he never knew we were there, but I'll always remember that time. In fact, I could take you to the very tree we were sitting against when the "Primp Queen" got me good. It remains one of my favorite moments in the woods.

Another time my daughter used her gift of making her old dad smile deserves a mention, but the occasion was far more emotionally intense than a battle of wits with a mature gobbler. Heidi needed a C-section to birth her second baby. Without knowing it, a small portion of the placenta was left in her uterus, resulting in some dangerously excessive postbirth bleeding. The medicine she was given seemed to have solved the problem, but about a week later, while at our house, she began to bleed profusely. Her husband, Emmitt, was out of town on a quick business trip, and I'd assumed the responsibility of rushing her to the hospital if necessary.

I called ahead and asked her doctor to meet us there. Heidi was growing weaker by the moment, and when we arrived at the hospital, she was immediately given an IV of fluids and placed in a wheelchair to be taken to the surgery floor. The doctor didn't want to wait on a uniformed assistant, so she handed me the IV bag and instructed me to hold it high and run alongside Heidi.

We were hurrying down a hallway headed toward an elevator that would take us to the operating room when Heidi suddenly fainted. Dead to the world, her feet went straight out and dug into the carpeted floor, stopping her forward progress. Her doctor quickly reached inside her pocket, pulled out a packet of smelling salts, broke it open, and waved it under Heidi's nose. She roused briefly, and I was able to get her feet back up on the footboards of the wheelchair. We took off running again. When we reached the elevator, the doctor pushed the button several times, hoping to hurry its arrival. Finally the door opened, and we quickly went inside.

Heidi's head was back with her face toward the ceiling. I was glad to hear and see her stir a little. The doctor and I looked back and forth, moving our gaze from Heidi to the changing red numbers above the elevator door.

Heidi's enthusiastic voice broke the silence. "I see a bright light!"

My heart jumped into my throat. My assumption was that Heidi's life was fading away. Every muscle in my body tensed, and I was speechless. I looked at the doctor and noticed that her face had paled. She was staring at her patient with a look of sheer panic.

Then Heidi spoke again. I feared it might be her last words.

"Bright light, ya'll. Right there! See it? It's in the ceiling!" Then she pointed at the recessed florescent lighting above us and laughed. She lifted her head up and looked at her two victims, waiting for our reaction.

Her doctor offered a relieved chuckle and then gave a good-natured scolding to her patient for taking several years off her life. All I could do was sort of laugh. The level of joy I felt when I realized Heidi was feeling good enough to bring a little humor into the situation was monumental. She'd gotten us—and good.

We were still laughing, albeit a bit worriedly, when the elevator door opened.

The nurse who met us there seemed a little puzzled as to why we were smiling, especially when she noticed the considerable amount of blood that was present. She took the IV bag from me and helped the doctor whisk my girl away to an operating room.

Needless to say, the time crawled by agonizingly slow. It seemed like hours as I waited for the doctor to reappear and give me the latest update. I stood quietly at a window and looked out at the city of Nashville. The tears rolled down my cheeks at the thought of losing Heidi. Thankfully, the outcome was positive. The portion of residual placenta was removed, and Heidi's condition improved quickly. I am so blessed to still have her around to "mess with my head" every once in a while!

As many parents have discovered, when it comes to getting a reminder of how precious our children are, there's hardly anything more effective than living through the trauma of nearly losing them or, worse yet, actually losing them. The gratitude I have that Heidi is still around is deep and rich. Though we don't get to do as much adventuring together as we used to enjoy, we still do the annual birthday "rack" hunt. The only difference now is that Heidi and Emmitt's three little "hunterettes" tag along. And believe me, they also are becoming incredible rack hunters. After all, it's in their DNA too! And it's becoming more and more apparent that the girls inherited Heidi's humor gene. We're in for quite a ride!

26

Mountaineer Memories

by Steve Chapman with George Ferrell

One of the most interesting song titles I've ever heard is "I Don't Like Half the Folks I Love." It's amazing how so few words can imply so much. It's my understanding that the songwriter thought of the "hook" and penned the lyrics after going to a family reunion. I can't help but wonder if he left the event beat up and scarred emotionally and/or physically. For whatever reason the song was written, I'm very happy to report that I would not have come up with that title, because it doesn't fit anyone in the Chapman family, immediate or extended.

A Chapman family reunion always takes place in the town of Chapmanville, West Virginia. Yep, you read it right. The town is named after my family. The gathering is invariably fun. Besides a yard full of delightful relatives to connect with who come from various parts of the country, there is plenty of well-cooked food and some newborn Chapmans to dote over. There is also lots of singing and some of the best clean joke telling on the planet.

All these great features make our reunions memorable occasions. But there is one more I have to add that has made the gathering even more of a treat. It's seeing the gleam in the eyes of my Uncle Jimmy. Jimmy Ferrell was married to my dad's sister, Daisy. At our gatherings, he'd talk about going hunting with his son, George, and his grandson, Travis. Sadly, Jimmy's face won't be in the pictures that will be taken at future reunions. His passing and absence will leave quite a void in the group shot, but we have our memories of him to enjoy.

I invited my cousin George to contribute to this book. I figured he could provide memorable tales of being with Uncle Jimmy in the hunter's woods. Not only did I want to honor the memory of my uncle by including him, but I was also eager to hear the stories dear to my cousin's heart. I hope you enjoy these tales based on one deer hunt George went on with his dad.

The Bobcat

My first deer hunting trip with Dad was when I was nineteen years old, just prior to my going into the Air Force. We went to the big mountains of Pendleton County, where Dad had hunted for several seasons with his buddies. On the Saturday before opening day on Monday, we were biding our time by squirrel hunting. As I sat under a huge oak waiting for a bushytail to show itself, I spotted a bobcat quietly sneaking through the timber. I had a Winchester Model 37, 20-gauge, "poke stock" shotgun. I managed to move around and take a shot. The bobcat dropped in its tracks.

When I got back to camp with the cat and told the story, Dad listened with a big smile. I'll never forget how good it felt to hear him tell me how proud he was that I was able to maintain enough composure to outsmart the eyes of such an intelligent animal, as well as let it get close enough to get the job done with a short-range scattergun. As a nineteen-year-old who was about to leave home to do military duty, I needed the boost in self-confidence Dad provided that day. I carried his encouragement with me into the Air Force and the rest of my life.

The "Ten" That Got Away

I didn't have my own hunting rifle for deer season, so for my first experience at chasing West Virginia whitetails, Dad borrowed a .30-30 Winchester from his brother for me to use. I loved the feel of Uncle David's gun, and I cradled it in my arms like I would a newborn puppy as we left camp on opening day. The November weather was clear but bitterly cold. Dad and I split up to find our places to watch for deer.

For a reason I can't explain other than feeling it would be best to be elevated as I watched the woods, I picked a large pine tree to sit in. It turned out to be a bad idea! Sitting up on a pine branch like a roosted turkey in frigid winter weather isn't an ideal place for anyone to be, especially a newbie deer hunter like I was. Being high enough to be exposed to biting wind made it doubly difficult to sit still and feel secure and safe. Still, I stuck to my pine perch and waited for daylight to come.

It wasn't long after daybreak that I saw a deer walking along the ridge some three hundred yards from where I sat. I remember two distinct feelings as the deer wandered out of range. My body felt frozen on the outside, but inside I was totally fired up by the sight of a deer. What happened next surprised me. I shivered uncontrollably. I couldn't tell if it was the cold on my skin or the deer in my vision that was causing it. Experience has since taught me that either one can start a fellow shaking, but I didn't know at the time that seeing a deer could cause the onset of a bone-rattling condition veteran hunters refer to as "buck fever." All I knew was that I couldn't hold still.

The relentless shivering didn't serve me well with what happened a little while later either. As I fought not to shake, I heard something that sounded like footsteps coming from my right. I couldn't believe my eyes when I saw a nice ten-point approaching. The sight kicked my nervousness into high gear, and my body shook so much I had to concentrate to stay seated on the pine branch. My dad's words came to me amid the mental chaos. *Be calm, breathe deep, don't get too excited.* I could almost hear his voice as the words filled my head. I wondered what he'd think if he could hear my thoughts as I responded to the echo of his coaching: *Yeah, right. What a load of crock that is!* I figured I was doing well to remember to draw my next breath, much less think about staying calm, cool, and collected. I'm sure the entire pine tree was shaking by then, and the gun felt like it weighed a hundred pounds.

To this day I can't explain how I managed to move the .30-30 around to rest it on a limb, how I took aim at the big buck, and how I pulled the trigger. My first-ever shot at a deer was dead on! I whispered, "Bull's-eye!" Man, was I wrong. The deer raised his head up, and without a moment's hesitation took off like the wind. I worked the lever like the Rifleman did on the old 1960's TV show. Using the buck's white-furred butt as a target, I took a second shot, a third, and then a fourth. I seriously thought, *How can an animal keep running with that many holes in it?*

Suddenly the buck stopped and stared back in my direction. I had one more round to throw at him, but lo and behold, my gun jammed. I frantically tried to unjam the action, constantly looking back and forth from the gun to the deer, from the deer to the gun. The deer remained standing in the woods about 250 yards away. I finally removed the stuck cartridge and loaded a couple of shells into the magazine. I hurriedly rested the barrel on a nearby limb. I aimed and fired one more shot. The leaves flew up under the buck's belly. With that, he ran over the ridge and out of sight.

I immediately came down from my perch. Within a minute or two, I found drops of blood in the leaves. It wasn't much, but I followed what little I could find in the thick laurel. As I tried to guess where the next evidence of my wounded deer would be, a shot rang out just down the hill from me. It didn't require a lot of deer-hunting experience to know what had happened. Though I didn't want to face the reality, I was sure the buck had escaped me and gotten into the sights of another hunter's gun. As it turned out, I was sadly right.

I stood there on the mountainside for a while, hoping against hope that the ten-point might have dodged the other bullet and decided to come back up the hill. But it didn't happen. I faced the music and headed back to camp. Dad was there already. When he saw me, he could see right away how disappointed I was. He told me he'd heard the shooting, and he just knew I'd killed my first deer. Like a good friend, he listened as I told the details of what had happened. When he learned that the big buck had likely yielded bragging rights for another hunter, he offered some reality by schooling me on one of the most important but unwritten laws of the deer woods.

"George, whoever brings the deer down gets to put the tag on it. It's just the way it is. It might not feel fair, but keep in mind that someday you might be on the receiving end of the deal. If so, you'll have more compassion on the guy who sent the deer to you, because today you sent a deer to another hunter."

Learning that law didn't lessen the disappointment I was feeling, but what did help tremendously was simply talking to Dad about it. I've heard it said that "with a true friend, joys are doubled and sorrows are halved." That day I learned how accurate that statement is. Telling Dad how hard it was to have been so close to getting a trophy but losing it made the painful weight of loss feel much lighter.

While I returned to the woods and hunted that evening, Dad went over to another camp to visit a couple of old buddies he'd hunted with through the years. He told them what had happened and described the location where I'd taken the shots. His friends informed him that a ten-point was hanging in the next camp down. His buddies reported that the fellow who'd killed the massive animal heard a noise in the brush and shot into it. (That riled Dad pretty good since it was such a foolish and unsafe thing to do.) They'd heard the guy's deer already had a few holes in it when it was taken down.

When Dad gave me that news later that evening, he was patient as he heard me rant about the outcome of the day. Then he calmly talked me off the ledge of depression and back into a willingness to get up the next day to try again. He was always good at doing that kind of thing for me.

The Blessed Bullet

On the same hunting trip where I got the bobcat and lost the ten-point, I learned an even greater lesson. As if enough hadn't already happened to talk about for the rest of our years together, later that evening in the camper Dad had an opportunity to teach me something that had life-saving potential. After watching me clean the exterior of Uncle Dave's .30-30, he offered me some advice.

"George, one of the most dangerous things a man can ever do is clean a gun. You just never know what might be in it."

As he spoke, I worked the lever and pulled the trigger to prove that I was cleaning an empty gun. Thankfully the gun was pointing toward an uninhabited area. Dad flinched. After making sure I understood how mindless it was to drop the hammer of a weapon while inside and without checking the chamber, he talked to me about how incredibly important it is to make safety the top priority of hunting. I apologized for putting us at risk and worked the lever again to do some cleaning inside the chamber. When I did, much to my surprise and Dad's, out popped an unexpended cartridge.

I immediately realized what I'd done. I'd failed to remember the two extra rounds I'd loaded that morning after shooting at the buck. I had used only one of the two, and the lone bullet was still in the gun when I'd reloaded and went back to hunt that evening. When I got back to the camper, I thought I'd ejected all the shells before going inside, but I hadn't. It could have been a deadly oversight.

When the cartridge came tumbling out, Dad instantly sat up straight in his chair, his back stiff and his eyes wide. I sat motionless as the shell bounced on the linoleum floor. My heart beat like the thumping of a kick drum. Finally Dad leaned over and picked up the bullet. As he turned it in his fingers and looked at it closely, he turned a strange shade of pale. Without saying a word, he turned it around and showed me the bottom of the cartridge. What I saw made my blood run cold. The primer had a dent from the firing pin when I'd pulled the trigger a few minutes before. Thankfully the shell hadn't fired.

We both knew one of us could have died that evening or, at the least, both of us could have lost our hearing. We had no one to thank but God in heaven for protecting us from such a disaster. Dad kept the shell for two reasons. He used it as a very effective way of illustrating to his grandkids just how dangerous using and cleaning a gun can be, and he kept it as evidence that sometimes supernatural intervention is required to shelter us from harm.

Success at Last

We hunted Tuesday but didn't see anything. Wednesday started the same as Monday. I figured since the pine tree had yielded some action, I would visit it again. This time, however, I had a different gun. I figured if a .30-30 couldn't close the deal, a 12-gauge shotgun with a heavy "punkin' ball" would do it. Dad had suggested his old, dependable, slick-barrel gun. He said that if I used it at a close enough distance, it would provide all the knockdown power needed. About ten o'clock that morning, I put his claim to the test.

One of our friends shot at a six-point higher up on the ridge, and after the report of his gun, all I could hear was crashing as something came down the ridge through the timber toward me. Suddenly a deer jumped over what appeared to be a ten-foot-high laurel and headed straight toward me. It passed close enough I could almost see the whiskers on its nose. From my pine limb location, all I had time to do was swing the gun like a pistol from one side of the branch I was sitting on to the other. I finally took desperate aim and pulled the trigger. I found out that a 12-gauge takes meat on both ends of the gun because my shoulder nearly broke with the heavy recoil of the stock. But that wasn't half the damage the punkin' ball did to the deer. The bullet sent the buck down to his knees. I pumped another shell in and braced myself for the evil that my shoulder was about to endure and pulled the trigger again. The second shot found the deer's neck, and the deed was done.

I climbed down out of the pine tree faster than lightning and ran over to the lifeless prize. Without concern for anyone else hunting on the mountain, I let out a victory whoop that probably still echoes there today. Dad was near enough to hear my yelling and hollered back to let me know that he knew what had happened. He told me later how big he smiled when the sound of my celebration reached his ears. He mentioned what a chuckle he got out of assuming the rest of West Virginia had heard it as well.

More than once through the years, I reminded Dad that I took more off the mountain that week than just my first deer. From feeling the strength in his affirmation after I took the wily bobcat to learning to embrace the unwritten "law of hunting" after the big ten-pointer got away, from seeing the evidence of God's protection in the dented primer of the .30-30 shell to achieving success in the field, our game bag was full of tales to pass on to family, especially grandkids and great-grandkids, and friends.

Needless to say, I miss Dad more than words can tell, but never more than when the opening day of hunting season comes in West Virginia. The old camper just doesn't feel the same without him in it with us.

The Hunt Is Over

Daddy's old truck, smell of coffee in his cup
And how the highway seemed so empty at four a.m.
These are things I remember as we headed to the timber
We were off to chase the whitetails again

Cold November stand, golden sunrise on the land
And how the big ones could appear just like a ghost
The sun going down, that's when I'd hear the sound
Of Daddy's words he knew I dreaded most...

It's time to go, the hunt is over
Throw that old Winchester gun across your shoulder
I know it's been good, son, to be here in these woods
But it's time to go on home
The hunt is over

When I got my first deer I thought I saw a tear
Running down that smile on Daddy's face
He said, "You might pull the trigger someday on something bigger
But, son, this is one you can't replace"

He lived for the seasons, and I lived for the reasons
He would take me back up to those hills again
Just to be up there together, thought these times would last forever
But today the good Lord said to him...

"It's time to go, the hunt is over
Throw that old Winchester gun across your shoulder
I know it's been good, son, to be here in these woods
But it's time to come on home
The hunt is over"[14]

27

A Big Ol' "Atta Dad!"

Most of us who are sons will agree there's hardly anything as sweet sounding as an "atta boy" from the lips of our fathers. Whether it comes after a base hit at the Little League diamond, or a job well done on the mower, or an improved grade in math class, it's always nice to hear a father's pride put into words. But have we ever thought about how our dads would feel if we turned the picture around and gave them a good, healthy dose of "son" pride? The following story is based on a dad named Phil and his nineteen-year-old son, Jamey.

Jamey's walkie-talkie buzzed in his pocket, and as he dug to retrieve it, he checked the field carefully to make sure the buck he was hoping to see hadn't stepped into the open. He pushed the talk button and responded to the call. "Dad, what's going on where you are? See something?"

Jamey had the volume turned down low so the noise wouldn't spook anything in the area. He quickly put the radio close to his ear after he spoke. He smiled as his dad's voice delivered some great news.

"I just arrowed a monster over here, son. He's at least a twelve, maybe bigger. I didn't take the time to count. He came in fast, and I only had a few seconds to get to full draw and pull the release trigger. All I know is he's the best deer I've ever shot with a bow. I'm shaking all over. And the best news is that he's down within sight of my stand."

Jamey heard the thrill in his father's voice and pushed the talk button to congratulate him. "Way to go, Pops! You get a big, ol' 'atta Dad' today! While you recover, I'll call Mom on the cell and tell her that her Mr. Phil just added a taxidermy job to his Christmas list."

Phil smiled at his son's response to the news about the buck. "Thanks, Jamey. I'm gonna wait about twenty minutes and then dismount. I'll start the cleaning process while you keep hunting. I'll call you when I'm done, and you can come help me drag this brute to the truck. It'll probably be about an hour from now."

"Are you kidding, Dad? I'm already packing up and just about ready to head to the ground to come to you. I can't wait an hour to see the prize you're taking home today! I'll see you in a few."

As Jamey topped the hill and saw his dad leaning over the huge body of a buck, his eyes widened. When he got to his dad, he circled him and the deer and slapped his hip in amazement. "Whoa, Pops! That thing is huge. One, two…four…five…ten…fourteen…fifteen points?"

Phil grinned big. "Yep! Fifteen points for scoring. One for every year I've been hunting with a bow. How about them beans, my boy?"

Jamey threw his arm around his dad's shoulder. "Give me a Pope and Young hug, man! This is an awesome buck! I can't wait to tell my friends about this. We gotta get some pictures. This is gonna be big news in these parts, and I'm the son of the one who flung the arrow at this trophy. You da man, Pops!"

With every sentence Jamey delivered, Phil's grin grew bigger. He couldn't remember ever being so gloated over by his son. He'd given Jamey plenty of "atta boys" while he was growing up, but they'd never been returned—until now. Phil enjoyed the accolades.

"Dad, I'm proud of you for maintaining enough calm to get a shot off at this buck."

Any other time Phil would have said, "Young man, stop talking and sharpen your knife. I can use your help." But this time he didn't want to stop his boy.

"It had to take some steady nerves to even get the string back, much less remember where to put the sight pin. I'm not sure I could have done it. I'm impressed, Pops! I'm totally impressed."

I believe that deep inside those of us who have children is an unspoken hope that we will hear something similar to what Jamey told his dad that day. No doubt a father like Phil would carry his son's words in his heart like a priceless pearl and wouldn't take a farm in Montana for them. What dad wouldn't feel the same way?

As I listened to Phil and Jamey's story unfold, I thought of the first time I offered my dad some praise. It didn't involve a deer hunt, but I remember the look of satisfaction on his face when it happened. That moment was just as huge to him as if he'd taken a fifteen-pointer.

My dad was a self-taught preacher, and he pastored a congregation of believers in Christ in the town of Point Pleasant, West Virginia. I watched him head to the basement of our house many times to spend hours preparing sermons to deliver to the people. My mother, sister, and I would always be in the pews when he stood at the pulpit to encourage the saints as well as "call the sinners home." The meeting would end, and our family would all go back to our house, usually without saying much about the service or the sermon except a comment or two from Mom.

Dad didn't seem to require compliments from the attendees or his family to keep delivering the truth. Sunday after Sunday he was faithful to God's call to preach. And service after service we would listen and go home. It was rather routine to me, and sometimes a bit on the mundane side of the fun spectrum. That is until one Sunday when I really listened to what Dad was saying in his message to his congregation.

As he preached that morning, I was so grateful for something he'd said that I suddenly got an odd thought. *Have I ever thanked Dad? No, I've never thanked him for a single sermon he's preached in my seventeen years of being his kid.* I decided at that moment to compliment him on the well-prepared and inspiring message he was delivering that morning.

When the service was over and we got home, I got out of our car and walked beside him up the sidewalk. I put my arm around his shoulder and simply said, "Great sermon, Dad. I enjoyed every word."

I'll never forget how he looked at me in that instant. His eyes shone, and a smile lit up his face. He almost acted like a teenager when he bypassed the first two concrete steps of our front porch and jumped straight to the landing in a single bound. It was easy to see that he felt lighter on his feet from the compliment. He was even a little more talkative at the lunch table than he normally was after an emotionally draining Sunday morning service.

I was convinced that day that my simple but sincere "atta Dad" had pleased my father in an unusually special way. And it felt really good on my part to be such a source of encouragement. After all, he'd been doing the same for me all along. I determined to offer more "atta Dads" in the future, and I followed through.

A few years ago, I documented my appreciation for his life in a song lyric. This is the highest compliment I can pay to the greatest preacher I've ever known and the best sermon ever preached. I hope you enjoy it.

Daddy's Best Sermon

Daddy was good at preaching the Word
About the best I've ever heard
He could help a sinner know he was lost
Then lead him home by the way of the Cross

He could help a saint want to hold on tighter
Say the right thing to make a burden feel lighter
But of all the sermons Daddy ever preached
The one that meant the most to me…

Was the way he loved me and my sister
And how he held our mama's hand, and the tender way he kissed her
Who he was on Sunday afternoon
With just us in the living room
Yeah, Daddy's best sermon, he preached at home

I remember growing up sitting in the pews
While Daddy brought the Good News
I could almost see the angels smile
When sinners cried and walked down the aisle

People came to hear him from all around
I never knew him to let them down
'Cause he was good at breaking the bread
But my soul had a hunger that he always fed

It was the way he loved me and my sister
And how he held our mama's hand, and the tender way he kissed her
Who he was on Sunday afternoon
With just us in the living room
Daddy's best sermon, he preached at home[15]

As a son who encouraged his dad and enjoyed the benefits, I can confidently say that if you'll take the next opportunity that arises to give your dad some heartfelt praise for something he's done or does, you too will enjoy what can happen. You might get to see your dad smile in a way you've never seen before. And his steps might get a little lighter too. And someday the bread you cast on the waters of his heart could very well come back to you.

28

Dream Hunt

People fortunate to hunt with their dads might not understand how deep the longing can be in the hearts of those who haven't experienced such a blessing. Although the following story doesn't reflect my personal experience, it does reveal what many men have shared with me over the years.

With our backs against the thick trunk of a fallen red oak tree, Dad and I quietly talked as we waited for daylight to come.

"Son," he whispered, "it's gonna be a great morning. I can feel it in my bones. Something is gonna come through this area. Before they make coffee at the diner back in town, I'm thinkin' we'll have one down and cleaned and be on our way to do some braggin' with the boys over a plate of biscuits and gravy."

I loved hearing my dad talk with me in such a confident and excited way. The flood of deer-hunting adrenaline that filled his soul was pouring over into mine. I was smiling inside and out. I was exactly where I wanted to be and where I needed to be.

Within twenty minutes the sun had once again resurrected on our side of the planet. There was plenty of light to see down the ridge we were monitoring and into the deep ravine we were sitting above. Dad had used his keen understanding of whitetail behavior to pick out a travel route the local herd regularly used. There were several trails within fifty yards of where we sat that led from some nearby cornfields to one of their favorite bedding areas.

Dad was so sure we were in a "hot spot" that he reminded me to keep my gun in position so I'd be ready for a shot with the least amount of movement. I gladly followed his instructions. Several minutes ticked by without conversation. We were too busy turning our heads slowly from side to side like oscillating radar as we scanned the area for deer.

I was looking off to the left when I got a gentle nudge in my ribs from my father's elbow. He'd taught me not to snap my head around quickly when he wanted my attention because that was a type of movement easily seen by the alert eyes of deer. With a slow, deliberate motion, I turned my face toward him. Finally, in my peripheral vision, I could see his left hand resting on his leg. He was pointing to my right with his index finger.

I followed the line of sight and, sure enough, there stood a timber monster. The buck was as big as I'd ever seen in our part of the world. On first glance, I could see he sported at least ten and possibly twelve points and had gnarly drop-tines falling from his main beams.

I was sitting close enough to Dad for our camo overalls to be touching. The closeness was intentional on my part. I felt more connected to him when we were touching, and I'd noticed that all morning he'd never tried to pull away. Because we were so close, he could feel my body tense the moment I saw the deer. While maintaining a visual on the buck, he whispered some encouragement.

"Stay calm, son."

When I heard how tense his voice sounded, I knew the presence of such a massive rack had rattled him as much as it did me. But his experience with moments like we were facing helped him control his nerves, and in turn, he helped me work through the heebie-jeebies.

We waited for the huge buck to drop his head and nose the leaves for some breakfast so we could take deep breaths. Once more I felt the thrill of being next to Dad and sharing such intense and enjoyable emotions. This wasn't something

I stopped and thought about very often or for very long. Instead, it was an instantaneous, warm sensation that shot contentment through my soul. And knowing he wanted me beside him intensified the joy.

After a standoff with the cautious buck that seemed to last a full minute, the creature finally lowered his head and searched for acorns. Dad slowly motioned his index finger, lifting it up and down, telling me to raise my gun and get the deer in my sights. I had to shoot across his lap to take aim, and he carefully raised his knees for me to use as a rifle rest.

Moving his arms slower than the drip of honey on a cold day, he got his hands to his ears and covered them as I drew a bead on the deer's chest.

"Take 'im, son. It's now or never," he whispered.

The .30 caliber bounced on dad's knees after the shot, and a whiff of smoke drifted from the barrel. We watched as the buck ran about thirty yards, stopped, and then stood still for a few seconds. Dad and I whispered almost simultaneously, "Down! Go down!"

As if the mature buck heard our pleading, he weaved back and forth. Dad glanced over at me, showing an expression of sympathy for the mortally wounded animal. The look on his face revealed that somewhere in his hunter's heart was a soft spot. He didn't seem at all embarrassed by the feeling, and I didn't see it as a weakness. Instead, I saw his pained expression as a sign of the kind of strength I wanted to have and be comfortable enough with to show.

As the life drained from the buck's body, he stumbled to the left, and then his legs went out from under him. By then we were both out of our seated positions and on our knees. It was hard to believe that such a massive deer was not just down, but it was ours to claim, to take pictures of for posterity, and to retrieve for the freezer.

Dad stood up and reminded me to put the gun safety on. Then he reached for my hand and pulled me up. He gently took my rifle and leaned it against the fallen oak. He turned to me and wrapped his big arms around me. The bear hug we were in lasted at least ten seconds—a long time for two guys. But I didn't mind at all. We were releasing the effects of the unbridled excitement we'd felt as a team. When Dad pulled back and looked at me, I noticed tears forming in his eyes.

"You are the man, son! You are the man. Perfect morning, perfect weather, perfect spot, perfect buck, and—most important—perfect shot."

I would have to create a new language to adequately describe how happy my dad made me feel in that moment. He kept his hands on my shoulders as he continued bathing me in words of affirmation and congratulations. As he talked, I could feel something watery forming in my eyes and running down my cheeks. I wanted to fight the flow, but I figured if Dad was man enough to let it happen, I could too.

I started to say something back to Dad, but for some reason nothing would come out. I couldn't think of what to say, so I just stood there looking at him, drops of salty water running down my face...

And that's when I woke up.

I'm not sure what time it was, but the blackness through my bedroom windows told me it was still nighttime. I sat up, swung my legs over the edge of the bed, and rubbed my eyes. They were damp. The darkness hid the quivering of my chin as I faced the reality that the hunting trip with my dad I'd always dreamed of was just that—a dream.

The pool of tears in my eyes got deeper the more I thought about the fact that going hunting with him was a wish that would never be filled. He'd left our family when I was five years old. The few memories I had of him only whetted my appetite to see him, hear him, touch him, and be with him again. I sat there in the unlit stillness and once more fought the anger over his longtime absence. The same questions I'd asked through the years came back to torture me. *Why would he leave us? What did I do wrong to drive him away? Did he ever love me? Why doesn't he connect with me?* And, like before, the answers never came.

I lay back down and rested my head on my pillow. I stared into the night and prayed for my dad, wherever he was. I asked God for the grace to be forgiving toward him. Then my thoughts went to the little boy who slept right above me in an upstairs bedroom. I softly whispered a promise: "Son, with God's help, I'll do my best to make sure your dream hunt comes true!"

29

"He Walked Here!"

In all honesty, as one who passionately loves the pursuit of the whitetail deer, I can't say that I am a "rack hunter." Instead, I consider my primary purpose in the enjoyable challenge of deer hunting to be the harvest of a great source of meat. One average-size doe here in Tennessee can yield more than forty pounds of boned, tasty venison. That proportion cannot be found in a single carcass of a smaller species, such as squirrel or turkey, even though the animal or bird may be preferred for the table. I venture to say that it would take ten to fifteen turkeys to equal one deer in terms of volume of meat. I appreciate the economy of the kill when it comes to comparisons between whitetail and the rest of the legally hunted, edible animals.

Furthermore, in my experience, the overall taste of doe meat is generally better. I'll admit that early archery season males can be less "gamey," but after an old buck has been whipped by the rut and is drenched with the hormones that drive him crazy, it requires far too much spice to cover the wild taste. If the goal is to see the smiles on the faces of family and friends as they sit with their feet under my supper table and take in the animal I worked hard at harvesting, then bringing home an antlered deer can be risky. Besides, no matter how thin you slice them, no matter how long you boil them, antlers never soften up. A fellow can break a tooth gnawing on a tine.

If my position on this issue were a sermon, it would be entitled, "The Virtue of

Going Antlerless." It is a message I have preached for years. When I see the covers of hunting magazines that exclusively feature the trophy bucks and their rocking-chair-sized antlers, it makes me wonder if the overemphasis on the big, bruiser bucks only furthers the notion that does are not worthy of hunters' time and skills. Perpetuating this attitude in the media has the dangerous potential of sending the wrong message. Consequently, many immature hunters feel less than accepted and successful if they fail to connect with an antlered deer. The harmful result can be that far too many spikes that would have grown to be well-antlered adults are killed merely for the sake of saying, "I got a buck!" Where is the wisdom in that?

These are the feelings I strongly held on to. Then…one day it happened! Something took place in a recent season that fiercely tampered with my convictions. I confess that I was sorely tempted to retire from the pulpit where I have sermonized about the dangerous doctrine of "rack worship." What happened? I saw *him*!

I took my son, Nathan, who was home from college, to a stand I had prepared along the edge of a massive, cut soybean field. He faced south, and I was just across a small creek facing north watching a smaller meadow. I was not toting a weapon since my goal was to help Nathan fill a tag. The wind was blowing across us, and the sun was peeking over the horizon.

Suddenly, at about a hundred yards to my right, in the openness of the field I was monitoring, I saw a deer approaching that I can only describe as…uh… well…diabolical.

If my belief that hunting primarily for meat was a virtue, then I must confess I sinned—big time! His body seemed twice the size of any of the three "slickheads" I had already sent to the processor. And atop his head was the most beautiful, perfect set of antlers I had seen in a long, long time. They must have boasted at least ten points. His gait was confident and majestic.

I whistled softly to Nathan to sneak across the creek and join me. The buck, without knowing we were nearby, turned ninety degrees and headed toward the timber on the far side of the field. Nathan arrived at my side just in time to scope the heavy deer and get a fleeting glimpse of its head gear. All the while I had him in my binoculars, and I must admit that my heart had nearly stopped.

The massive and obviously dominant buck disappeared into the high grass and brushy edge of the woods. The two of us, still shaking, sat motionless, hoping he would reappear further down the field. After about thirty minutes of wishful waiting, we resigned ourselves to the likelihood that he was gone for good.

I had hunted that farm for several years and had not seen the size of deer I had suddenly encountered. I'm not sure where he came from, but his arrival spelled trouble for me. For the rest of the season, I became a…forgive me…rack hunter. My tightly wound philosophy about being mostly a food hunter came completely unraveled by the sight of the stately creature. My nights were filled with dreams about him. The days when I couldn't sit somewhere on that farm and watch for him were hard to endure. I longed to see him again. I was pitiful!

Perhaps the meeting with such a wondrously gorgeous animal had an alternate purpose—besides squelching my excessive pride about being satisfied with doe hunting. For one thing, I began to acquire a new appreciation for those who have an unbridled passion for taking bucks with record-book potential. Because of my "rendezvous with greatness," I was able to pull off the road of resentment and embrace their quest.

Second, I had a good start toward understanding hunters who key in on one huge deer. These folks have some serious challenges to contend with. They are the ones who, for example, sit in church pews on Sunday mornings wishing they could be listening to the sermon by cell phone as they monitored a scrape on some distant ridge. As the pastor pours his heart out with the text from a sermon he labored over for days, the hunter of a specific and massive buck is sitting there in a trance. He may look like he's intently listening to his preacher, but in his mind he's thinking, *If I set up on the north side of that thicket and let the wind work for me, I'll have a better chance when he comes in to bed down. Then again, he's got to be hungry now that the rut is winding down. If I set up in the evening along that winter wheat field, maybe I'll see him as he's coming out to graze.* Thoughts about a big buck consume him. The obsessed hunter suddenly returns to reality when his wife elbows him sharply in the ribs and announces, "Hey! They asked you to pray the benediction! Wake up, Bubba!"

I am now able to sympathize with this man all because of one brief sighting of the animal he dreams about. If for no other reason than that, it was a good season even though it ended without another glimpse of "my" buck. I can only hope he survived the eyes, arrows, and bullets of other hunters. Maybe next year!

Besides seeing the buck that occupied my attention so intensely, the most memorable part of trying to track him again was discovering the sign he left behind. His "scrapes" were broad, and the licking branches were high. His rubs destroyed some young cedar trees that were well beyond sapling stage. The does in the area seemed extra skittish, and the young males were a bit more nervous.

But of all the signs that revealed the big buck's presence, his hoofprints provided the most evidence of his enormous stature. I dare say one hoof would cover a good portion of this page. It was deep and wide. I guessed his weight to be 200 to 230 pounds. The sight of his tracks alone did more to lead this meat hunter astray than any of the other markings that bore witness to his existence. I memorized them. I studied them. And I wanted him!

One day as I walked beside a line he had taken from one side of a plowed field to the other, probably just the night before, a thought came to my mind: *He walked here!* The mystique of being on the very ground that the great beast had occupied just hours before was overwhelming. I stopped and dropped to my knees in the dirt. I spread my index and middle fingers apart about two and a half inches and slipped them down into the depression left by the buck and said again, "He walked here!" I was mesmerized by the connection I felt to that deer.

As I remained in a kneeling position and took in the size of the tracks, I suddenly had one of those thoughts that cross not just the mind but also the heart. *Just as these prints testify to the presence of that majestic buck on the earth, there are signs on this planet that provide proof that God has been among us—and still is.* I whispered the revelation audibly but softly: *"He* walked here!"

I began to think of the deep and impressive tracks He had left to reveal His presence. They can be found in the lives of men and women...even hunters. My heart, which once had been filled with darkness and confusion, was now flooded with the light of His great love and the clear understanding that He had purchased my salvation through the work of His Son, Jesus. That sign of Him having been among us left a deep, permanent impression in my spirit. And I thought of the children God had given to Annie and me. I was there in the delivery room when they were born. To witness the unbelievable miracle of birthing a human life left an indelible mark on my heart and is one that definitely testifies that *He* walked here!

As I scanned the field of my heart, I saw other signs of His having passed by. There in the soil of my flesh was a small scar located on the index finger of my right hand. It was left there by an eight-inch meat cleaver when I was just a child. My Grandpa Chapman was cutting a watermelon with his sharp butchering tool, and after he sliced one piece, I reached for it. At that very same moment he came down with the heavy cleaver to cut the second slice, and it intercepted my hand at the top of the melon, burying it into the lower portion of the rind. When I pulled my hand back. I thought I would find a bloody stub. Fortunately, the soft melon had cushioned the blow enough to result only in a severe cut across the outside of my finger. God knew that my future would include playing the guitar and that I would need all my digits. The scar is, in my opinion, a track left there by a loving and merciful God.

God walked here! The phrase echoed in my head as I stood and looked toward the timber. I peered at the edge of the field for a moment and then lifted my eyes toward the sky. The words floated freely toward heaven: "Thank You, Father, for reminding me through the big buck that roams in this territory and whose tracks I stand beside that because of the signs You have left in my life, I can assuredly say to others, 'God walked here!'"

Today I am a convert. Though I still firmly believe that a doe is a wonderful trophy, I can also say that I am now a rack hunter...but for more reasons than just the antlers!

30

"Are You Sure, Dad?"

The game was squirrel. The players: Nathan and me, a father and a son. The stakes were high. If the critter won, we would go home empty-handed. If we won, supper was served. The bushytail in the distance was the only one we had seen that evening, and the sun was headed to its hiding place behind the trees.

Nathan was a young outdoorsman, about eleven years old at the time. He was fresh out of the hunter's safety course and a novice at handling a gun. But he had shown great aptitude in learning the skills necessary to be a responsible participant in the hunter's woods. In fact, I was so impressed with how quickly he understood the rules of the game that I surprised him with a challenge as we sat against the big oak and watched the solitary squirrel on a limb about fifty yards away.

"Nathan," I whispered, "see if you can sneak over close enough to get a shot at that squirrel." His youthful eyes widened when he heard my offer. He knew very well that the stealth required to get within range of the skittish critter was reserved for more mature woodsmen. With a look that seemed to question my good judgment, he asked, "Are you sure, Dad? If we're gonna take something home this evening, don't you think you ought to go after him?"

I could hear two feelings in his voice. The first was the hopefulness that I would not withdraw the challenge. His excited demeanor as he answered told me he cherished the prospect of bagging a squirrel on his own. How well I remember the first time I sat alone in the woods with a friend's 20-gauge/.22 caliber, over-under style single shot. I was an anxious thirteen-year-old. I can still feel the tight grip I had on the wooden stock of the gun as I waited for the sighting of my first squirrel. The thought of being by myself with such a powerful instrument was intensely exciting. It was the day I took a giant step toward manhood.

Though Nathan would be only twenty or so yards from me when he got close enough to shoot, at his age he would feel like he had gone to Montana for the hunt. My heart was filled with joy that he was about to taste the responsibility of independence.

The second emotion I detected in his question was a level of doubt. The slight tremor in his voice informed me that even though he was grateful for the challenge, he wasn't totally sure he could rise to the task. It hit me that he truly did want to know if I thought he could do it. All he needed was a nod of assurance from me. I realized I was his source of confidence. He had little on his own.

I understood his hesitance to attempt something so monumental. After all, I was the fellow who, one Sunday night in my early teens, was on my way to the stage with my mom, my dad, and sister at a church our family was visiting.

We were invited to sing, and my mother always played the Gibson guitar used to accompany the four of us...until that night. She had taught me some chords and coached me as I played for the family, but only in the privacy of our home. However, when we got up out of our seats and started down the side aisle to make our way to the front of the sanctuary, she suddenly turned around, handed me the guitar, and whispered, "Here. You play it tonight."

My reaction that night was exactly the same Nathan gave when I charged him with the task of "bringing home the bacon." I said to my mother, "Are you sure, Mom?"

I remember the mixture of fear and joy that overwhelmed me. I was afraid my brain would not send the signals to my fingers that were needed to form the G, C, and D chords. I was afraid of failing and making a fool of myself. On the other hand, I was overjoyed at the thought that she deemed me an accomplished enough guitarist to play for the family in public.

We were only a few paces from the steps that would lead us up to the stage area when my mom whispered, "I know you can do it, Steve!" That was all I needed. Our little quartet gathered around the podium, I carefully strummed a G chord, Dad started singing, and we were on our way. I strummed along. It was a scene that took place more than forty-five years ago, and I haven't stopped playing since. To this day the guitar is one of the main tools of my trade.

Would my mother have presented her young son with so great a challenge if she didn't think he could do it? I seriously doubt it. It would have jeopardized the impact of the song. She believed I was capable to do the job. Did I believe Nathan was responsible and skilled enough to go after his prey using such a lethal weapon? Of course I did. Otherwise I would have never suggested he do it.

And do it he did. Though the leaves were dry and crunchy like fresh cornflakes, he slowly turned to begin his stalk. As he leaned forward out of the sitting position to get onto all fours, I said, "Son, if you get close, don't forget that when you draw a bead on that squirrel you'll probably get so excited it might be tough to hold steady. If you let yourself get too rattled, you'll miss the shot. You've gotta control yourself. You can win the battle against your nerves. You have to be in charge of them in order to hit your mark."

With that little speech, he crawled away. I watched him and also kept an eye on the squirrel sitting on a limb working on a hickory nut, silhouetted against the sky. Nathan kept his movements slow and deliberate, producing minimal sound in the noisy leaves. Within three or four minutes, he had significantly closed the gap between himself and the squirrel. My heart pounded as I watched him slip along the ground. He wisely kept his eye on the furry form above him and paused each time the squirrel stopped scraping its teeth on the hard shell of the nut.

Finally I saw him stop and slowly raise the shotgun skyward. As he lay in the prone position, he quietly pulled the hammer back and took aim. The distance of the shot, from where I sat, seemed to be about thirty yards. I wondered if the full choke pattern of the buckshot would find its target. I waited to see if Nathan would win the battle with his nerves.

Even when it's expected, a gun blast always makes me jump. When the report of the 20-gauge suddenly boomed in the big timber, I reacted with a startled jerk. I quickly recovered enough to see the gray squirrel fall sideways and plummet to the earth. Nathan looked back at me, and I gave him a firm thumbs-up signal accompanied by a smile that nearly broke my jaw. He sat up on his knees and reloaded. Then he stood up and carefully approached the downed prize. After making sure it wouldn't come to life and bury its teeth in his leg, he picked it up by the tail, turned my way, and held it high. I could see the beam on his face as he started toward me. There was a certain confidence in the way he deliberately crunched across the leaf-covered floor of the woods.

Later that evening, the gray squirrel became one with us along with some fried potatoes, sliced tomatoes, and a big glass of sweet tea. (Excuse me while I drool!) The taste of success was delicious, thanks to Annie and her culinary talents. The day may have ended, but the memory of it will live on in my heart.

Since then I have asked my son and my daughter to do other things that have stretched their comfort zones. As I have done so, I have tried to be careful not to challenge them if I felt they were not up to it. I was also mindful that they needed to start with small responsibilities before moving to greater ones. For example, when Heidi was a little girl, she was terrified by the simplest of things, such as going to the counter at a fast-food restaurant to ask for ketchup packets. For some reason, she resisted the chore until one day I asked, "Heidi, what are you afraid of? This is a prime opportunity for you to learn an important social skill. I believe you can overcome your fears and master your emotions."

That little sermon might have been a little heavy for a seven-year-old, but there was enough assurance from Dad that soon, getting ketchup packets was no problem for my daughter. As time went on, she moved to weightier concerns. One of them was singing before an audience. She eventually took charge of her fear and dread of performance, and now she now regularly sings with great confidence in front of auditoriums filled with people.

Of all I have ever set before my kids to do, I know the very hardest challenge they will face is to be in control of their moral behavior. I can only hope that the more manageable tasks, like sneaking up on bushytails or asking for ketchup packets, have provided a good foundation for their confidence. As they fight the fierce battle between good and evil, right and wrong, perhaps the simple "rehearsals" I was able to help them through will benefit them.

In the same way that I made sure they were sufficiently equipped to do a task before I asked them to, God does the same for mankind, especially in the area of inner character. A vivid example of this truth is found in His words to Adam and Eve's son Cain. This young man was not happy that his offering was ignored by God, and he grew jealous of the attention that Abel, his brother, was getting for his sacrifice. God saw that Cain's attitude was less than acceptable, so He presented him with an incredibly demanding task. Genesis 4:6-7 records God's words to Cain:

> Then the LORD said to Cain, "Why are you angry? And why has your countenance fallen? If you do well, will not your countenance be lifted up? And if you do not do well, sin is crouching at the door; and its desire is for you, but you must master it."

Question: Did God think Cain was able? Was Cain equipped to refuse jealousy? The answer is *yes!* Otherwise God would not have demanded he do it. Did Cain respond positively? Unfortunately, no. Cain allowed evil to win, and his decision led to the murder of his brother. How incredibly tragic.

For those of us who live in this age of rapidly dwindling morality, we must ask ourselves, Does God think we are equipped to rule over our flesh and all of its selfish desires, such as lust, greed, envy, malice, and jealousy? The answer is found in 1 Corinthians 10:13: "No temptation has overtaken you but such as is common to man; and God is faithful, who will not allow you to be tempted beyond what you are able, but with the temptation will provide the way of escape also, so that you will be able to endure it."

Yes, we are able! If we weren't, we wouldn't be asked to be people of high standards. While maintaining self-control is an enormous challenge, we can do it. What do we need to help us rise to the task? What on earth can help us when we look heavenward and desperately ask, "Are you sure, God?" We need the same thing Nathan needed when he was deciding whether to go after that squirrel. We need what Heidi needed as she looked toward that busy counter at the burger shop. And we require the certitude I longed for as my mother handed me the guitar those many years ago. We need that divine nod of assurance our Father in heaven offers that tells us we can indeed face the battle for personal virtue…and win. We can do so with confidence because He thinks we are capable. And remember, to see that sacred, heavenly nod, we can look at God's words to Cain: "Rule over it." The truth is clearly implied: *God thinks we're able!*

31

It Takes One to Hunt One!

There is something about being called a turkey that falls somewhere between a humorous dig and a derogatory comment. For whatever reason, it never really offends. It just "hangs out there" and meets a need. The one who says it feels better, and the one who hears it is not left feeling devastated.

I'm not sure when or how it happened that the turkey became a laughingstock. To my knowledge, it never did anything harmful to anyone. In fact, there was a day when it was treated with much more respect. When commenting on the bald eagle's appearance on the Great Seal, Benjamin Franklin famously called the turkey "a much more respectable bird." Why he preferred it or why it never received that place of honor would be interesting to know. I'm sure one could dive into the archives and find out, but why do that when it's a lot more fun to guess? (I know...I just lost the good graces of the history teachers, but hey, men rarely stop and ask for directions!)

Starting with the reasons for rejection, I can think of only two possibilities. One, it's just not the prettiest bird on the planet. With a face like that on our dollar bills and presidential emblems, it would be tough to look at them for very long and find patriotism welling up inside. Instead, we'd just sort of gag. The poor thing was not graced with handsomeness. The male, especially, got a serious whack in the kisser with the ugly stick. And to the die-hard lovers of the wild turkey, I'm sorry but that thing—that wattle—hanging off an old gobbler's face is really gross. I think they make medicine for that! I will admit though, from the neck down, it's a beautiful creature, which could be said of a lot of humans. (Don't look at me like that!)

Second, the flight of a wild turkey does not match that of the final choice, the bald eagle. There's something about the high-flying ability of the eagle that stirs in us a desire to rise above things such as ignorance and poverty. It moves us deep in our hearts. On the other hand, the soaring of a turkey is basically limited to getting in and out of bed, which could also be said of some people I know.

On occasion, broad-breasted turkeys must take to the air to escape danger, but they don't sail very far. Though pretty in flight as they leave the roost at daylight and whoosh overhead on their way to their kitchen table, they just can't get to the heights that an eagle can. Of course, if an eagle was packing enough food on its breast to feed a family of five, it too would have a hard time flapping its way into the stratosphere. The wings are there, the wind is waiting, but the "pot breast" of a turkey gets in the way. (This human resemblance to the wild turkey is getting a little too close to home!)

For whatever reason, you won't find the heavy, homely, and horrifically ugly face of a turkey on your silver dollar. Nor will it ever grace the banners that wave over this nation. The two birds in question have a lot to offer, but the bottom line is that *flying* was chosen over *food*. And that's fine with me.

Regarding the possible reasons that Benjamin Franklin presented the turkey as a good representative of America's positive traits, there are a few that seem logical. Could it be that the turkey was initially considered because of the food source it was to the people who lived here and for those who eventually settled on this continent? In my experience as a turkey hunter, there is a consistency about the breast meat that is both tender and tasty. As for the rest of the bird, I have given up on trying to nibble my way through the drumstick simply because the tendons and ligaments are akin to eating rubber bands and microphone wires. Forgive me, but I normally don't include that portion of the harvest in the cooking skillet. The domesticated, commercialized turkey does not seem to have this problem, probably because they don't get the exercise wild turkeys get in the forest.

Besides the food source, perhaps the wild turkey was looked at as our favorite fowl because it was plentiful. Their numbers, by ratio to the population, were far greater than today. Yet there seems to be plenty around in many regions for the modern hunter to pursue.

There were practical uses for certain parts of the bird. For example, those who fashioned their own arrows were more likely to use the feather of a turkey for fletching than any other type available. The length and strength of its quill and the width of the plume added to the arrow's durability and accuracy of flight. Furthermore, arrow making was more than the construction of a practical tool for hunting and self-defense. It was a work of art. Because of that, turkey feathers were often used as vanes on the shaft since they held ample color and eye-catching marks. This was true then and remains so today.

Of all the reasons the wild turkey should have gotten the votes needed to occupy the office of top bird, I can't help but wonder if Mr. Franklin's main reason for putting the *Meleagris gallopavo* on the ballot was rooted in his love for hunting it. I have a feeling that after many frustrating attempts to harvest a turkey that ended in failure, he had developed a level of respect for the bird that was similar to the amount of esteem others gave him as a leading citizen of the nation. It seems reasonable to believe that he had some exciting encounters with the incredibly effective eyesight of a turkey. And it's conceivable that he had discovered how nearly impossible it is to see a bird that stays on the ground through the daytime, feeding beneath the underbrush well below eye level of the average-sized man. As far as I'm concerned, if Franklin's feelings about the turkey were grounded in his sincere regard for its elusiveness, that alone is good enough for me. I say it's not too late to call for another vote!

I admit there was a time when I wasn't as excited about hunting turkey as I was about hunting deer. The reason was simple…I had never tried to bag a turkey. Then one day, my friends Don Scurlock and Eddy Richey talked me into going along for a hunt during spring season in Tennessee. They warned me that I would never be the same after the attempt and offered me a chance to back out. I had noticed that when springtime arrived, they were a little different from the rest of earth's inhabitants, and I'd often wondered why. But it was not until I yielded to their invitation that I discovered what made them look so wild-eyed and seem so skittish, especially during the months of April and May.

That first hunt was unforgettable. Don and Eddy instructed me that two things were extremely important. One, camo cover for every part of the body was absolutely necessary. Don even covered his eyes. And following his example, I shrouded my pump shotgun with camo tape. Without the proper concealment, there was no way to blend in with the surroundings and fool a turkey's highly sensitive peepers.

Second, they told me that when the bird is coming in, the slightest movement would likely spook it and send it scampering. The blink of an eye or a trigger finger sliding around to push the shotgun safety button could ruin the opportunity. I was cautioned that my shooting position had to be established before a gobbler fixed on a hen call and decided to approach. Otherwise I would blow it.

There was enough exciting emotion in just the instructions Don and Eddy gave to cause my heart some considerable palpitations. I wasn't sure if the real thing would be survivable. Nevertheless, I ventured on with them to the fields that morning on my first turkey hunt. As we walked on the dirt road well before daylight, we kept our talking to a whisper. Don had "put the birds to bed," meaning he watched them from a distance the evening before and knew where they had flown to roost. Knowing they were overhead in the trees on a bluff nearby, we had to take care not to disturb their slumber.

In the darkness, Eddy put two decoys out in the field, and then the three of us took our places along the tree line. Just after first light, Don began using a gift he possesses that is nothing less than remarkable. He had studied and practiced the wild turkey's language so well that he, with his man-made devices, could speak to them as if he were one of their own. (Imagine what Joy, his wife, would think about that compliment. And imagine what she's had to endure!) With a light, dainty clucking sound, Don broke the morning silence.

His "waking up" call initially got no response. But he knew what he was doing. He waited a minute or two and with the flat, waterproof mouth call made of tape and latex rubber, he spoke again. Behind us, a bird responded. I froze. Eddy was motionless. Don slowly looked over at me, and though I couldn't see his face behind the mesh camo mask, I could tell he was smiling. It was the way he held his head that told me his heart was racing faster than the pistons in a screaming Indy car.

Suddenly, I heard my very first sound of the swish of turkey wings in flight as a bird sailed off the bluff and glided down into the field. The grace of its soaring was impressive. So was its size. I didn't realize how tall a wild turkey stood. I wouldn't have noticed had I not been crouched low against a big oak. From where I was sitting, the eyes of the hen that had landed in the meadow appeared to be looking down at me. It was an awesome sight.

I was already in the shooting posture and had been there since we sat down. I took the instruction about minimizing my movement very seriously and was trying to be a good student. The problem that arose was excruciating, however. After about twenty minutes in one position, my body started to protest. My derriere had lost its feeling, and the numbness was creeping up my back and was on its way to my brain. But to move would have spelled disaster. Although my arms wanted desperately to shake, I forced myself to hold steady and hoped relief would come quickly.

Finally a bearded bird descended into the field. The male is the only legal game allowed during the spring season, and the sight of one was welcomed. As he landed near the hens, they briefly scattered. It was as if they knew he came around only when he wanted "something." (Good grief! This man-turkey comparison thing is starting to hurt.) He had, indeed, shown up for the "ladies." Except for this special time in a gobbler's life, when "love" is all they are after, they usually stay away from the females and travel in bachelor groups.

Finding himself around several attractive hens, the male began his ritualistic strutting. With his tail at full fan, his head changed colors from pale gray to a brilliant red, along with some white and a hue of blue. It was a sight to behold. The problem for the three of us who were waiting for the chance to send him to turkey heaven was that he was too far away. Don was careful not to talk too much with his calls for fear of saying the wrong thing and causing the gobbler to run off. All we could do was sit by and hope he meandered over within range.

Suddenly things started falling into place. They were working their way around the field to where we sat. By then, the mixture of painful numbness and explosive excitement had started doing weird things to my entire body. I was an emotional and physical mess. Knowing I couldn't move, yet wanting to shake like I had grabbed hold of a live electric wire, I began to wish I had worn some plastic underpants. I was loving this new experience. In the stream of pure adrenaline that was rushing through my brain, I saw a reflection of the future. In it I could see all the seasons of springtimes yet to come, and I knew where I wanted to be when they arrived (if I was still around). I wanted to be at the edges of fields, tucked away in my camouflage among the leaves and branches, doing what I was doing at that very instant. Before I had ever pulled the trigger on one of these birds, I had become a bona fide, no-holds-barred turkey hunter. I had been "spurred."

As it turned out, none of us were able to score that morning. When the gobbler got within about fifty yards, he saw something he didn't like and scampered off to another part of the farm in search of companionship. The three of us gathered our decoys, seat pads, and wounded egos and tried another spot.

Before ten o'clock came, I had managed to completely embarrass myself in front of one of the greatest turkey hunters alive. Don called in a huge, mature gobbler in another field, but I was much too anxious with my shot and missed the bird entirely. My friend was gracious and kept his ribbing to a minimum... at least until Eddy showed up. I have not been allowed to forget that blunder—and rightly so. I displayed the worst case of "feather fever" anyone has ever had. The bird should have been mine. It really is hard to draw a good bead when intense emotion makes my head spin around wildly on my neck! I hate it when it does that.

As an avid deer hunter, there's one thing I especially appreciate about turkey season. When the fall and early winter hunting seasons come to an end, the law demands that we deer hunters drop our weapons and surrender to things like our jobs and families. We start to experience withdrawals around late February. The index fingers of gun hunters, usually the one on the dominant hand, start to twitch, and one eye closes involuntarily. (Bowhunters' twitches are far more profound and more embarrassing in public.) Then, when we face the disheartening reality that our legal return to the hunter's woods is several months away, we enter a certain type of depression. Talking intelligently becomes a chore unless, of course, someone asks about the deer we might have taken during the past season. We can be a pitiful sight in mid to late winter.

However, at about the time our loved ones are making arrangements to check us in at the local asylum for the depressed and troubled, something strangely wonderful happens. I warn you that it could occur at any given moment. For example, it might happen one day as you sit in your convalescent chair staring dejectedly at the linoleum. A caregiver walks into the room and asks, "Would you like a *turkey* sandwich for lunch?"

Like an alarm clock, the word "turkey" rings a bell. Suddenly you lift your face and look toward the window. A bright light begins to shine on you, illuminating the entire room with an indescribable glow. Unexplainably, you stand up, raise your arms, and scream loudly, "Spring turkey season is only six weeks away!" Your family members get the call that you have recovered. You are back among those who embrace life as a wonderful thing. The doldrums are gone, spirits are renewed, and the smile returns to your face! That, my friend, is why turkey season is made for the deer hunter.

Don Scurlock would reverse my theory about the order of hunting seasons and the rehabilitative benefits they offer. He would say that deer season is therapy for the serious turkey hunter. And I fully understand his position now that I have had the privilege of joining him and Eddy in the gobbler game. In either case, we all profit emotionally by both seasons.

Some final observations about the wily old gobbler. I have to admit I have a lot in common with him. For one thing, that old bird might be ugly, but he's smart. (Did I just insult myself?) And there's another thing that impresses me about him. It's in his nature to run at the very first sign of danger, and I have never seen one ignore that attitude. A mature male turkey is just that because he doesn't stay around for one extra second if he thinks his life or safety is in jeopardy. Like a wise old buck, he's out of there. I've arrowed a lot of deer because they stood there a moment too long after detecting trouble. I got the best of their curiosity. Not so for a woods-wise gobbler. He's gone at the first hint of trouble.

In the same way, to spiritually survive, I must understand that when an enemy (such as lust, for example) reveals itself in my heart, if I don't flee immediately, I get in real trouble. To hang around is a mistake. For instance, if I'm in a hotel room alone and far from home, I might be flipping through the TV channels. Suddenly I come upon a station that features smut. To momentarily pause and entertain a thought such as *I can handle this for a second or two* is a grave mistake. I know if I don't immediately turn the thing off or go to another channel, I run the risk of getting shot right in the eyes with a deadly round of eroticism. However, the smart move is to "flee [dart away like a turkey] from youthful lusts" (2 Timothy 2:22).

I deeply admire the gobbler's attitude of willingness to forego the next grub worm, a juicy bug, or even a fleeting, extra glance at the source of danger. He knows it's the key to his survival. I want to be like him. May I never forget that quickly running from the enemy of fleshly, unholy pleasure is the first step in avoiding the "flaming arrows of the evil one" (Ephesians 6:16).

With that worthy goal in mind, I will consider it a great compliment the next time spring season arrives in Tennessee and my sweet wife, Annie, looks at me in my boyish get-up of head-to-toe camo and facetiously says, as she often does, "Turkey—it takes one to hunt one!"

32

Number One Arrow

Whenever the month of July rolls around, a switch is flipped on somewhere in my being. It opens the circuit to a whole array of signals that bring to life the mechanisms inside me designed to pursue the elusive whitetail deer. As if on a timer, at 12:01 a.m. on the first day of the middle month of summer, my mind begins to search through my memory banks for the whereabouts of the items I will need to use during the coming archery season.

My quest leads me to the shed out back where there are large, clear plastic bags that contain the camo I will need to wash with unscented soap, let dry in the sun, and store again in bags of old leaves I saved from the year before. Also hanging securely on nails above them are my portable tree stands that need to be sprayed off and aired out to free them from the smell of gasoline fumes from my mowers.

Then, with great care, I will remove my winterized compound bow from its case, readjust the tension on the limbs, check all the screws and hinges, cams, cables, rest, and sight pins. Then I will examine the nocking points for tightness, make sure the peep sight is unobstructed, and wax the string. Once I have determined that the bow is in good working order, I will go back to the shed and dig out my "bag of rags"—perhaps the ugliest range target that ever received a piercing.

I will then carry my bow and arrows to the area of the backyard that everyone in the Chapman household knows not to approach when I am practicing. There, I will exhale a deep breath of excitement as I get ready to pull the string to full draw for the first time in much too long. And the enjoyable journey to opening morning of season begins.

Summer preparation is a treasured ritual for me. It's a time of year when I let my mind wander into the future and enjoy the fantasies of how my pulse will race and my senses heighten as the leaves begin to fall. And for a bowhunter whose desire for the heart-stopping excitement of seeing a takeable deer has not been satisfied for several months, July is a timely reprieve. It is the medicine needed to regulate an advanced case of acute buck fever.

As the season draws very near, around mid-September, my preparation for opening day intensifies. By this time I am a walking heap of anxious anticipation. I start to focus on the fine points of readiness, including adding a small drop of vegetable oil, which has no telltale scent, to certain moving parts of my bow and re-marking the adjustment straps on my tree stand with bright paint that can be more easily seen in the pale light of dawn.

The very last detail I usually cover is something I consider incredibly important—so much so that I do it with a great deal of deliberation. It is the process of choosing my number one arrow. I don't care at all to go into the woods on the first morning of archery season with less than full confidence in the flight and accuracy of my "string bullets." Nothing can dampen the high hopes of a successful hunt quicker than not knowing exactly how and where an arrow is going to sail once it leaves the bow. After weeks and months of scouting and practicing, not to mention the expense, why mess up the moment of truth with anything less than complete assurance that all systems are go?

Knowing I will mount only four arrows to my quiver, I begin the painstaking process of selection. With "spin checks" already out of the way and the undesirable shafts culled out, I reduce the number of possibilities to a dozen. Then I replace all damaged plastic fletching. After that I shoot each one at least a dozen times. As they leave the bow I watch them fly. Amazingly, even though they look and feel precisely the same from one to the next, the arrows have their own character. Once I have picked out six arrows that seem to excel in terms of flight quality, I start the process again. When I am down to four arrows that have convinced me they are "aces in my air force," I then begin a very discriminatory search for the one that will get the honorable position of top gun.

At this point I put the broadheads on the arrows. Knowing the three thin blades might slightly alter the way an arrow will fly, I go back to step one and start shooting each shaft at least a dozen times, one after the other, at a target specially made for broadheads. I try to observe how the arrow slides off the rest as well as any unusual or excessive movements it might make, such as fishtailing or porpoising.

Each year I have found that one arrow outperforms all the others. Its consistency at flying to the spot my sight pin covers is noticeable, and its behavior during release feels right. Three other excellent flyers are chosen as alternates. I then take my Scripto permanent ink pen and mark the odd color vane on each shaft with their rank. I start with last of the group and write "#4" and the year of the season. Then I mark number three and two. At that point I stop.

As I hold the arrow in my hand that I consider to be the best among all the rest, I always feel a little melancholy. I think to myself, *This is the one I will depend on to do the job. This "faithful friend" has consistently shown it is worthy of occupying the first slot in my quiver. I will protect it, and from this point on, I will limit its testing to one shot per day just to make sure it is still number one.* With that, I mark it, set it aside, and continue my wait for opening morning.

This tedious process has not been fruitless. I have collected a good number of arrows that are either bent or broken, but they are also covered with dried blood! The plastic vanes on most of those successful shafts are marked "#1." If I am fortunate enough to find them after they are used to take a deer, I never throw them away. Somewhere among all my souvenirs from seasons past are the remains of these "top guns." They are like old soldiers who are retired and deserve a safe resting place.

One day as I was going through some hunting memorabilia in my garage, I found a former number one that had been slightly bent as a result of an encounter with a whitetail's rib. It had been put away for memory's sake, and the "#1" badge was still visible in black on the bright orange vane. I held it for a moment and recalled with joy the hunt that it represented. Then I whispered a familiar compliment: "Well done, thou good and faithful servant." As if the arrow had become a mirror in my hands, I held it up to eye level and asked, "What about me? Am I a number one arrow?"

The question was loaded with an abundance of implications. As I pondered it, I thought about my life as a husband and dad. I couldn't help but wonder, *Is my behavior in the presence of my family displaying the straightness of important virtues like honesty, integrity, and devotion? Am I worthy to be their leader?* It was a sobering moment of self-examination.

Then I thought of even more serious questions. *As a man who claims to belong to Christ, am I a servant He could hold in His hands and confidently write on my heart, as He has done on others through the ages, the inscription "#1"? Could He trust me to do whatever He asks of me? And if I'm called upon to be launched at only one target, am I willing to be bent and broken for that single cause?*

These questions gripped my emotions that day. They inspired me to reassess my willingness to be tested. I wondered if I would ever make the mistake of being satisfied to be less than the best I could be in His hands. As I allowed the impact of the analogy to continue its work in my heart, I thought of what I sometimes do to turn an aluminum arrow that is a little wobbly into one that flies with greater stability. From time to time, a careful spin test will reveal the shaft is straight but the broadhead is sitting just off center, taking away its ability to spin perfectly. To correct this problem, I apply heat to the area where the screw-in insert is mounted to the shaft. After the glue melts, I can adjust the broadhead and then spin test it once more. If needed, the flame is applied again and again until the arrow spins without the slightest waver.

This corrective technique is a vivid picture of what the Lord often does to His own arrows. When He needs to readjust us, He applies the heat. In 1 Peter 4:12, we are exhorted, "Beloved, do not be surprised at the fiery ordeal among you, which comes upon you for your testing, as though some strange thing were happening to you." God works on us because He loves us and wants to help us "straighten up and fly right." The flame He applies can come in the form of anything from persecution by an evil world to a close family member who grates on our patience. And just as I must heat and reheat my metal arrows, He will take us to His workbench as often as needed. Why? Because He needs us to be in the best condition when our divine moment of truth arrives. To be less than an accurate arrow for Him would be a sad waste of life.

When all is said and done and those I love hold the memory of me in their hands, perhaps in the form of a picture or something written on paper, I deeply long for them to be able to say, "He was a good one. He 'flew' well!"

More importantly, may I strive to be faithful in allowing God to test me the way He wills in order to make me more effective for His purposes. In order for the right adjustments to be accomplished in my life, I know I must allow Him to examine me in the way Psalm 139 puts it: "Search me, O God, and know my heart; try me and know my anxious thoughts; and see if there be any hurtful way in me, and lead me in the everlasting way."

Not by any means in a haughty attitude nor with a wish to outdo another, I want to be one of God's number one arrows. Someday I want to hear Him say, "Well done, thou good and faithful servant" (Matthew 5:21 KJV). That lofty goal is one only He can help me meet. I know this to be true because of the benediction found in Jude 24:

> Now to Him who is able to keep you from stumbling, and to make you stand in the presence of His glory blameless with great joy, to the only God our Savior, through Jesus Christ our Lord, be glory, majesty, dominion and authority, before all time and now and forever. Amen.

May each of us be willing to let Him do what it takes to test us, adjust us, and write on our hearts "#1 servant."

33

A Time to Laugh

A cheerful heart is good medicine" (Proverbs 17:22 NIV), so my ear is always open to hearing a humorous story, especially one about the thing I like to do the most—hunt. Assuming you share my appreciation of stories about the lighter side of the fair chase and the medicinal value it can yield, I'll pass along two of my favorites. And for the record, because I have no idea who originated these tales, I don't know who to credit if you find them funny or who to blame if you don't.

Three Hunters, One Deer

A lawyer, a doctor, and a preacher headed to the woods one midday to hunt deer. They left their vehicles and started walking side by side through a big field on their way to a spot where each one would go his way and take an evening stand. Suddenly, not far from the road, a big buck that was bedded in the high grass jumped up and ran to escape. The trio of hunters immediately raised their guns and shot simultaneously. The buck rolled to the ground and expired instantly.

The three hunters took off running to the deer and arrived at the same time. They quickly examined the body and discovered only one bullet hole. The size of the rack on the buck would bring some serious bragging rights, so it didn't take long for an argument to erupt about who could claim the trophy.

As the three men stood around the heavy carcass and engaged in a heated discussion about the ownership of the beast, a game warden drove by and spotted the men. He could tell by the flailing of their arms that an argument was in process. Worried that a group of apparently upset men with guns could yield an injury to someone, the game warden pulled over and cautiously headed to the fracas in the field.

When he approached the hunters and asked what the problem was, they stepped back and revealed the hefty whitetail that lay at their feet. When asked what was going on, the lawyer spoke up and explained why they were arguing.

The game warden asked the three guys to give him a minute to inspect the deer to see if he could settle the debate. Less than thirty seconds later he stood up and said, "Gentlemen, I have no doubt about whose deer this is."

The three shooters listened intently, each one hoping his tag would be punched and his wall would display the mounted prize. What they heard the game warden say made only one of them happy—and a little miffed.

"This is the preacher's buck."

In unison the men asked how in the world the warden was able to come to that conclusion.

"Oh, it's easy," he said with a smile. "The bullet went in one ear and out the other."

Double Deer-ception

It was the fall deer archery season and the first year for Jack to hunt in the state he had moved to during the summer. Not yet having private land to hunt, he opted to give it a go on some public land. Any concern he had about the potential overcrowding on state land was offset by the fact that the bag limit in his new state of residence was three antlerless deer per day.

During some preseason scouting, he had located a hollow that seemed to be a good spot, and he headed to it on opening morning. He was especially pleased with his choice of portable stand placement when, about a half hour after sunrise, he heard the adrenalin-inducing sound of footsteps in the dry leaves to his left. Sure enough, it was a sizable doe—just what he was hoping to put in his freezer.

With one fluid motion he drew back the taut, muscle-testing string and peeked through the peep sight. He found the bright green twenty-yard pin and moved it to the deer's lung area. When he let the arrow go, it instantly sailed through the deer and stuck in the ground on the other side of its body. The doe kicked high and ran back in the direction it came from—but not far. Jack could hear the death crash and congratulated himself on remaining calm enough throughout the shot not to mess it up.

As he processed what had just happened, he heard the same crunchy sound of steps to his right. He slowly turned to look over his shoulder and saw another doe approaching. It was smaller than his first doe, though not small enough to keep him from instantly deciding that he shouldn't pass on another chance to stock his freezer.

Moving as slowly as he could, he removed a second arrow from his bow-mounted quiver, nocked it to the string, and quietly waited for the opportunity to come to full draw. The doe didn't seem to be aware that just a few yards away, one of its own kind lay lifeless on its side. She seemed to be determined to go somewhere and walked with a steady pace under Jack's stand. Just beyond the tree, the doe stopped, unaware that she had presented the hunter above her with a high-percentage quartering-away shot.

The leaves seemed to explode under her hooves when she responded to the arrow that found its mark. She didn't run more than thirty yards and stopped abruptly. As though she was quickly deciding which way to go, she looked left and right. But as she did, she began to weave side to side, back and forth. Seconds later, she toppled over and was down for good.

Jack could hardly believe that within a few minutes, he had accomplished a serious meat feat. It was a double-deer day, and he couldn't wait to tell the tale to his buddies—but the story would only get better.

As he removed his backpack from the hook on the tree, a sobering reality suddenly occurred to him. He stated the obvious out loud with a deep sigh: "Two deer to field dress and drag back to the truck. This is the day I might die of exhaustion."

He knew that the fifteen-minute walk from his vehicle to his stand represented a much longer drag since it included a few upward grades. But not being one to shirk a challenging task, Jack field dressed both deer, attached his dragging rope to the neck of one of them, and began the strenuous trek back to his truck.

After about twenty minutes of huffing and puffing through the woods with the lifeless doe carcass, he stopped to take a brief rest. As he surveyed his surroundings, he realized that because he was only partly acquainted with the lay of the land, he wasn't totally sure about which direction the truck was parked. His worry, however, was interrupted by a familiar sound.

"Pssst!" It came from the sky.

He looked up, and in a tall, straight tree sat another hunter in a climber stand. Sounding frustrated that his hunt had been disturbed, the stranger said, "Are you lost?"

Jack answered with an apology and an explanation about his inadvertent intrusion. "So sorry, man. I just arrowed this doe, and I'm heading to my truck with her."

He dreaded to admit that he was indeed a little unsure about where the gravel road was, and he didn't want to further engage the man in conversation, but knowing he had no choice, he continued.

"Hey, man, I'm new to the area and still learning it. Can you tell me which direction the road is?"

The fellow above him gave an unfriendly grunt and simply pointed to his left and said, "Dude, it's that way."

Feeling a little scolded and fighting back the urge to thank the man loud enough to alert the local deer of their presence, Jack simply whispered, "Thanks," and proceeded toward the road.

It took forty-five minutes to complete drag number one. With his bow, backpack, and deer securely stored inside his lockable truck bed, he headed back to get the second deer. As he walked away from his vehicle, he mentally mapped a return drag via a different route to not disturb the hunter again. However, when he thought of the guy's gruff demeanor and apparent unwillingness to accept the fact that bumping into other hunters is a part of the challenge of hunting on public land, he suddenly got an idea that he just couldn't say no to. He turned on his heels and went back to his truck.

He put his pack back on, got his bow, relocked the bed lid, and smiled as he once again started back to his second deer. He couldn't wait to do what he was about to do.

Making a wide sweep through the woods to keep away from the other hunter, Jack made it back to his other deer. He tied the dragging rope to its neck and began his final trip for the day. The previous trail of disturbed leaves that he had made with deer number one was easy to follow, and just as he'd hoped, it led him right back to where the stranger was still sitting in the tree.

All the extra effort and sweat it took to reappear below the guy was worth it to Jack when he saw the look of shock on his face. To top off his act of "double deer-ception," he could hardly keep from laughing when he looked up and said, "Dude, I can't believe you'd guide me wrong about where the road is. I've been dragging this deer now for nearly two hours. Thanks a lot…and this time I'll find my truck on my own."

As he dragged on Jack thought to himself, *Never has so much effort felt so good.*

34

The "Here's How" List

The top drawer of my chest of drawers in our bedroom doesn't hold my socks, undies, or T-shirts. Instead, it's the catchall drawer for things like my Navy dog tags, my late father's Social Security card and driver's license, some coins from countries outside the USA, and a ziplock bag containing the map used while walking some of the Appalachian Trail with my daughter.

Because most of the contents are memorabilia, I don't open the drawer often. But when I do, I always enjoy a walk through some good memories. Such was the case when I had a few extra minutes to peruse the contents and found an item that reminded me of my son's first deer.

Nathan's introduction to hunting took place when he was about eleven years old. It was an exciting and unforgettable October morning for both of us when a gray squirrel scampered along the treetops and came into range of his single-shot .410-gauge shotgun. With the pull of the trigger, the blast of the gun, and the lifeless gray's head-over-tail tumble on the way to the ground, the hunting hook was set in Nathan's soul.

After a couple more hunting seasons that yielded some successful small-game outings—and more important, some valuable experience with firearm safety—I felt confident that Nathan was ready for the big game contest when the next season came. To make sure he would be "well-weaponed," I forked out the cash for a brand-new Marlin .30-30 rifle that summer. The Model 336 lever action was the perfect gun for our part of the world. Best of all, the smile on my boy's face when he held it for the first time was worth every dime I'd spent. It wasn't easy to wait until the Saturday before Thanksgiving, when the time would come to chase the whitetail deer. But there was a problem.

When I looked at our state's hunting calendar and compared it to my concert schedule with Annie, I was heartsick to see that we had scheduled events on the opening weekend of the season. I would be gone on Friday and Saturday and wouldn't fly home until noon on Sunday. I was totally crushed by the thought that I would be out of town on opening morning of rifle season, especially because I had so looked forward to being there with Nathan and showing him how to prepare for his first walk into the woods as a licensed deer hunter.

Determined to not let the unfortunate circumstances of my absence prevent Nathan from experiencing the thrill of opening weekend, I called a friend who owned a sizable farm with a nice cabin and asked him if he would host my young first-timer on his property for the two days. He happily agreed but alerted me to his need to miss the Sunday morning hunt due to a commitment at his church. I told him I would extend grace to Nathan to hunt alone that morning, and he offered to help him get up in time to get to his stand if he hadn't tagged a deer on the first day. I assured my friend that as soon as we landed, I would get to the farm as quickly as possible and check on him. Though it was not what I wanted, at least we had a plan in place.

As I wrestled with the disappointment that I would not get to be the doting guide on that first day of the season, I thought of the next best thing I could do. I wrote a detailed "Here's How" list for Nathan to carry with him to my friend's farm. That was the list I came across as I was exploring the memory drawer. I sat down on the bed and read through it—and the memories flooded my heart.

I had written my list on a five-by-eight manila envelope. I remember I used it because I thought the heavy-duty paper would endure being handled a lot. The envelope was still folded four times—just the right size to fit in a shirt pocket. The edges of the folds were a bit frayed, indicating it had indeed been in and out of my son's hands and his pocket.

The blue ink on the heavy paper had faded only a little, and thankfully, the writing from the early 1990s was still legible. Using both the front and back, I provided Nathan with a numbered, step-by-step set of instructions to study and apply on opening day. Here is that list.

Saturday Morning

1. <u>Bathe with baking soda</u> (in yellow plastic bag), use in hair, <u>do not use deodorant</u> or aftershave.

2. Put clothes on outside cabin or at the barn. Don't forget gloves and face mask. If you have to pee, <u>do it now</u>!

3. Before walking to stand, <u>put fox pee on your boots</u> with sponge or put it on the ground and step in it with heel and toe of each boot.

4. <u>Load gun</u> without shell in chamber at truck until in stand. If you see deer as you approach the field, quietly lever a shell in. Take note of safety button—fire or safe?

5. Cautiously go to stand. Watch for deer!

6. <u>Before</u> climbing in, open ziplock—fold top over bag and cover entirely with leaves.

7. With foot (boot), dig out leaves like a scrape to expose the smell of the ground.

8. Get into stand. At top of stand, put <u>brown duct tape</u> on ladder for your boots to be quiet and not squeak.

9. If in ladder stand, check out closely the areas open for taking a shot. Rehearse raising the gun and possibly using your knee to hold steady. Be cautious while doing this—deer could appear any time.

10. Check behind you slowly. Practice left-handed aim.

11. Shift slowly when seeking comfort for your butt. Before moving, check all around you.

12. If deer comes into view, don't look for just one deer—check around it for others. When you raise gun to shoot at one that's not looking, another one could be nearby and see you and spook. Raise gun slowly. Check safety first and make sure button is off.

13. When you shoot, carefully watch direction deer runs and listen for either stopping or falling.

14. Wait about ten minutes and go find deer. Keep your gun ready to fire (not with hammer back).

15. Field dress near the barn. <u>Take pictures first</u>.

By the time I finished reading the nearly thirty-year-old list, I was mentally back at the airport on that Sunday morning, the second day of Nathan's first deer season. I was remembering how anxious I felt about grabbing our luggage and heading to my friend's farm where Nathan was hunting. After dropping Annie off at the house and hurriedly getting in my truck, I took off and within thirty-five minutes was driving down the lane that led to the cabin. It was just after noon when I rounded the last turn of the lane and saw my son standing in the front yard. He was still in his camo.

Not having cell phones at that time prevented me from knowing what the hunt had yielded for Nathan. I studied his face as I pulled up and turned off the motor. He seemed a little down. I opened the door and nervously asked the inevitable question.

"Well, how'd it go?"

Nathan just shook his head side to side and pursed his lips as if to imply it had not gone well. Then he said six words that are forever etched on my heart.

"It's been a real drag, Dad."

My sympathetic response was exactly what he had hoped for.

"Well, that's okay, son. The season lasts into January. We'll close the deal soon enough."

Nathan said it again, but a little louder and a little slower. "Yep...it's been a real *drag*." Then he smiled in a way that indicated he was waiting for me to get it.

After several seconds of processing his report, I finally realized he had gotten me good. I grinned big and responded to the great news that was tucked away in his veiled message. "Where is he?"

"He's a six point, and he's behind the cabin!"

The memory of our big hug in that moment, represented by the handwritten list I held in my hands, was as enjoyable as the day we had lived it. And knowing that my experience, passed on to him via the list, had helped yield his first deer brought great delight once again to my heart.

That treasured and worn manila envelope has been refolded and put back in the box where I found it. As they say about other valuable items, I wouldn't take a farm in Georgia for my "Here's How" list. And though the memory my son and I share about his first deer is precious to both of us, there's one other reason I consider the list to be priceless. It's a great picture of another "numbered list" that was written for my son to use, but not one I composed.

I'm referring to the Scriptures, God's written Word. It is the divine "Here's How" that provides every step needed for my son, my daughter, Annie, me, our son-in-law, our daughter-in-law, our grandchildren, and all who live and breathe to live successfully and fully, holy and pleasing to the One who inspired it. It's the list of written instructions that will help everyone find the trophy of God's saving grace. Here are just a few items from God's "Here's How" list from Romans 10 (NIV).

> 9 If you declare with your mouth, "Jesus is Lord," and believe in your heart that God raised him from the dead, you will be saved.

> 10 For it is with your heart that you believe and are justified, and it is with your mouth that you profess your faith and are saved.

> 11 As Scripture says, "Anyone who believes in him will never be put to shame."

> 12 For there is no difference between Jew and Gentile—the same Lord is Lord of all and richly blesses all who call on him,

> 13 for, "Everyone who calls on the name of the Lord will be saved."

35

So Much More

The long ascent up the steep Montana mountain was easy for me but not in the least a casual stroll for the horse carrying me. His rhythmic, heavy breathing sounded locomotive-like as he labored to climb toward the high, grassy meadow where my son, our guide, and I would dismount and wait for daylight. I felt bad for my horse straining under my weight, but I was grateful for the lift. Even though I knew he couldn't understand my words, I patted his muscular neck from time to time and verbally blessed him for the ride.

Thanks to the strength and endurance of all three horses, we reached the mountaintop well before the skies began to turn that unique gray-blue that announces the sun's rising. As a result, we would get an unexpected chance to view one of the most stunning sights my son and I had ever seen.

After riding through the dense cover of the timber for well over an hour, we broke out into an open meadow. Simultaneously, we looked up and gasped in utter amazement. Above us was the stariest sky that a couple of suburban lowland dwellers from the east had ever seen.

The complete absence of ambient illumination from cities or any other light source created a pitch-black backdrop that sparkled with what seemed to be at least a million white specks of light. Some were a little larger than others, some appeared to dance, and a few even had hints of color. We couldn't take our eyes off the heavenly scene.

Prior to seeing such a spectacular display of the Montana night sky, we were anxious for dawn to come and light up the mountains so we could begin glassing them for bull elk. But as we strained our necks to stare skyward, we both would have been satisfied to take in more of the breathtaking view above us. In fact, the awesome sight would eventually inspire part of a song lyric that I'd like to share—but first I want to tell you what happened during our hunt for the mighty ant-lered elk.

We tried hard to locate a shooter bull on the first day of our five-day trip, but it didn't happen. In no way were we disappointed. It meant that the next morning, we'd get to remount our four-legged transports and do it all again in Big Sky Country.

As we had hoped, the trio of horses delivered the three of us back up the mountain to the eight-thousand-foot "viewing station" in time to enjoy another indescribable experience. Once again we were in total awe and wishing the rising sun would hold up for a while somewhere over Tennessee to allow us a little more time for stargazing. But again dawn arrived on schedule, and we took our seats to glass for elk.

After we had spent the early hours on the peak without spotting game, our guide decided we would ride around the mountain on an old logging road to check out a huge open area where elk tended to graze in the afternoon. Around four o'clock, the action started when we found a herd below us. About thirty cows and at least two good bulls were slowly grazing their way up the hillside.

As any father with a son on his first elk hunt would do, I insisted that he would be the triggerman. Nathan mirrored our highly skilled guide as they belly-crawled side by side to a spot where they could carefully look over a little rise and see the ascending herd. I crawled behind them with my video camera in hand but didn't try to get into a position above them to film a shot if it was taken. I knew if I did, I could risk revealing myself to the elk and send them thundering away. I resolved to be satisfied with only rearview footage. As it turned out, it was the right thing to do.

From about seven yards behind the pair, I watched through the viewfinder of my camera as my son slowly slid his rifle onto the backpack the guide had quietly placed in front of him to use for a solid rest. Though he was in a prone position facing away from me, I could see that he was working the bolt and chambering a cartridge. My heart raced. Moments later, it appeared that he was lowering his head to the scope to take aim. I could feel my pulse in my temples. I rechecked to make sure the red recording light was on in the camera viewfinder and waited and hoped.

I wasn't quite sure what our guide was saying as he softly coached his teenage hunter, but it sounded like, "Wait…wait…let him turn a little more…" Ten seconds later the earth beneath my chest thumped with the blast of my son's rifle. Almost instantly, and with the guide's guidance, he chambered another round and fired again. About fifteen seconds of silence followed the second shot, and then our guide suddenly threw his arm across his hunter's back and started vigorously patting it while congratulating him with the sweetest words a young first-timer in the elk world (and his dad) could hear: "He's down! Great shot!"

We waited until the remainder of the herd moved on, and then we descended only fifty yards to get to the six-by-six's final resting place. I was not aware of how close we all were to the bull when the shot was taken. It made me extra glad that I chose to hang back, resisting the temptation to get the kill on film. And I was happy that my son was blessed with a closer shot than the one I would face two evenings later.

When the moment came for me to put the crosshairs on a six-by-six bull, he was standing broadside about 250 yards away. The wind was whipping across the hillside at a bullet-path-bending speed, and consequently my first shot didn't even come close. His lack of reaction to the report of my rifle indicated that the sound was drowned out by heavy wind and that he didn't hear the impact of the bullet slamming into the dirt somewhere below him.

The second shot, which was aimed several inches above the bull's vitals, found its mark but wasn't immediately lethal. When I pulled the trigger, the bull was facing some heavy timber about two hundred yards in front of him and directly above us. Without hesitating the guide said, "Let's go!"

The plan was to stay out of sight inside the timberline and quickly head up the mountain to see if we could intercept the bull before he disappeared into the thick, massive stand of spruce trees. Fortunately for me, the wounded animal stopped at the edge of the timber. When we reached the flat he was on, we saw him struggling to walk at about seventy-five yards. I dropped to my knee and took aim. The third shot was fatal.

I enjoyed the congratulatory high fives from the guide, who candidly admitted he was worried that the bull could have easily been lost in the dark, dense timber had he escaped into it and had we not rushed up the mountain to close the deal before sunset. I confessed to him that it was well worth nearly spitting up a lung as I gasped for air, trying to keep up with him during the hurried climb.

While the kudos from our guide were great to hear, the hugs and "atta boys" I got from my son were even sweeter. The celebration we had that evening remains a treasured memory that I return to often, and when I do, I also remember that first morning of the hunt when we encountered a star-studded night sky and how we couldn't wait till each of the next mornings to see it again.

As I mentioned, the scene would later become part of a song. It came to mind several years later as I attempted to capture the idea that what we can see of nature, as vast and as awesome as it is, is merely the edge of the unfathomable depth of our Creator's greatness, a mere taste of His eternal power and divine glory. The innumerable stars we saw while atop the mountain are just a hint of what else exists in His universe. There's so much more!

Each time I sing the verse in the song that refers to the stars, I'm mentally transported back to Montana, where my son and I sat on our horses next to each other at 8,000 feet, worshipfully looking heavenward. It's a place I love to go in my heart.

So Much More

When I look out on an ocean
From a high and rocky shore
Beyond the waters I can see
I know there's so much more
And it's just like the Lord

When a clear night on a mountain
Seems to open heaven's door

Beyond the million stars I see
I know there's so much more
And it's just like the Lord

So much more
Beyond what I can see of Him
There's so much more
Of all He is there is no end
This world He made
Is just a taste
Of all He has in store
I am sure
With the Lord
There's so much more

When I look into the pages
Where His glory is revealed
I know beyond that book of hope
Is glory greater still
There's so much more![16]

36

The Archers of Ephraim

Being a hunter has taught me a long list of beneficial lessons, and many of them are a result of noticing things in the outdoors and connecting them to imagery found in the Bible. One example comes from my early days of hunting antlered deer. I've included it in a couple of my books because of the positive impact it can have on men.

It didn't take long to learn from observing whitetail deer that during the rut, or mating season, males can make a fatal mistake: abandoning their usual cautiousness for the sake of being with a female. Many "love crazed" bucks have lost their lives at the hands of hunters like me who take advantage of that uncontrolled trait.

This "buck and bubba" comparison has its limitations because the bucks are only doing what comes naturally to them, and their actions can't be categorized as sinful. Yet their untimely demise due to setting caution aside has motivated me to remember the fair warning in 1 Peter 5:8: "Be alert and of sober mind. Your enemy the devil prowls around like a roaring lion looking for someone he may devour" (NIV).

Being spiritually consumed by the devil is a fate I want to avoid, and for that reason I am determined to keep a cautious attitude when it comes to women.

Recently, while reading the Bible through my "hunter eyes," I discovered another helpful and life-changing "outdoor insight." I was drawn to a reference to archery in Psalm 78. I noted that it, too, contains an alert. Though not as direct as Peter's warning about the roaring lion, the verse offers an important heads-up: "The men of Ephraim, though armed with bows, turned back on the day of battle" (Psalm 78:9 NIV).

On first reading, I wasn't sure what the lesson was, but the imagery immediately pulled me into the picture because I have often been armed with a bow—while hunting, of course. And I could relate to the words "turned back on the day of battle." I'm referring to those late-September days when I left the woods sooner than I planned because I got tired of dealing with the frustrating and ever annoying warm-weather war with gnats and mosquitos. Or in the spring, as turkey season progressed from the coolness of late March into the rising temperatures of late April and early May, the midmorning attack of the blood-sucking flying pests prompted an earlier-than-planned trek back to the safety of my truck.

Obviously, the circumstances I have faced as a hunter aren't nearly as serious as the challenges confronting the men of Ephraim, but at least I could understand the imagery of giving up and heading home. But what meaning does the connection have for me?

The next few verses of Psalm 78 reveal that the men of Ephraim turned back from the battle because they forgot what God had done for them. "They did not keep God's covenant and refused to live by his law. They forgot what he had done, the wonders he had shown them" (verses 10-11 NIV).

What did they forget? Among other amazing things God had done on their behalf, He supernaturally delivered them through the Red Sea, He fed them in the wilderness with heavenly manna, and He provided water from a rock while they were in the desert. You have to wonder how anyone could overlook or dismiss those miracles. Verse 8 gives us the answer: The people's hearts "were not loyal to God," and that led to their forgetfulness and disobedience. There's the connection.

I don't ever want it said that I forgot what God has done for me. To put it mildly, knowing now that forgetting His great works in my life can lead to disobedience, I would be a fool to do so. For example, if I didn't treasure the fact that He took my place on a sinner's cross, was buried in a cold and dark grave, yet rose again to give me eternal life, I'd be insane.

That miracle alone is beyond anything I deserved. But He has continued to do amazing works on my behalf. I think of the fact that He provided a helpmate in Annie. That He gave me the humbling privilege of being wed to her is nothing less than a miracle. I admit without reservation that I would be an absolute, total, worthless slob if not for my dear wife. Plus, she appreciates my enjoyment of hunting. What more can I say!

Then there are our two children, who have given us such immeasurable joy. Add to them the blessing of their spouses, who are the finest of people, and our half-dozen lovable and adorable GrandChaps.

I could continue the list of wonderful works He has done for me, but I'll stop here to avoid being a total bore. Suffice it to say that when I face the battles of life—struggling with health, finances, disappointments, or any other enemy that comes against me—my goal is to not be like the men of Ephraim. Instead, I want to grip my spiritual bow tighter, check my quiver to make sure it's full of arrows from God's Word to use against the enemy of my soul, and stay in the fight—all the while remembering God's past faithfulness so I don't become faithless to Him in the future.

Because of the LORD's great love we are not consumed,
for his compassions never fail.
They are new every morning;
great is your faithfulness.

LAMENTATIONS 3:22-23 NIV

37

The War Is Over

"Deer: 8 / Hunter: 0"

Those are the words I whispered to myself as the evening light faded and I gathered my gear in preparation to dismount the deer stand I had been occupying for the previous three hours. I had made eight trips to the woods in an effort to fill a tag, and I had zero deer to show for it. I was frustrated with the score, but I knew I had to accept it and hope for a better outcome the next morning, when I'd head back to the woods.

I didn't know things would get even worse.

After arriving back at the seventeen-foot ladder stand I had exited the evening before, I paused at the bottom of the steps, cocked my crossbow, slid the safety lever to green, attached it to the pull-up string, climbed up, sat down, and checked my watched. It was six fifteen—at least twenty minutes before legal shooting light would come.

The tree that my stand was attached to was a huge and healthy oak that was dropping October acorns like rain. The ground around the massive trunk was so covered with "deer candy" that walking under the tree sounded like my grandkids walking on bubble wrap. I could only hope the local deer didn't hear the pops and crunches under my boots as I approached the tree in the predawn darkness.

After the many additional duties were completed—storing my backpack, pulling my crossbow up to my lap, loading a bolt onto the flight groove, detaching and stowing the quiver, and putting on my facemask and gloves—I was finally able to sigh deep and say the welcome words "Now…let the hunt begin!"

I enjoyed watching the subtle light of dawn slowly illuminate my surroundings. The light growing in the eastern sky was making it easier by the minute to see well into the field to my left. The interior of the woods to my right, however, remained nearly black. I kept my eyes on the field.

About fifteen minutes later, the light was sufficient for legal shooting, and my anticipation meter was registering high. As I basked in the glow of being blessed to be in a deer stand once more on such a clear, crisp October morning, I saw movement in the field through the openings in the green foliage remaining on the long, thick branches that angled downward at their outermost tips. A sizable doe was walking toward my stand. She was an early arriver—and just what I was looking for.

I was excited to say the very least. It always happens when deer come near, even a "slickhead." The situation was testing my nerves as I slid my right hand onto the grip of my crossbow and placed my thumb on the safety lever. At the same time, I tightly squeezed the foregrip with my left hand as though I was choking it. The lone doe continued toward me, and I could almost hear the thanks from the family that would receive the venison I was about to harvest.

Once the doe reached the drip line of the tree, she started feeding on the acorns, and I prepared to make a shot. The problem was that she was facing me. For a high-percentage placement of the bolt, I needed her to turn broadside. She finally did, but before I could raise my bow and aim, she began a clockwise path around the tree that led her behind a smaller tree near the base of my ladder stand. She stopped there (of course!). I could see part of her body and her face at about fifteen yards, but the rest of her was concealed behind the leaves that still hung on the smaller tree. Then she lifted her nose and began to sniff, indicating that she was getting a little nervous. I was sure she had detected the aroma of something she didn't like— namely, me. And I was bracing for the likelihood that I was about to get busted.

I debated about what to do until I noticed that her vitals were visible through a five-inch opening in the foliage. I instantly thought, *I probably shouldn't wait…I can do this!* I put the peep site pin on the right spot, pushed the safety lever upward to red, and pulled the trigger.

The bolt slipped through her with lightning speed. She kicked high, ran about twenty yards, and stopped. I watched and waited for her to topple over, but she didn't. Instead, she walked away and disappeared into the timber far across the other side of the field. I feared the worst.

When I descended the stand and retrieved the bolt, my suspicions were confirmed. On the shaft was not blood. It was wet with debris from her paunch—a softer way of saying she was gut shot. I couldn't believe it. I was sick with regret as I looked toward the woods where she had wandered out of sight. I knew what was ahead. There probably wouldn't be a blood trail to follow. Instead, it would likely be a body search. Sadly, I was right.

For the next four hours I walked every hollow and thicket I could check but didn't find her. As I searched, I replayed the shot over and over in my head and finally decided that something in that opening of leaves—something too small for me to see—must have that made the arrow go off course. There was no comfort in that possibility. It was only a nagging, logical deduction.

I can't forget the moment I finally admitted to myself that it was time to stop searching. I was physically exhausted and emotionally spent. If I refused to yield to better judgment and continued expending energy and sweat, someone would probably have to come looking for me. When I reluctantly admitted that I had lost the deer, it was like surrendering in a war in my soul. It was a conflict between ego and humility.

It was hard to do, but I turned slowly on my heels and began the long, empty-handed walk back to my truck. The stark contrast between how high I had soared that morning on the wings of anticipation and how low I was feeling as I drove away from the farm was hard to process.

As I have discovered time and again through the years, when something not so good happens in the hunter's woods, there may be something good to be gleaned from it. In the case of the unrecovered doe and the resulting inner war that erupted between my ego and the humbling but wise choice of "giving in to giving up," I saw a similarity to another time in my life when choosing to end a war was the good and right thing to do. It involves my decision to face my pride-driven search for lasting peace, which I thought I could find in this world, and admit that I would find it only by yielding my life to Christ. Quite honestly, it wasn't a war that was easy to end, but doing so was by far the smartest thing I've ever done. The following song lyric describes that memory.

The War Is Over

Almighty God on heaven's throne
I've been fighting You far too long
But the blood of Your only Son
Has brought me here to say Your love has won
And the war is over

I'm leaving this battleground
Laying my weapons down
All my doubt all my pride
Kept me on the losing side
I want peace
Between You and me
I surrender
The war is over

It's by Your grace You have forgiven me
Even though I've been a soldier for Your enemy
I've been his fool
But those days are gone
You have my heart and soul
From this moment on

I know You could have taken life from me
Instead You gave me life abundantly
That's why…

I'm leaving this battleground
Laying my weapons down

All my doubt all my pride
Kept me on the losing side
I want peace
Between You and me
I surrender
The war is over[17]

Notes

1. Steve Chapman, "The Arrow and the Bow," © 1987 Shepherd's Fold Music. Administered by EMI Christian Music Group. All rights reserved. Used by permission.

2. Steve & Annie Chapman, *Gifts Your Kids Can't Break* (Minneapolis, MN: Bethany House, 1991), 51.

3. Steve Chapman, "Seasons of a Man," © 1987 Shepherd's Fold Music / Dawn Treader Music. Administered by EMI Christian Music Group. All rights reserved. Used by permission.

4. Steve Chapman, "The Key," © Times & Seasons Music / BMI. Used by permission.

5. Steve Chapman, "The Pocket," © 2000 Times & Seasons Music / BMI.

6. Kenny and Donna Johnson, "Playing Baseball with Jesus," used by permission, www.kenny-anddonnajohnson.com.

7. Steve Chapman, "Don't Unpack Your Bags," © 2005 Times & Seasons Music / BMI.

8. Steve Chapman, "Psalm 91:7."

9. Steve Chapman, "Blessed Sorrow," © 2004 Times & Seasons Music / BMI.

10. Steve Chapman, *A Look at Life from a Deer Stand Devotional* (Eugene, OR: Harvest House Publishers, 2009), 40.

11. Steve Chapman, "The Tangled Web," © 2009 Times & Seasons Music / BMI.

12. Frank E. Graeff, "Does Jesus Care?" 1901.

13. Steve Chapman, "That's a Call," © 2012 Times & Seasons Music / BMI. All rights reserved. Used by permission.

14. Steve Chapman, "The Hunt Is Over," © Times & Seasons Music / BMI. All rights reserved. Used by permission.

15. Steve Chapman, "Daddy's Best Sermon," © Times & Seasons Music / BMI. All rights reserved. Used by permission.

16. Steve Chapman, "So Much More," © 2018 Times & Seasons Music.

17. Steve Chapman, "The War Is Over," © 2018 Times & Seasons Music.

More Great Harvest House Books by Steve Chapman

365 Things Every Hunter Should Know
The Hunt for Faith
The Hunter's Cookbook (with Annie Chapman)
The Hunter's Devotional
A Look at Life from the Riverbank
My Dream Hunt in Alaska
One-Minute Prayers® for Hunters
Stories from the Deer Stand
Tell Me a Huntin' Story (with Don Hicks)
I Love You and I Like You (with Annie Chapman)
Down Home Wit and Wisdom
Wasn't It Smart of God to…

To learn more about Harvest House books and
to read sample chapters, visit our website:
www.harvesthousepublishers.com

HARVEST HOUSE PUBLISHERS
EUGENE, OREGON